# *Belief policies*

# CAMBRIDGE STUDIES IN PHILOSOPHY

*General editor* ERNEST SOSA

*Advisory editors* J. E. J. ALTHAM, SIMON BLACKBURN,
GILBERT HARMAN, MARTIN HOLLIS, FRANK JACKSON,
WILLIAM G. LYCAN, JOHN PERRY,
SYDNEY SHOEMAKER, BARRY STROUD

## RECENT TITLES

# Belief policies

### Paul Helm
King's College, London

**CAMBRIDGE**
UNIVERSITY PRESS

Published by the Press Syndicate of the University of Cambridge
The Pitt Building, Trumpington Street, Cambridge CB2 1RP
40 West 20th Street, New York, NY 10011-4211; USA
10 Stamford Road, Oakleigh, Melbourne 3166, Australia

First published 1994

Printed in Great Britain at the University Press, Cambridge

*A catalogue record for this book is available from the British Library*

*Library of Congress cataloguing in publication data*

Helm, Paul.
Belief policies/Paul Helm. Cambridge Studies in Philosophy
p.   cm.
Includes index.
ISBN 0 521 46028 X (hardback)
1. Belief and doubt. I. Title.
BD215.H439   1994
121'.6 – dc20                     93-32409
                                              CIP

*#288 90929*

ISBN 0 521 46028 X (hardback)

TS

*to Bill Iddon*

For no one believes anything unless he has first thought that it is to be believed. For however suddenly, however rapidly, some thoughts fly before the will to believe, and this presently follows in such wise as to attend them, as it were, in closest conjunction, it is yet necessary that everything which is believed should be believed after thought has preceded; although even belief itself is nothing else than to think with assent. For it is not every one who thinks that believes, since many think in order that they may not believe.

St Augustine, *On the Predestination of the Saints*

# Contents

# Contents

# Contents

# *Preface*

I should like to use this opportunity to thank various people whose help in bringing this book to the light of day has been indispensable. My Liverpool colleague Nicholas Nathan kindly offered to read a draft of the book and I was able to take advantage of almost all of his valuable comments. The suggestions of the reader for the Press, Tim Crane, resulted in the avoidance of many mistakes, and in a strengthening of the work as a whole.

Chief among those who have guided the text through several of its various resurrections and transfigurations is Joan Stevenson, my secretary for the four years during which I was seconded from teaching as Director of Staffing Services at the University of Liverpool. More recently Lourdes McGunigle has also provided assistance.

Part of chapter two first appeared as 'Belief as action' (*Cogito*, 3.2, 1989, 127-32), and part of chapter three as 'On Pan-critical Irrationalism' (*Analysis*, 47.1, 1987, 24-8). The bulk of the book was completed during a period of study leave in 1992-3 generously granted by the University of Liverpool.

# Introduction

In epistemology there is a tension between considering what people believe and know, and prescribing acceptable ways of believing and knowing. This tension is understandable; after all, an epistemologist, given that he is not a complete sceptic, can hardly avoid taking note of the fact that we actually do know and believe certain things, as well as taking account of what we know, and of how we know, or at least claim to know. This is most obviously true in the case of natural science, where it would be folly not to take account of scientific success and progress, and not to record that those who have achieved this success cannot have been following a wholly mistaken method of acquiring beliefs. But what is true of science is true of other more mundane perceptions and beliefs with which scientific beliefs are sometimes continuous.

At the same time it cannot be the task of the epistemologist merely to codify practice. The history and sociology of knowledge and belief must not be confused with the critical, reflective task of the philosopher. It is also the epistemologist's task to reflect on what ought to be the case, on how epistemic endeavours ought to be prosecuted, on tools and methods and standards. Much of what appears at first sight to be descriptive and reportive in the work of epistemologists turns out, on closer inspection, to be prescriptive and recommendatory. This study is a contribution to epistemology of such an overtly prescriptive kind.

Many reasons are given for adopting and abandoning beliefs, reasons to do with personal well-being, with the achieving of power, success, freedom from temptation, and much else. Philosophical reflection on these reasons is appropriate but, because such reasons are, by themselves, not evidence-centred, the study of them has more to do with action theory and ethics than with epistemology. Where they arise as a result of inadequacies in a person's evidence, its absence or

1

indifference, then such reasons may be epistemically relevant, but only then. Otherwise they are not to be regarded as truth-centred because they do not have the discovery of truth as paramount, but the quelling of certain disquiets or the achieving of other non-epistemic goals.

We shall be concerned with those beliefs about matters of fact the prime motive for adopting which is the acquiring of truth through evidence; or, more weakly, where sufficient evidence has been sought in vain. We shall not consider either beliefs about oneself, or beliefs formed on testimony alone.

In the case of beliefs about oneself there is controversy over whether such beliefs can be based upon evidence, or whether they are instances of immediate awareness. Such beliefs are notoriously intertwined with self-interest and self-image. If it is not easy to formulate belief-policies about matters of fact concerning the world around us, it is certainly not easy to formulate such policies to cover beliefs about ourselves.

In the case of testimony there is an additional philosophical issue that I am unwilling to take sides on. Some philosophers (such as Elizabeth Anscombe (1979) and C. A. J. Coady (1992)) maintain a non-reductive thesis about testimony, claiming that its epistemological value is not equivalent to the inductive evidence supporting its reliability. Others, notoriously Hume, maintain the reductive thesis. Obviously the reductive thesis presents no problems that inductively acquired evidence does not present. But a non-reductivist would need to supply a distinct set of belief-policies regarding testimony, (see Coady 1992, pp. 190ff.). Because this work is agnostic on the reductive thesis I make no attempt to set out such belief-policies.

Let us call an inquirer who strives to base any belief on evidence alone an evidentialist. We shall be concerned with the evidence that a human inquirer actually possesses or is likely to possess, and with the ways in which such evidence or the lack of it bears on the warranting of belief. While such an approach cuts out much, it still leaves much to be discussed. For, while the evidentialist claims that a person discharges his duty to truth and falsehood by being concerned only with issues of evidence, there are many variations on this theme. It is part of the purpose of this book to highlight these variations, to argue that such variety is not so much desirable as inevitable, and to show that this inevitability is of epistemological importance in that it necessarily introduces non-evidential considerations.

The mesmeric word 'rationality' has various senses. For example, it can refer to the structure of reason–giving, or to the sources of the reasons given. Yet, whatever the appropriate structure of reason-giving for the beliefs we justifiably hold, and the sources of such reasons, there are still questions about the degree to which those sources are to be applied, questions of stringency and thoroughness. Though this study is not an investigation of the first two senses of rationality it is an attempt to open up the question of the third sense in a systematic and reflective way, and in so doing to give support to a positive account of the place of the will, of decision, in epistemology.

It would be an unwarranted assumption to suppose that all evidentialist positions hold that all beliefs are to be determined only by sufficient evidence, or even that such a claim – let us call it 'sufficient evidentialism' – is clear. The unwarranted assumption is that there is one obvious answer to the question of what adequate evidence amounts to. So the various views to be introduced and outlined later on in the book (particularly in chapter four) are contributions to how beliefs ought to be formed by reference to evidential considerations, or by other considerations when evidence fails. They are not contributions to the criteria of belief-formation more generally.

Although this book is an attack upon sufficient evidentialism, it is not a direct attack. It will not be argued that this 'ism' is to be rejected in favour of another 'ism'. And I shall most certainly not be arguing that to raise questions about sufficient evidentialism is to defend irrationalism. The claim is that built into the standard accounts of evidentialism is one common assumption. It is the main purpose of what follows to inquire what the consequences are if that assumption is questioned.

The assumption is that sufficient evidentialism is clear and obviously true, perhaps because it is self-announcing or self-certifying in character. I shall argue, in due course, that sufficient evidentialism is one evidentialist belief-policy among many others. I shall also argue that the choice of even an evidentialist belief-policy, like any choice, involves the will. It is in this rather indirect way that the will plays a significant and crucial part in the formation of justifiable beliefs, because the will must inevitably be involved in the choice of a policy or policies each of which functions as a person's standard of what is to count as adequate or sufficient warrant for belief for that person.

The classic forms of rationalism and empiricism have been foundationalist in character. It will be assumed that strong foundationalism is not rationally compelling, perhaps because, as Plantinga has argued, it is self-referentially incoherent, or for some other reason. The fact that there is no rationally compelling theory of knowledge is another reason for supposing that the will must be involved in a significant way in the acquiring of justified beliefs. In the absence of rational compulsion believing becomes a matter of recognising certain duties, or having certain ends, or cultivating certain virtues. The term 'belief-policy' has been chosen to indicate this voluntaristic element in believing, while at the same time remaining strictly neutral as between whether believing is best thought of in terms of fulfilling duties, attaining ends, or cultivating virtues.

Still, it might be objected, the fact that what has been called strong foundationalism is self-referentially invalid does not usher in an era of epistemic anarchy. To see this, and to emphasise the point, it is perhaps helpful to distinguish between the formal and the material conditions of epistemic rationality.

The acceptance of certain formal conditions of rationality is not a matter of their being self-evident to any rational man, but it must be couched in terms that are more personal or subjective. Richard Foley (for example) elaborates this rationality in terms of a set of conditions necessary for the personal effective pursuit of goals 'of what a person would have to do in order to pursue his goals in a way that he would believe to be effective, were he to be carefully reflective' (Foley, 1988, p. 5). According to Foley it is epistemically rational for a person to believe a proposition if there is a way of arguing for the proposition that is uncontroversial for him (Foley, 1988 p. 14). The epistemic goals are to believe what is true and not to believe what is false now. It is a further, non-epistemic question as to how these goals are to be integrated with other, non-epistemic goals. The formal character of Foley's account is brought out in the following way:

What I am claiming is that it is epistemically rational for a person to believe a proposition just if there is a way of arguing for the proposition that is uncontroversial for him . . . An argument has uncontroversial premises for a person just if careful reflection would reveal to him no good reason to be suspicious of their truth, and the premises of an argument support its conclusion in a way that is uncontroversial for a person just if he would think that the argument is likely to be truth preserving were he to be carefully reflective. (Foley, 1988, p. 14).

What is and is not controversial for a person, what is or is not suspicious for a person, is not something that a theory of epistemic rationality can disclose or dictate. For what counts as uncontroversial or unsuspicious for a person relates to standards of another kind than the merely formal, overarching standards of rationality, the need to check evidence, to be consistent, and the like. Foley touches upon considerations of a more material kind. He points out that the uncontroversial nature of A accepting a conclusion which is based upon premises which are uncontroversial for him depends upon the absence of 'defeaters', propositions the acceptance of which would defeat the inference by undermining support for the conclusion.

Foley also draws attention to the fact that the rational goal of now believing truth and not believing falsehood is not equivalent to the goal of maximising truth; and this introduces the notion of epistemic risk and of the agent's attitude to such risk, which is

not something that we impose on him. He on reflection must decide for himself whether in his search now to have true beliefs and now not to have false beliefs, it would be appropriate for him to believe the conclusion of an argument whose premises he believes make the conclusion likely to a certain degree. (Foley, 1988, p. 21).

Using Foley's language, in this book we shall be concerned to argue that the existence of different kinds of defeaters, and different attitudes to risk, manifests the existence of differing epistemic standards which are personal in character and which, as with ethical standards, the will has a significant part in forming and sustaining. So our concern in what follows are some of the different ways which a person may have of discharging his commitment to epistemic rationality.

Foley goes on to claim that

there is nothing in the formal part of the theory that guarantees that our simplest and most fundamental beliefs about the external world, the past, and the future, are likely to be epistemically rational for us, but the formal part of the theory together with plausible assumptions about our nature as believers does imply that such beliefs are likely to be epistemically rational for us. (Foley, 1988, p. 111).

On what grounds are these assumptions to be made? If they are assumptions, what makes them plausible assumptions? Are there other, equally plausible assumptions? Later on in his treatment Foley appeals to the naturalising of epistemology. But the weaknesses of appealing to what is natural are notorious, and it is not easy to see how the chasm between the requirements of the formal conditions of epistemic rationality, and the material conditions, can be bridged in any such way. It will later be argued that the only way in which it can be bridged is by a person adopting or retaining some belief-policy or other.

Foley claims that both a formal and a material epistemic rationality are required in order for a person to fulfil his epistemic goals. Alvin Plantinga, who prefers to think in terms of epistemic duties, distinguishes between objective and subjective epistemic duties (Plantinga, 1988 and 1990). This distinction is an important one and, as Plantinga argues, it is necessary to discharge both sorts of duties. But, as in the case of Foley's proposal, it is difficult to see how the gulf between them can be bridged by an appeal to function (as Plantinga proposes) any more than by an appeal to what is natural. For there are many different accounts of what it is for a human being to function in a proper epistemic fashion. I shall try to show later that there are different epistemic choices made by those who there is no reason to think are not functioning properly when they make them.

Plantinga may say that appealing to function, or to the ontological ground of such functioning (Plantinga, 1991) does not *settle* epistemological differences, but that it does *display* them. Different epistemologies derive from different ontologies. What follows in this study could be regarded as making the parallel proposal that different epistemologies are grounded in different projects, strategies or policies; not in nature, but in will.

Foley considers the contrast between subjective and objective foundationalism as that between two rival views. No doubt this is one way of dividing up the field. But objective or classical foundationalism may also be considered to be the limiting case in a spectrum of such cases. The only alternative to basic or classical foundationalism (within the foundationalist camp) is some form of personal or subjective foundationalism, of which there are very many versions. And perhaps, as Foley argues (Foley, 1988, pp. 93ff.), personal foundationalism incorporates some of the advantages of coherentist views of justification.

Foley's is but one version of subjective foundationalism. One reason for this variety is the fact that there are many different considerations that make *p* non-controversial for different people, according to their differing epistemic standards. A slightly weaker position than this would be to allow that all epistemic rationality has a foundational character, but that, once beyond a basic set of uncontroversial propositions, the principles of admission and rejection of other beliefs vary enormously.

While there is this difference between personal and objective obligation, following a belief-policy is not equivalent in a straightforward way to discharging one's epistemic obligations. As Alston has shown (Alston, 1988), there is a divergence between internalism, the view that the grounds for justification must be those that the subject himself is aware of and believes to be adequate, and issues of epistemic obligatoriness or blameworthiness. One may not have the time or the requisite cognitive power consciously to formulate a belief-policy, but one may have done sufficient to free oneself from blame and so to discharge one's epistemic obligations.

Consciously adopting or retaining a belief-policy is a form of internal justification of those beliefs which fall within its scope. I shall be arguing that, while the adoption of a belief-policy is necessary for the subjective justification of most of our believings, it is not necessary for the justification of belief *tout court*, since there are cases of instinctive and infantile beliefs which are justified. But it is precisely in such cases that the will is not, or only minimally, involved.

Some philosophers have thought that it is sufficient to diminish or eliminate the role of the will in belief to argue that it is impossible, either on logical or psychological grounds, to choose what to believe, just like that. It is claimed that the will cannot operate in this direct and immediate way, certainly not if the belief so chosen is intended to be evidentially supported. I agree with this observation, though not with some of the arguments that have been used to support it. The place that the will plays in the retention, modification, and adoption of belief-policies, it will be argued, is much more significant in estimating the relation between belief and the will. In belief-policies the will is concerned not with single beliefs, such as the belief that today is Wednesday, but with criteria for the acceptance and rejection of sets of propositions.

An attempt to provide an account of a belief-policy thus understood is a central feature of what follows, and the chief way in which an important connection between belief and the will is to be identified. The drawing of this connection is attempted in two main ways; firstly by providing a straight defence of a belief-policy as an important epistemological concept, and then by attempting to expound and, where necessary, to recast some standard epistemic positions in this voluntaristic mode. In some cases, as with the Clifford – James debate, no recasting is necessary, but in other cases an attempt will be made to show that several epistemological positions may be plausibly interpreted as invitations to adopt one or more belief-policies.

The various options represented in the text by certain historical and contemporary epistemologists are intended to be illustrative and supportive of the main thesis. They are not meant to constitute an argument from authority, nor are the case-studies exhaustive. There is no mention of the belief-policies of philosophers falling outside the Anglo-American tradition, no mention of Nietzsche or of Sartre, of Schopenhauer or of Bergson, for example, though there is a brief glance at Pascal; there is no attempt to discuss the contribution of the 'pure rational will' as claimed by Kant, or by the activistic or voluntaristic versions of post-Kantian idealism, aspects of which are treated in Code (1987).

Nor have I attempted to incorporate a detailed discussion of Bayesianism into the treatment of various belief-policies, since it is such a specialised area. For our purposes its formal account of how decision between rival hypotheses is to be made is to be regarded as one among several attempts to show how belief may be proportioned to evidence. In so far as the operation of Bayes' theorem depends upon judgements of prior probability, as Putnam has argued (Putnam, 1981, ch. 8) then it is at least possible that it will be infected with elements of non-evidentialism.

Voluntaristic philosophies are often thought to be anti-intellectual by definition. The argument carries (it is hoped) no such implication. It does not constitute an attempt to demonstrate the worthwhileness nor even the inevitability of anti-intellectualism, but to show that in the acquisition of justified beliefs the intellect functions, at the most basic level, in terms of norms about evidence which are not purely evidential. Further, the appeal to the will is not to a mere volition, to a reasonless choice, but to choice by reference to considerations which cannot be purely evidential. The intellectual is not to be identified with the evidential.

Voluntaristic epistemology has a tradition which goes back through Descartes to Augustine as is seen, for example, by the place Augustine gives to the will in perception (Augustine, 1873, XI, 2–3). And I would be happy to think that Augustine's response to scepticism in his *Contra Academicos* was, in essence, the adoption by him of a belief-policy to the effect that evidential sufficiency is not necessary for rational belief.

If belief-policies are ways of forming believings in accordance with certain preferred epistemic norms, then one obvious question is: on what basis can a decision to prefer one of a competing set of belief-policies be made? It will be argued that, as in ethics, there is no compelling reason to think that because choices have to be made any such choice must be arbitrary, a mindless operation of the pure will.

It was stated earlier that one consequence of believing being subject to the will in any significant sense is that it takes upon itself some of the characteristic features of an action. If this is so then one would expect some, at least, of the significant philosophical issues that arise in connection with action to replicate themselves in the case of believing. It is the purpose of chapters six and seven to attempt to display some of these ramifications of believing, in two significant areas.

It is a notorious feature of human action that weakness of will can intervene. A person can know what ought to be done, and yet do what ought not to be done. That is, it is characteristic of actions that there can be both failures of will and occasions of self-deception. In chapter six it is argued that as weakness of will may occur in the case of action so it may also occur in believing; a person may know that a particular proposition ought to be believed, but not be willing to do so because of an unreasoned, but wilful, retention of another belief-policy.

It is generally held that a person is responsible for those actions performed at will, without duress or undue constraint, however such factors are defined. If believing is subject to the will it is reasonable to suppose that a person is responsible for such believings. And so in chapter seven it is argued that to the extent that people are responsible for their actions they are, *ceteris paribus*, responsible for their believings. The consequences of this doctrine for toleration are then explored.

In the final chapter an attempt is made to apply a number of the foregoing results to an interesting area in the philosophy of religion, fideism, which has been central in discussions of belief and the will in the past.

# 1

## Belief, knowledge, and norm

It is a philosophical commonplace that belief is conceptually tied to truth. In believing that $p$ A takes $p$ to be true. The taking of $p$ to be true is distinct from whether $p$ is desired or feared or admired or whatever.

### BELIEF AND ITS STRENGTHS

Taking $p$ to be true can have varying degrees of strength. Sometimes philosophers and others have attempted to offer a measure of that strength in terms of the odds that the putative believer would be willing to take on $p$'s truth. But it does not follow that because a person is willing to take odds on a proposition's being true that the proposition is strongly believed. There may be propositions which a person is prepared to take odds on to which only minimal assent is given. At a more theoretical level, degrees of belief in $p$ can be separated from expected utilities if $p$ is true, so that betting can play a more convincing role as an index of the strength of a belief (Ramsey, 1990; Mellor, 1971). L. J. Cohen defends the view that a belief is a disposition to feel, and hence denies that it is like a disposition to bet (Cohen, 1992, pp. 5–6).

In 'Consciousness and Degrees of Belief' (Mellor, 1980) Mellor argues that taking odds is what he calls a case of assent, having a belief about a belief. Gambling may measure or express such assent, and beliefs about beliefs are no doubt fallible, though often reliable. I might be mistaken about the strength of my belief, which might be better evidenced in action. Belief, as opposed to preparedness to bet, shows itself in a variety of ways, depending upon the sort of belief it is. It may show itself in action or in a willingness to believe other propositions connected with what is believed or, as Cohen claims, as a distinctive feeling. So, while preparedness to bet may be a sufficient sign of the strength of a belief, it is not necessary.

The idea of beliefs having strengths basically implies that the belief to some degree that $p$ does not exclude belief to some degree that not-$p$. With respect to a large numbers of inconsistent empirical propositions we each believe them to some positive degree. The question 'Do you believe that $p$?' is often rightly taken to be equivalent to 'Do you overall believe that $p$?', 'Do you believe $p$ more strongly than $q$?' A person's array of beliefs is in a state of continuous and potential flux.

But what is it to believe a proposition, or to take it to be true? One prominent answer, offered by Swinburne (Swinburne, 1981) is: A person believes $p$ when $p$ is found to be more probable than not-$p$. This is unsatisfactory in that it prevents by fiat any believings against the evidence or where evidence is positive but weak. A person may recognise that air-travel is the safest way to get from A to B and yet believe that she ought not to travel by air. A person who is brainwashed into believing that the Aryans are the master race is not a contradiction in terms. There are multitudes of hunches, guesses, and opinions held in which the holder has not considered the question of the probability of what is believed. So, even if Swinburne's view is acceptable as an account of rational belief, it is not a good account of belief *simpliciter*. In the same way, a person may believe $p$ to a degree, but believe $q$ more. Joe may believe overall that his honey will win the prize, but also believe that it is more likely that Fred's honey will win than Bill's will.

Swinburne claims (Swinburne, 1981, p. 5) that anything with a probability greater than one-half is belief-worthy. But surely this is too low. Suppose that there are slightly more colonies of bees that swarm each year than do not. Nevertheless, if Joe knew this it would be unwarranted for Joe to believe that his hive will swarm.

Is Swinburne offering the connection between belief and probability as a conceptual thesis or not? Is it analytic for him that belief is tied to probability? He says 'Normally, to believe that $p$ is to believe that $p$ is more probable than not-p' (Swinburne, 1981, p. 4). This suggests that it is not an analytic claim, as does his later remark (Swinburne, 1981, p. 5) that the rules for the application of the concept of belief are not sufficiently precise. Then he goes on to express an analytic thesis about belief, but what is analytic is that belief that *p* is the belief that *p* is more probable than not, not that it must be significantly more probable than not. If so it must be possible to believe that *p* without believing that *p* is more probable than not-*p*; perhaps because the probabilities have not been considered. This is not to say that it is possible to believe that *p* when *p* is taken to be *im*probable, though some have argued this.

So if it is not analytic, what are Swinburne's arguments? His only argument is that if a person does not believe that *p* is probable, he cannot believe that *p* is true (Swinburne, 1981, p. 4). Is such impossibility causal or logical? Swinburne suggests that in order to have the concept of belief I must have mastery of some of the concept of probability. But a child may believe what its mother says because it knows no different. A person may have a reason for thinking that probability does not apply to what is believed; for example, the belief that there are other minds.

Another case is where a person simultaneously believes *p* and not-*p* (which is not equivalent to believing both *p* and not-*p*.) Such a person is in two minds; he half-believes *p* and he half-believes that not-*p*.

Thus there are degrees of belief, and believing is a more diverse phenomenon than philosophers such as Swinburne argue.

In a book which aims to show a philosophically interesting and important connection between belief and the will it may be thought important that any account of belief should avoid stressing the part that evidence may play in the holding of a belief; and also that the dispositional aspects of belief should be downplayed. However, in the sort of relationship between belief and the will that is to be proposed, neither of these points matters a great deal.

It has been widely thought that the fact that a person possesses grounds for his belief, evidence of a certain sort, say, inevitably reduces the scope that the will plays in belief. For the evidence, or what is taken to be evidence, invariably constrains the will so that given that A takes there to be preponderance of grounds for *p* (whatever those grounds may be) A cannot believe another proposition incompatible with *p*. (On some accounts, A's taking it that there is more reason for *p*'s being true than for *q*'s being true just is A's believing that *p*.)

However, the forthcoming argument about belief-policies, and hence for the place of the will in belief, does not depend upon there being a relative absence of evidence for the belief in question.

13

As we have noted, widely differing accounts of the nature of belief have been given. On some accounts a belief is a disposition to behave where speech in included in behaviour, on others a disposition to feel. It may seem that a voluntaristic account of believing should favour a non-dispositional account of what a belief is, since it may seem natural to argue that the more dispositional the account of belief the less place is left for the will. It is obvious that while a single act of believing may (without begging any questions) be subject to the will in a ready and straightforward sense, there is less place for the will in the modifying of dispositions. So a thesis which stresses the place of the will in belief must also play down the dispositional aspects of belief.

The argument to follow does not depend upon treating belief as an occurrence and not as a disposition. To see this we need only compare believing with a typical action. Since actions are certainly subject to the will, what is true of actions should, if beliefs are subject to the will, be true of them also. Actions which are habitual or are in other ways the outcome of dispositions may be as intentional as single episodes. Further, the will may have a role in altering such actions via the long-term modification of the dispositions of which a particular action is an expression. In the same way the will may have a role in the modification of the dispositions which particular believings presuppose and express.

A parallel argument may be mounted against a behavioural analysis of belief. I happen to think that any behaviourist analysis of belief is mistaken. But even if such an analysis were correct it would not rule out a positive account of the place of the will in belief, since behaviour can, in appropriate circumstances, be modified by the will. It may be thought that a behaviourist account of belief would be more congruent with recognising a place for the will in the formation of belief.

Belief or believing is a basic concept, irreducible to any other, a simple idea of the mind. In the face of difficulties with any such account certain philosophers have resorted to analogies to provide an understanding of the concept. For example, Peter Geach proposes that believing should be understood on analogy with saying that. From the point of view of relations between belief and the will there can be no objection to such an analogy. After all, saying is an action that it makes perfect sense to suppose is affected by the will. But the analogy can only be an analogy, as it is perfectly possible to say that $p$ without believing that $p$.

Cohen makes a sharp distinction between belief and what he calls acceptance, 'a policy of mental action' (Cohen, 1992, p. 12). At first sight, it looks as if the voluntaristic aspect of acceptance would help my thesis. But, according to Cohen, acceptance is a hypothetical, contractual phenomenon, which has the following features. Acceptance, unlike belief, is active rather than passive, it is linguistically formulatable, it is not available to non-human animals, and it is a matter of degree (Cohen, 1992, pp. 15-16). Acceptance may lead to belief (Cohen, 1992, p.18).

Cohen has identified an important conceptual distinction. But it is not clear that belief lacks all the features Cohen claims for acceptance, nor that what are often taken to be the voluntaristic aspects of belief can be fully accounted for by Cohen's notion of acceptance. In his endeavour to make the distinction between belief and acceptance as sharp as possible Cohen has neglected the extent to which our beliefs, as well as our acceptances, are revisable by procedures in which the will figures prominently. So that, for example, on my view belief-desire explanations of action do not necessarily treat people as animals or infants, despite Cohen's claim (Cohen, 1992, p. 49), since the intervention of a belief-policy introduces reflection and responsibility which his account of belief excludes. Having belief-policies by means of which earlier beliefs are corrected is a distinctively human trait, because of the degree of self-awareness, and the use of language, that it involves. It is partly for this reason that I think that Cohen is incorrect in supposing that one cannot systematise one's beliefs (Cohen, 1992, p. 105). A perceived inconsistency, if it flouts a belief-policy (as it is likely to do) is a reason for dropping or modifying one of the beliefs in question

On some accounts, Plato's for example, knowledge is wholly distinct from belief, because the sort of thing that is known cannot be the sort of thing that is believed. Knowledge treats of unchanging essences, belief of shifting appearances. On other accounts, most of those that are currently favoured, for example, knowledge and belief can both be of the same thing. Knowledge involves belief, but more than belief: it involves evidence or grounds or reasons, whatever produces justification.

Not just any propositional attitude which falls short of being justified and true is, for our purposes, a belief. People may speculate as to whether $p$ is true, or have an idle hunch that it is; or they may accept (in Cohen's sense) that *p* or when asked, express the opinion that it is true. In all such cases the propositional attitude may be said to be conceptually related to truth, and so such cases may be said to qualify as *bona fide* cases of belief. In the same way the expression 'wish that' may be said to be conceptually related to truth in that if A wishes that *p* then he wishes that *p* is the case, is true. Yet a person may wish that bees did not sting while knowing (and so believing) full well that they do. Obviously so, for typically we wish for things that we believe are not true and which may never be true. What applies to 'wish' applies also to other propositional attitudes such as 'hope', 'wonder whether', 'consider', and 'forget'.

The connection between belief and the will is only worth discussing in the case of those beliefs which have some significant degree of conviction attaching to them. Otherwise, if 'belief' embraces whimsical and off-hand beliefs there is going to be a prima facie case for saying that the will is involved in such believing, correspondingly little to argue about, and little that is of philosophical interest. The more challenging and interesting objective is to take cases where the will is not prima facie involved, and then to show that, despite these appearances, there is a significant sense in which it is involved.

The remainder of this chapter has the limited aim of starting to map out such a more fruitful approach to the issue of belief and the will by considering the normativity of belief. If it makes sense to appraise only those aspects of human behaviour which are, in some significant sense, under our control, and if belief (or believing) can be appraised, then this provides a reason for thinking that belief is, in a significant sense, subject to the will. The remainder of the book will be devoted to exploring what that sense is.

So what is meant by the claim that belief is subject to the will is no more or less what is meant by saying that actions are subject to the will, i.e. that it is possible for choice to affect what is believed in the same way as choice may affect what is done. Though the manner in which choice affects belief may be different from the way in which it affects action.

### BELIEF AND APPRAISAL

If the idea that all bees die in the winter is incredible, this means not that such an idea cannot be believed, but that it ought not to be. It cannot mean the first, because some people do believe it. They believe it, but they ought not to. Such people are gullible, they believe things which they ought not to believe. They may have reasons for believing that all bees die in the winter, but these reasons are not good reasons, for the idea that all bees die in the winter is not worthy of belief. Anyone who sincerely maintains it is holding a belief for which there is no justification.

What is interesting about the use of such expressions – incredible, gullible, having good reasons, being justified – is that they are all terms of appraisal. They express or presuppose standards of some kind or other. If there are positive ways in which knowledge, belief, and such normative matters are related, this may be because believing is often an action, as eating and drinking are actions.

This normativity is at the heart of rationality, of the idea of having reasons for belief, of debating what a person should believe, whether he should abandon a belief, and so forth. The reasons which give rise to a belief may be causal, but they are also justificatory.

Let us suppose, with the tradition, that if a person knows that the bees are about to swarm then it follows as a matter of logic, or is a conceptual truth, that the bees are about to swarm. Some other conditions are required for knowledge besides belief (and truth). These other conditions may be called 'evidence'. Furthermore, not just any amount or kind of evidence is sufficient for a true belief to be knowledge. There must be enough evidence, and the belief must be upon that evidence.

To suppose that there is, as a matter of fact, never sufficient evidence of the right kind is to be committed to some version of scepticism. To suppose that there never could be is to suppose a scepticism of a deeper, less eradicable (but perhaps for that reason more harmless) kind. We shall not make either supposition.

The philosophical debates about what constitutes evidence or sufficient evidence in the analysis of knowledge are debates about what is to count as knowledge. When someone knows something, he is not simply in a certain subjective state. This is true, with appropriate modifications, even where what is known is some truth about the knower's own state. To know that I am worried about the bees it is not sufficient to believe that I am, for I may believe mistakenly. I must also have certain evidence about myself. Otherwise self-deception would be impossible. Whatever the exact philosophical analysis of

17

knowledge ought to be, it is agreed on all hands that evidence and truth ought to figure in it. Knowledge is to be understood in terms of certain standards of evidence. Nothing that is knowledge could fail to meet these standards whatever the standards may be.

No one supposes that in the analysis of knowledge it does not matter what the standards of evidence are, that, say, a person knows $p$ if $p$ is true, he believes $p$, and $p$ was the first thing he thought of on waking up. What is wrong with this criterion of knowledge is that it is related to evidence in a purely accidental way. The critical debate about what constitutes knowledge is over what is to count as being in possession of that degree of evidence which, it is reckoned, is necessary in order for someone to know.

As we have already noted it is possible for human beings to believe almost anything. People have, from time to time, believed that it is possible to square the circle, that mental illness is caused by the influence of the moon, and that there are mermaids. Ungrounded and self-contradictory beliefs are no less entitled to be called beliefs than those that are well grounded, beliefs based on evidence and the appropriate investigative procedures. All are beliefs, for in all such cases the agent takes some proposition or set of propositions to be true. For a belief to be genuine, no standards of evidence have to be met, nor (more controversially perhaps) do those who believe have to believe that their belief meets certain standards, for the belief genuinely to be one. There are plenty of examples of self-consciously whimsical or capricious beliefs. A person may believe, against all the evidence, that the bees have not swarmed while realising that this belief is against all the evidence. It is no less a belief for being ill-supported.

If belief is compared with knowledge, what do we find? The ideas of irrational or ungrounded knowledge are conceptual oddities, themselves self-contradictory concepts, or perhaps expressions that embody category-mistakes. What could a case of ungrounded knowledge be, if we exclude possible but controversial cases of self-guaranteeing or self-evident propositions? To speak sensibly in this vein it is necessary to speak of irrational knowledge *claims*, self-contradictory knowledge *claims*, and the like. If some cognitive state is ill-grounded, then it can at best be a claim to knowledge, not knowledge. With belief there are three possibilities: the belief may be true, the belief may be false, or the belief may be merely a claimed, and not a genuine, belief. With knowledge there are only two

18

possibilities: either knowledge, or claimed knowledge. There cannot be false knowledge.

As we saw, certain hypotheses are regarded as belief-worthy, others as not. Certain reasons for a belief may be judged to be good reasons. These expressions introduce the fact that there are different standards of believing, and the appropriateness or otherwise of a particular standard. But it is not possible, in the same way, to raise the question of different standards of knowledge. To attempt to do this would, in effect, be to offer one or another analysis of knowledge. If the sceptic says that nothing that is possibly false can be known, he is not recommending a certain standard of knowledge, his remark has to do with a certain analysis of knowledge, with what knowledge is, what 'knowledge' means. The issue between the sceptic and his opponent is not over preferences about two sorts of knowledge, one strong and one weak, but about two rival, incompatible concepts of knowledge. If the sceptic is right about knowledge, then nothing else could count as knowledge. Whereas, if it is said that we ought only to believe what our senses tell us, and someone else denies this, the disagreement is not over the concept of belief, for both sorts of belief are regarded as being genuine cases of belief, but over the appropriateness of certain conditions for belief, of standards of acceptance for propositions.

It has been argued by Cohen, in support of the distinction between belief and acceptance (Cohen, 1992, p. 26) that, if these considerations about normativity support the idea that belief is subject to the will, then, by parity of reasoning, they support the view that emotions are subject to the will, and this is absurd. But is it? It is absurd to suppose that some token feeling of despondency could have had a different origin than it did, or that such feelings can be switched on and off at will. (What human states can be thus switched?) Even the overt manifestations of such feelings cannot unfailingly be switched off and on at will. But it is surely not absurd to suppose that a person might have a policy about feelings of jealousy, to try to quell or channel their occurrence, let alone their overt expression. Cohen allows that we can indirectly influence feelings, but claims that they are not any the less involuntary when they arise (Cohen, 1992, p. 27).

Let this be granted. Nevertheless, the concession is an important one. Bees sting, but it seems unnecessarily fatalistic to conclude that because bees sting one cannot prevent oneself being stung by a bee. For one can control one's exposure to bees. One can have a policy

19

about such exposure. And in a parallel way (I shall argue) one can have a policy about exposure to evidence or to whatever else causes belief. It is the fact that we all believe in accordance with such tacitly held but revisable policies which provides a reason for the normativity of belief, as well as for the normativity of emotion and action.

These ways of marking the distinction between knowledge and belief provide one way into the web of issues that have to do with belief and the will, without it being necessary to make any direct claim about the place of the will in the formation of single beliefs. The difference between knowledge and belief, and the fact that there are rival standards for the believing of some proposition, or for the believing of some proposition to a greater degree, is an argument for the conclusion that there must be a sense in which at least some cases of believing are subject to the will in which no cases of knowing are.

So, although for the same person at the same time there can be beliefs of different strengths, some justified, some not, and yet all of them genuinely beliefs, this is not true for knowledge. There are not different kinds of knowledge where 'knowledge' is being used in the same sense. The only sense that can be attached to different kinds of knowledge is that of there being knowledge of different kinds of things – knowledge by acquaintance versus knowledge by description, perhaps, or knowledge of persons versus knowledge of things, or knowledge of arithmetic versus knowledge of astronomy. In such a sense, knowledge is clearly subject to the will. A person can decide that certain kinds of knowledge are more worthy of attention than others. The significance of such choices will be discussed later on.

What Norman Malcolm says (Malcolm, 1952) may appear to be a denial of this view. He distinguishes 'know' in the strong sense from 'know' in the weak sense, claiming that if a proposition is known in the strong sense then there can be no evidence in the future that would prove that a mistake had been made. 'Know' in the weak sense does not carry this implication.

Even if Malcolm is correct about this distinction, what he is drawing attention to is two strengths of truth-entailingness. He is not claiming that there is a sense of 'know' in which it is not conceptually tied to truth. In the strong sense, if Jones knows that $p$ then it is not possible that he is mistaken, while in the weak sense it is. But in both senses if Jones knows that $p$ then $p$ is true. Nevertheless, if knowledge requires belief, and all belief is normative, or contains an essential normative component, then to that extent knowledge is normative too.

There are philosophers who would not accept the analysis of knowledge given earlier, even to the extent of denying that if A knows that $p$, then $p$ is true. So in this sense there can be different and competing concepts of knowledge. How then does the situation about knowledge differ from that regarding belief? In this, that in the case of the different concepts of knowledge the different concepts are competing, while in the case of belief it cannot be denied that there are *bona fide* beliefs of different strengths and levels of credibility. The raw data of human cognitive activities are such that no account of belief that denied the fact that beliefs have such varied strengths and levels could survive.

However, I am not arguing that beliefs have strengths whereas knowledge does not. Rather, any belief of a given strength might itself be governed by different normative considerations. Two people may each believe $p$ with the same degree of strength, but have different reasons for doing so.

So whatever analysis of knowledge a philosopher is disposed to defend, it must also be recognised that there are beliefs fulfilling different standards. Yet it is not quite true to say that, while normative questions about what a person ought to believe can be raised, such questions can never be raised in connection with knowledge. For certain philosophers have explicitly raised these questions in attempting to construe the concept of knowledge as itself a normative concept. It is widely agreed that such attempts fail, but they are not without interest. They provide the first of several different possible ways in which it has seemed plausible to establish connections between epistemology and norms.

## BELIEF AS NORMATIVE

Can belief be defined or analysed in normative terms? This question raises two separate issues: the issue of whether a given proposition ought to be believed, or whether it is belief-worthy, or is warranted or justified, and the issue of whether or not a person's believing that proposition is warranted or justified. A proposition may be warranted, but a person not warranted in believing it because of not being in a position to appreciate or recognise the evidence in question. Joe may believe that his bees are about to swarm, and there may be evidence that they are, but Joe may believe that the bees are about to swarm not because of the evidence, but because he wants them to swarm.

Since a person's being warranted in believing *p* logically depends upon that proposition's being warranted, a consideration of propositional warrant is logically prior to a discussion of warrant for belief. So can propositional justification or warrant be analysed in normative terms? There are numerous difficulties with supposing that it can be. To start with, from the fact that a proposition is warranted it does not follow logically that it ought to be believed. The proposition that Joe's bees are about to swarm may be warranted, but perhaps Joe ought not to believe this, otherwise he will panic and suffer a heart attack. No obligations follow logically from facts, not even from facts about evidence. Alternatively, someone might say that a proposition *p*'s being justified is to be understood as: *p* serves some normative goal. But the same sorts of problems arise here as before, namely that there are normative considerations that may incline one to believe propositions that are unwarranted by the evidence.

Perhaps a translation of epistemic into normative terms may be approached from another direction, using the concept of an epistemic duty. It might be claimed that each of us has duties not only to each other, but also to truth and to evidence. Supposing there are such duties, what are they? To believe only propositions for which there is sufficient evidence? Might there be duties to believe justified propositions which are not recognised to be justified and which, if they were believed, would be being believed irrationally? Perhaps, as a last resort, epistemological notions could be analysed in terms of a person's duty to the truth. Could we say that what *p* is justified means is that A ought to believe *p* if A's only duty is to the truth? The central difficulty is this: if A's duty is only to the truth, and it is the case that a justified proposition may be false, then it does not follow that A ought to believe *p* if *p* is justified. So there are formidable difficulties in the way of analysing propositional warrant in normative terms. (Firth, 1956, 1959, 1978; Heidelberger, 1963).

## THE ETHICS OF BELIEF

Even if, as we have been arguing, there is no such thing as an ethic of belief in this sense, there may nevertheless be an ethic of belief in another sense or senses, and so an alternative way in which belief and the will are connected. For the example one may raise the question of what standards or norms are appropriate for belief. The ethics of belief is not now a proposal about what 'knowledge' or 'belief' mean, but an inquiry into the norms or standards which ought to govern believing.

Ought one to believe solely upon the basis of the evidence regarding the truth or falsity of the proposition under consideration? Or are there other kinds of considerations, non-evidential considerations, that may or must operate in the case of rational belief-formation? Are considerations about pain and pleasure, or about comfort and discomfort, or about being able to reckon with the world satisfactorily, relevant to whether or not one ought to believe a given proposition? Are there situations in which considerations about evidence are not only not sufficient to justify belief, but are not necessary either? Are there situations, in other words, where belief is justifiable by reference to non-evidential types of consideration?

Another related question has to do with the relation of evidence to belief. Granted, for the moment, that belief ought only to be upon evidence, there is the question of whether the degree of belief ought to be proportional to the evidence, or if it ought to bear some other relation to the evidence. And this in turn raises the question of how evidence is to be measured. How is a person ever in a position to know that there is more, or less, evidence for a proposition? Can evidence have degrees of strength, as beliefs can? How are degrees of strength of evidence to be measured?

The drawing of such a sharp distinction between belief and knowledge might be challenged on the grounds that philosophers cannot assume that there are cases of knowledge, but must establish on rational grounds that there are. One of the tasks in doing this is to provide a definition of knowledge which is rationally acceptable, to set rational epistemic standards that are necessary and sufficient for knowledge. What is knowledge is not given to us, handed down. It has to be forged by the rational intellect. So that in this sense philosophers do decide what is known, for they formulate or identify an acceptable concept of knowledge. Having established this, then what counts as an individual item of knowledge is in no sense up to them. It might further be argued that this is also the case with belief.

Even if the general point holds, it is not sufficient to produce an exact symmetry between belief and knowledge, because any concept of knowledge is going to be a distinct concept from that of belief. One condition of this distinctness is the truth-entailingness of knowledge, and it is the truth-entailingness of knowledge which ensures that what is knowledge is not up to us.

This objection makes a philosophical assumption that is by no means self-evident, that the way forward in epistemology is by the provision of a general theory, a general theory of knowledge and belief, which our ordinary expressions of knowledge and belief should then be judged in terms of. What else could be meant by saying that philosophers must establish a concept of knowledge on rational grounds? To attempt this is to adopt the strategy of the 'methodist', in R. M. Chisholm's terminology (Chisholm, 1982, p. 66). There is also the strategy of the 'particularist' to be set alongside it. The particularist does not begin with a general argument, laying down a universal criterion or test for knowledge, but with an appeal. That is, the particularist appeals to particular cases of knowledge, to things that we indubitably know, and begins from these to construct a general account of knowledge.

There are many things that quite obviously we do know to be true. If I report to you the things I now see and hear and feel – the chances are that my report will be correct. I will be telling you something I know. And so, too, if you report the things that you think you now see and hear and feel. To be sure, there are hallucinations and illusions. People often think they see or hear or feel things that in fact they do not see or hear or feel. But from this fact – that our senses do sometimes deceive us – it hardly follows that your senses and mine are deceiving you and me right now. One may say similar things about what we remember.                                        (Chisholm, 1982, p. 69)

Chisholm's remarks obviously raise far-reaching questions about the nature and programme of epistemology, but it is sufficient for present purposes to say that the claim that it is the philosopher's job to forge the concept of knowledge *de novo* is by no means obvious.

This sense of the phrase 'the ethics of belief' comes to the idea that there are theories about the part of evidence in belief, or belief-policies with regard to one's commitment to the truth of a proposition, and that the questions 'Which belief-policy ought I to adopt?' and 'Which theory of evidence ought I to choose?' are central epistemic questions.

24

This suggests a parallel between the questions 'On account of what ought a person to commit himself to the truth of $p$?' and 'On account of what ought a person to commit himself to the rightness of A?' where A is some action or policy. There is a parallel between epistemology and ethics, in that both have to do with standards. If this is so then presumably it is possible to raise similar sorts of questions about belief and its warrant as about action and its morality.

Just as it is possible to ask, in ethics, if there are situations in which, though A is not obligatory it is permitted, so one may ask: are there situations in which, though a person need not believe $p$ (i.e. there is no evidential epistemic warrant to do so) nevertheless he may believe that $p$? Or are all situations such that either a person must believe that $p$ or refrain from believing $p$? Again, one can ask, can there be situations in which the evidence for $p$ balances the evidence for not-$p$, and in which, therefore, the rational course is to suspend belief, situations in which, in this sense, there is epistemic indifference? (Compare the situation for the utilitarian in which two possible courses of action have equal utility.) And what of situations that are epistemically indifferent in another sense, in which there is no evidence either for $p$ or for not-$p$? Are there such situations? Or does every proposition have either decisive evidence for or against it, just as with some versions of utilitarianism, every prospective action has some utility or disutility rating? If there are such cases of indifference, what is the rational attitude to adopt towards them?

Are there irresoluble conflicts between evidence, just as there are on some views of what ethics is? (Van Fraassen, 1973) Or are all considerations about evidence to be placed on a linear scale? Is there always an answer to the question of what a person ought to believe with respect to $p$ as there is, on some views of ethics, to the question, What ought I to do? Are there, in epistemology, the equivalent to acts of supererogation in some ethical systems? What would they be? Is it sometimes better to believe that $p$ even though one has no obligation to do so, where obligation is understood in terms of epistemic warrant? Is believing in these situations any more than credulity? What is the relationship between evidence which warrants belief and other sorts of considerations such as the importance of the belief? Is the case of believing that $p$ when there is no evidence for $p$ but when believing will bring certain benefits similar to acting to bring about certain ends when the action involves flouting the evidence, for example, acting to bring about the happiness of a person, perhaps oneself, when doing so involves telling lies?

Suppose that there are epistemic obligations. Do we all have the same such obligations? Perhaps a person with certain ethical or social obligations also has corresponding epistemic obligations (or permissions); and perhaps a person may have epistemic obligations in some situations that he does not have in others.

All these examples presuppose that belief is an all-or-nothing affair. But it may not be. As we have seen, belief to a degree that $p$ does not exclude belief to a degree that not-$p$. Faced with three roads, a person may believe to a degree that A is the correct route to X, have some conviction that B is, and not believe to any degree that C is. Similarly, just as a belief that $p$ may not totally exclude a belief that not-$p$, so acting towards the fulfilment of a goal or end is not incompatible with having some alternative action in reserve for the achieving of that end.

Finally there are adverbial parallels between actions and beliefs. As one can find it impossible to perform an act, or do it with difficulty, or take a long time doing it, so one may find it impossible to believe, or difficult to do so, or one may find that coming to believe is a lengthy process.

### BELIEF AND ETHICS

These questions arise from considering the epistemology of believing in a parallel way to the way in which certain normative questions are considered. They are justified by the fact that both epistemology and ethics have to do with standards. But there is a question which brings us to a consideration of another sense of the phrase 'the ethics of belief', namely, are the issues about standards of belief not only parallel to issues about standards in ethics, but also themselves ethical standards? Is it possible to speak of the ethics of belief in precisely the same way in which we speak of the ethics of human action?

It is important to see that the answer to this question could be 'No'. There is a contingent connection between the issue of standards and the issue of ethics or of ethical standards. Beehives must meet certain standards to function effectively, but a good beehive is not a morally good beehive. Epistemology involves standards, as we have seen, and so (as I shall argue) involves the will, but this does not entail that epistemology is a branch of ethics. The two reasons for this, have to do

26

with morality and metaphysics. Someone might argue, on moral grounds, that epistemology cannot be a moral matter because all moral matters have to do directly with issues of pleasure and pain, or with human welfare in some other sense, or with the revealed will of God, and epistemology has to do with truth and evidence, which is not the same thing. For believing to be a moral matter, on this view, it would have to be shown that it had inevitably and invariably to do with pleasure and pain or human welfare, and that one could set oneself the policy of believing those things that maximise pleasure and minimise pain.

It might be claimed that even to raise the question in this way is to misunderstand or to do violence to the concept of belief. Even if it could plausibly be argued that to believe those propositions for which one has evidence is also to pursue the policy that in the long run maximises pleasure and minimises pain, nevertheless to contemplate believing a proposition not because the evidence favoured it, but because it met some other standard is to do violence to the concept of belief, which is conceptually tied to truth. But utilitarianism is not the only conceivable ethic, and an ethic of belief (in the full sense) might well accord with an ethic that maintained truth-telling as an absolute principle, or an ethic that was agent-centred rather than act-centred. Then it might be maintained that in order to tell the truth it is necessary to believe what is true as far as possible, or that certain epistemic policies are logically necessary for carrying certain moral principles into practice, or for fostering certain moral virtues.

The metaphysical objection is that for belief to be an ethical matter believing must be an action. But, it is objected, believing is not an action. It is not something people do, but something that is true of them, either a state, or an event in which the mind is passive. It would be sufficient to answer this objection to note that belief is under our control.

Suppose we reflect upon this objection by beginning with an intuitive notion of what an action is. Sneezing is typically not an action, whereas blowing one's nose is. And blowing one's nose is an action because it is something that is under one's control, and also because it involves voluntarily bringing about changes in the state of one's body and in the world.

Following a suggestion of Michael Stocker's (Stocker, 1982) it will be argued later that believing is more like an action than is usually thought. Can I write at will? Obviously not, for writing requires writing materials, and I may not possess these, or be able to possess them at will. Can I stop writing when I am writing? Sometimes. Can I write while I am tying my tie? Obviously not, no more than I can believe that today is Tuesday when I know that it is not. Are there situations when I cannot help writing, as there are times when I cannot help believing? There may well be, and these are not invariably pathological. Are there situations when I want to write, have the materials, and yet cannot write? Clearly there are, as there are situations where I want to believe that *p*, when I possess the evidence that would warrant believing *p*, and yet cannot bring myself to believe. And so on.

Such parallels do not demonstrate that believing is an action; nevertheless believing is perhaps more action-like than is usually conceded. More importantly, the parallels may suggest that, though belief is not typically directly subject to the will, it may be voluntary in less direct ways.

## THE SEARCH FOR EVIDENCE

There is a final ethical or normative dimension to belief-formation to which some attention ought to be paid. Evidence does not usually fall into our hands out of the sky. It has to be sought. If rational belief depends (in part or in whole) upon evidence, and evidence must be sought, how thorough ought the search to be if the belief is to be a responsible one? If, say, beliefs ought to be formed in the light of the evidence, then how persistent ought an inquirer to be in searching for evidence? Such a question cannot be sensibly answered without recognising that the question of the truth or otherwise of some propositions is a more momentous issue than the truth or falsity of others. Obviously enough, some matters are more important than others.

Whatever the precise answer to these questions ought to be, the will is going to be involved in forming the determination to search for evidence. (Compare: it is wrong to act against moral principles; or, it is wrong to act illegally. Both statements may prompt the reasonable retort; but how neglectful of the moral principles, or of the law, may a person be? Ignorance of the law may not, in the eyes of the law itself, exculpate; nevertheless as a matter of fact a general knowledge of the law may be acquired. Whatever degree of knowledge is desired the will is clearly enough going to be involved.)

Suppose the view was taken that in order for a belief to be rational not only must the evidence that is available to that person support it, but that before that person could rationally believe *p* all the evidence that bears on the truth of *p* must be consulted. Such a requirement is obviously too strong. Not only is there always going to be some truth relevant to the truth of *p* that remains unconsulted, in order for the requirement knowingly to be fulfilled the person in question must know that all the evidence consulted to date is all the evidence that there is, and this generates a vicious regress. The person needs to know what the evidence for 'All the evidence that I have consulted to date that bears on the truth of *p* is all the evidence that there is', and precisely the same problem will arise in this case.

Even if the point of logic could be circumvented, the fact that there will always be some further observation that could be carried out means that the suggested requirement is obviously too strong as it stands.

A more attractive suggestion is that, before a person's belief can count as rational, he must make a reasonable effort to include as many propositions as possible which bear on the truth of *p*. The trouble is not that this suggestion is too strong, but that it is too vague. For what is to count as a reasonable effort? Either this requirement is interpreted strictly, in which case it is impossible to fulfil it, and no one rationally believes anything, or it is interpreted loosely, and so provides no help.

Perhaps what is lacking is some kind of social 'control' upon the acquisition of knowledge, the sort of thing envisaged by Thomas Kuhn in his notion of a research tradition, normal science conducted in the light of some controlling paradigm. 'Reasonable' might then be interpreted as it is interpreted in the law, as being what is typically or usually done or expected, in this case by members of some social group, the group of scientists pursuing normal science. So that for the belief that *p* to be held reasonably by someone, that person must have made the effort to acquire evidence for or against *p* with that degree of vigour and rigour that is appropriate to one's cultural or scientific circle, and to one's obligations within that circle.

There seem to be problems with this also, however. The critical standards which prevail in a particular scientific circle may be low, or inadequate in some other way. In appealing to the standards of one's cultural circle there seems to be a danger of providing a sociological account of rationality, of equating the rational with the socially acceptable. Which is to prevail, the cultural circle of astronomers or of astrologers? A second difficulty is that such a criterion takes no account of the unusually gifted, lone, solitary genius, or the person unusually well placed, whose evidence may be different from that which is available to others, or from that which others appeal to. It would be unreasonable to suppose that such factors alone should rule out any belief acquired by such a person as dogmatic, irrational, or sceptical.

These difficulties might be avoided by strengthening the conditions for epistemic rationality so that they become not conditions about the sort of evidence that an inquirer ought to have but a condition about the inquirer's attitude to the evidence. And so it might be held that one is epistemically rational if one has good evidence for $p$ and if, in addition, one has good evidence for the belief that if one had all the evidence relevant to the belief-worthiness of $p$ it would still be rational to believe that $p$. An inquirer may not have direct access to all the evidence but may none the less have a rational belief about it.

The trouble with this final suggestion is that it is implausible to suppose that the inquirer could have a rational belief about the character of the total evidence that was arrived at independently of the evidence that he has for $p$. And, naturally enough, if there is good evidence for $p$, evidence which justifies the belief that $p$, then this in itself is evidence that if all the relevant evidence were available it would still be rational to believe that $p$. For how could there be a a reasonable judgement about all the evidence that was not based upon an assessment of the evidence that is available? Any appeal to the character of the relevant evidence as a whole seems to be superfluous.

What answers one gives to these questions also depends on whether one is taking a verificationist or falsificationist approach to epistemic justification. If the approach is falsificationist, or at least naively falsificationist, the inquirer's search needs to be extended no further than the discovery of a single counter-example. Similarly, perhaps, if one holds an anti-evidentialist ethic of belief of the kind that some have suggested can be found in some of the writings of Kierkegaard.

Difficulties arising over the degree of thoroughness of any epistemic inquiry also arise over its termination. Suppose that a person knows that $p$. Then $p$ is true. It follows that any evidence that may come to hand against the truth of $p$ must be misleading, since such evidence supports the falsity of something that is known to be true. If a person knows that *p*, therefore, ought not evidence against *p* to be disregarded? Or may it not be? But does this not lead in turn to what Chisholm has described as a 'kind of dogmatism and infallibilism that is inconsistent with the spirit of free inquiry'? (Chisholm, 1976, p. 116).

This objection seems fair, if the right to be sure is the right to be sure that *p* is reasonable, and not the right to be sure that *p* is true. But then an inquirer may have the right to be sure that *p* is true and not know that *p* is true. So it is reasonable to maintain that if the inquirer knows that *p* (where 'knows' entails the truth of what is known) then that person has the right to disregard all future evidence. But if knowing simply confers the right to consider *p* as reasonable, then the inquirer in such a position does not have the right to disregard all future evidence.

In support of Chisholm it may be argued that in addition to having good evidence for *p*, and *p*'s being true, for it to be rational for a person to disregard any future evidence that person must be entitled to believe that there are no truths that would undermine the belief. If one justifiably believes that there are not such defeating truths then it is permissible, though presumably not obligatory, to ignore the possibility of extra evidence coming to hand which would defeat the proposition in question.

There are problems with this. For one thing, it is not easy to see how an infinite regress can be avoided. For the additional condition that the inquirer must fulfil – that there are not truths which would undermine his belief – is itself something that the inquirer must believe. But if it is a necessary condition of believing some contingent truth *p* that one rationally believes some other contingent truth *q*, then this simply transfers the problem to the rational belief of *q*. To be consistent, for that person to believe the additional proposition there must, on the analysis being offered, be a further proposition believed, and so on *ad infinitum*.

So it is not possible to provide a general answer to the question about thoroughness of inquiry. But the question is none the less an intelligible and an important one, and will be taken up in a slightly different connection in the later discussion, in chapter five.

# 2

## Belief and the will

Let us begin by distinguishing a strong from a weak sense in which belief is subject to the will. If A believes that *p* while knowing or believing that *p* is not evidentially warranted, then we shall say that A's belief involves an act of the will in the *strong* sense. One explanation for a belief in such circumstances might be that A wanted to believe that *p* and this want might, in turn, have one of a variety of explanations. For instance, believing that *p* makes him happy. Another explanation may be that A finds himself with a belief for which there could be no empirical evidence, for example, a metaphysical belief. Alternatively, A might find the evidence for *p* or not-*p* evenly balanced, and take the view that believing that *p* is permissible.

I will concentrate almost exclusively on beliefs about matters of fact, as opposed to moral or metaphysical beliefs, without forgetting that these classes of belief cannot always be clearly separated.

'Weak' belief, or minimal assent as I shall call it, covers a spectrum of cases. Suppose that A, a properly functioning person, comes to possess certain non-propositional evidence resulting in certain beliefs. For example, the presence of bright blue sky and bright light causes in A the belief that the sun is shining. What is minimal assent here? Simply whatever is involved in the recognition of the state of affairs described, involving sensory and conceptual application, and the intention to look. (If the evidence is regarded as propositional in character then minimal assent is the appropriate proposition functioning as a reason for immediately believing that the sun is shining. Immediately in the sense that no further reflection, or trains of reasoning, or further evidence, or the weighing up of alternative possibilities is necessary to cause the belief.) Perhaps outside interference with A's brain could cause such an immediate belief, but then the relevant evidence would not function as the reason why A believes that the sun is shining.

How does minimal assent differ from the occurrence of basic behavioural responses in non-human animals? In this, that while in each case evidence causes beliefs (if non-human animals have beliefs) human beings can become aware of their beliefs through language. So, though some evidence may be non-propositional in character (let us suppose) it can be given as a reason for belief.

Another case of minimal assent is as follows. If A believes that *p* because of the belief that *p* is evidentially warranted (whether or not such a belief is justified) then this involves an act of the will in minimal assent. For, given the sufficiency of the evidence for *p* in order to believe that *p*, A has to assent to *p*, upon that evidence.

It might be objected that in such cases A may not be able to help assenting, so that the will would not be involved, even in a weak sense. To this it could be replied that there is a distinction between possessing evidence and assenting, in that assenting involves the judgement; sufficiency of evidence does not psychologically force or compel assent; assent is given upon the evidence. Assent involves judgement. These replies might be adequate for certain cases, but not for all. There are momentary, manifestly involuntary beliefs. To take Cohen's example, under certain circumstances I cannot help believing that the car in front is going to crash (Cohen, 1992, p. 23). Would it not be absurd to say that the will plays any significant role in such a case? No, even in such cases the will is involved; compare the (admittedly unlikely) case of someone who sees all of the impending crash seen by his alert neighbour, but who at the time is day-dreaming.

Even where, like the car accident, belief seems forced, there are parallel situations where features of one's environment change so suddenly and unexpectedly that believing cannot keep pace. For every person who cannot help believing that an accident is occurring there is likely to be another who (as we say) cannot believe that the crash is occurring.

Even if this defence of minimal assent is unconvincing, I shall argue in due course that the fact that such beliefs are overwhelming, that no opportunity is afforded, or needed, to assess evidence by reference to belief-policies about evidence that a person holds, is no more an argument against the importance of such policies than reflex acts like blinking and blushing are evidence against the fact that we often weigh up alternative actions. Thus, *contra* Hume, and modern philosophers such as Swinburne (Swinburne, 1981, ch. 1) and Cohen (Cohen, 1992, ch. 1), not all belief is the natural effect of evidence impinging upon the senses and intellect.

<h2 style="text-align:center">REASONS AND CAUSES</h2>

At first sight it seems unlikely that the reasons why a person believes that $p$ can be the causes of that person believing $p$ because, typically, reasons are propositions and propositions cannot be causes. Joe believes that the queen-bee is dead because the worker bees are listless. What he believes – that the queen-bee is dead – is not an event, though it refers to a series of events, but a proposition. For causes are either states of a thing, or events that happen to a thing or that are initiated by it, and propositions are neither states nor events. Although the questions, what is a person's evidence for $p$? and, why does a person come to hold and retain the belief that $p$? are separate questions, they may be connected in that what a person believes (the particular propositions believed) may constitute for him the evidence on which another proposition comes to be believed. It is plausible to suppose that having evidence for $p$ is a reason for believing that $p$ and, following Davidson (Davidson, 1963) and others, it will henceforward be assumed that reasons are causes. So that, given real assent, having evidence of a certain strength might be causally sufficient for a belief.

To say that a belief is evidentially caused is to say that it is brought about by evidence alone (together with minimal assent). If evidence can be non-propositional, then it is the apprehension of the states of affairs themselves which is sufficient to bring about the belief; awareness of bright sunlight brings about the belief in an aware individual that the sun is shining. If evidence includes memory, or the testimony of someone else, then for a belief to be evidentially caused under such circumstances it has to be regarded as evidentially persuasive, and nothing (evidential or non-evidential in character) sufficiently dissuasive. As the reference to memory makes clear evidential causation may concern not only a person's evidence, but also whatever is mistakenly taken to be evidence, or whose strength is overestimated.

In considering causal accounts of belief, at least at this stage in the argument (an important qualification will be introduced shortly), attention is to be focussed upon the belief-states of the person, those beliefs that can form reasons for believing further propositions. The issue is whether or not belief is caused by evidence or supposed evidence alone, taking weak assent for granted. Is there a plausible alternative to such evidential determinism?

Are there belief-states which, together with the awareness of certain data and the ability to weakly assent to a proposition *p* upon those data, are causally sufficient for the production of the belief that *p*? If it can be shown that there are then it will follow with respect to that further belief that there is a perfectly familiar sense of 'will' in which that belief has not been willed, our strong sense. Whether the belief in question is evidentially determined depends upon how the weak assent is determined.

Showing that there are belief-states, which, together with the awareness of certain data and weak assent, evidentially determine further belief-states would not, of course, show that all belief-states are evidentially determined. In order to show this it would be necessary successfully to maintain that belief-states and weak assent, together with the awareness of certain data, are causally sufficient *and necessary* for the production of some further belief. If this could be shown then it would follow that no empirical belief could be subject to the will in the strong sense.

Cases of empirical beliefs being willed in the strong sense are clearly possible. Suppose a situation where the evidence for *p* and that for not-*p* is evenly balanced, but that a person must choose either *p* or not-*p*. Then it is coherent to suppose that that person is evidentially free with respect to *p* or not-*p*, though not free *simpliciter*. Given determinism, he is caused to believe by a set of circumstances, but not by evidential circumstances alone. It may be said that what is forced here is not the belief, but the action. No doubt this is a possible case. But it is overly dogmatic to say that this is what must happen in every case, that in all such cases action must run ahead of belief, which remains in a state of equilibrium.

When the evidence for *p* is equal in strength to the evidence for not-*p* the person could suspend judgement pending further evidence. Perhaps this ought to happen. But it is important to note here that such a claim is not self-evidently true; it is not obvious that the judgement ought to be suspended. Why may not the person opt for either *p* or not-*p* on non-evidential grounds? And in any case there are situations, made famous by William James, in which some belief or other is forced. Which course is followed in such circumstances seems to depend upon the operation of a policy for believing such propositions.

If a person has a belief-policy and believes that *p* in accordance with that policy, then he believes *p*, partly at least, because he wants to. Given the standards, the belief follows spontaneously, with no psychological compulsion. This is so even in cases where a person has standards which are accepted for good reason (as he judges), yet the standards are not those that he would want. Though he might be rather paranoid about the standards, yet given that he accepts them, belief follows spontaneously.

So if a person believes in accordance with what the evidence is taken to be, then he believes *p* partly as a result of wanting to. The belief is evidentially free in the compatibilist sense of freedom, evidentially spontaneous. Believing is satisfying a want of a certain sort based upon acceptance of certain standards of evidence. If beliefs are formed in accordance with a person's evidential standards or policies or mechanisms of belief-formation, then that person may be said to believe things as a result of wanting to, even though on occasion particular beliefs thus formed may be found to be in conflict with other wants for which evidence is not necessary.

So far we have considered the question of belief and the will as if it were a special case of a more general philosophical problem, that concerned with causation and free will. If believing that *p* is an action, like choosing honey instead of jam for breakfast, then the question of whether or not it is caused, and particularly whether or not it has been evidentially caused, can be raised, in the way in which a parallel non-evidential question about choosing honey can be raised, and answered in similar terms, with similar sets of considerations about the will being relevant. But there is more to be said.

When philosophers discuss the question of belief and the will they have in mind a set of issues besides those that dominate the free will–determinism issue. Such questions as: does evidence or apparent evidence, together with the power to weakly assent, determine the adoption of all beliefs, or can propositions be believed by an act of the will alone in the face of evidence or apparent evidence to the contrary? Behind these questions is the further assumption that evidence is something which cannot be chosen, only assented to or not.

## BELIEVING AT WILL?

Suppose that Joe believes himself to be surrounded by a swarm of bees and shortly afterwards feels a sharp jabbing sensation in his left forearm. Why could not this belief, together with the experience of jabbing, which is something which manifestly Joe has not willed, be causally sufficient together with weak assent for Joe to believe that he has been stung by a bee, assuming that he possesses the appropriate concepts? There are numerous instantaneously produced beliefs of this kind, beliefs about contingent matters of fact which are evidentially caused. The original beliefs, together with weak assent, are causally sufficient for the new belief, given Joe's continuing functioning as a cognitive agent with certain sensory and intellectual powers, and his experience of the jabbing. Perhaps Joe's belief that he has been stung by a bee has the following sufficient conditions:

  (i) Joe's initial belief state i.e. that he is surrounded by a crowd of bees;
  (ii) Joe's awareness of a jabbing sensation;
  (iii) Joe's thought that he has been stung by a bee;
  (iv) Joe's assenting to the evidence that he has been stung by a bee.

So there are plausible examples where a person may be said to have beliefs that have been evidentially caused by other beliefs, and the provisional conclusion can be drawn (with qualifications to come later) that in such cases there is an obvious sense in which belief is not subject to the will in the strong sense. Given that Joe has certain beliefs, that he continues to function as a cognitive agent, and that he assents to additional personal evidence, then he will acquire a further belief for which that evidence is the evidence. Of course one way in which Joe may fail to continue to function as a cognitive agent is by choosing not to.

Are there belief-states that are, together with minimal assent, causally sufficient *and necessary* for the production of some further particular belief? That is, are there beliefs such that they can as a matter of logic only arise by one particular causal route or recipe? If there are then not only are certain believings not subject to the will in the strong sense, but they could not be subject to the will, since for the production of such beliefs there could, as a matter of logic, only be one causal route.

It may be that there are such beliefs, but if so they will have a rather special character. In general it is not plausible to suppose that certain belief-states are causally both necessary and sufficient for the production of other beliefs. Take Joe's belief that he has been stung by a bee. This belief could have been produced by being stung by a nettle while believing that there are bees in the vicinity, or it could have been produced by being stung by a bee while believing that there are bees in the vicinity, or it could have been produced by being stung by a wasp . . . and so forth. Suppose that Joe's belief that he has been stung by a bee is true (while again leaving aside the question of whether or not it is a justified belief). What then? Can such a true belief have been causally produced in more than one way? Joe may have arrived at the correct belief that he has been stung by a bee by seeing the bee land on his forearm and feeling it sting him, or by seeing an insect which he did not know was a bee land on his forearm and sting him while being told by a reputable beekeeper that what had stung him was a bee, and so forth. So such true beliefs can be caused in more ways than one.

Perhaps this example suffers from being insufficiently specific. What about Joe's true belief that he has been stung by a newly flying Italian bee on the index finger of his left hand? Could such a specific true belief have more than one causal ancestry? Again, clearly it could. Joe could come to believe this by personal observation alone, or by a combination of observation and testimony, by seeing certain things happen while believing them, or by seeing certain things happen and being told authoritatively by someone else what was happening.

What about the matter of justification? Let us suppose that Joe has a justified true belief that a newly flying Italian bee has just stung him on the forefinger of his left hand. Could such justification arise in more than one way? Clearly, again, it could. Joe, knowing quite a bit about bees, might see the insect sting him. Alternatively, it could be that Joe, knowing little about bees, sees the insect sting him and is persuaded by someone else that it was a bee.

So the vast majority of beliefs can be produced in more than one way. Does this matter? Is this a weakness in the general case that many of our beliefs about matters of fact are not subject to the will in the strong sense? Surely not, for the following reason. By a previous argument it has already been established that if a belief is causally produced by personal evidence and minimal assent then that belief has not been brought about by an act of the will in the strong sense. To have shown that there are beliefs for which some belief-states are both causally sufficient and necessary would only strengthen this negative conclusion. In a sense, by establishing the weaker thesis we have established all that is necessary. For:

(1) This belief could have failed to have the causal ancestry that it in fact had

is perfectly consistent with

(2) All beliefs have some causal ancestry or other.

And it is some version of (2) that is needed in order to establish that a belief is not subject to the will in the strong sense.

It might be said that to establish (2) as true is of no positive epistemological interest, in that (2) could be true because some beliefs are due to auto-suggestion, and some other beliefs are due to self-hypnosis, and still other beliefs are due to wish-fulfilment, and so on. An argument about the causal efficacy of evidence is needed, it might be argued, in order to establish (2). For what is of interest is the place of the will in the beliefs people ought to have, and specifically the question of whether the awareness of evidence, together with minimal assent, exercises a causal role in the production of rational belief.

As was noted before, what is of concern is personal evidence. It is obvious that evidence that a person does not possess, and cannot come to possess at once, say, by looking directly in front, can be of no causal relevance in the production of rational belief, though a person's belief that it is impossible to possess any further evidence, or that certain crucial items of information are lacking, may be. So the question is whether a person's beliefs can be caused by the beliefs that that person already has. There is no reason to doubt that they can, if the conclusions of our previous discussions are correct. Take Joe again. He believes that he has been stung by a bee on the basis of believing that he has been stung and believing that there are bees in the vicinity. The two beliefs that, *ceteris paribus*, cause the belief that he has been stung, are both beliefs based upon Joe's evidence. So there is no reason to doubt that some beliefs are caused by beliefs about evidence, whether or not the beliefs turn out to be true or false.

There is a further problem, already briefly touched upon. Suppose that a person believes that *p* because *r* and *s* are already believed. Not all his beliefs can be caused in this way, for to suppose that they could would involve a regress. This is one aspect of the familiar regress of justification, couched in causal terms, on which foundationalist epistemologists trade. If this regress is to be avoided, then it must be allowed that there are beliefs which are not caused by other beliefs.

Even if it is allowed that there are beliefs, foundational beliefs, perhaps, which are not caused by other beliefs, this would hardly modify the place of the will in belief. It would have, at worst, a minimal consequence, for it is not likely that the will in the strong sense is more of a factor in such beliefs than in the less basic beliefs. It is likely to be much less so, for the following reason. Such basic or foundational beliefs are often regarded as being, if not self-evidently true, then unquestionably true. They are beliefs which occur upon having experiences which are sufficient for accepting the truth of propositions expressing them. If so, then in accepting such propositions there is the least possible scope for the will, nothing beyond minimal assent. The point about self-evident or unquestionably true propositions is that if a person gives his mind to the data they report then this is a sufficient condition for assenting to their truth.

If the will is to be involved in the formation of particular beliefs in any stronger sense it seems more likely that it will be involved during the operation of trains of inductive reasoning, and the collection of evidence, or in connection with propositions for which there is little evidence one way or the other, or with propositions with respect to which a person has a strong personal bias or interest in their being true rather than being false. By contrast, some of the formative accounts of self-evidence in modern philosophy stress the lack of the power of the will as a feature of such knowledge. In discussing what he calls 'intuitive knowledge', the knowledge of propositions such as white is not black, a circle is not a triangle, John Locke says

Such kind of truths the mind perceives at first sight of the *ideas* together, by bare *intuition*, without the intervention of any other idea; and this kind of knowledge is the clearest and most certain that human frailty is capable of. This part of knowledge is irresistible and, like bright sunshine, forces itself immediately to be perceived, as soon as ever the mind turns its view that way; and leaves no room for hesitation, doubt, or examination, but the mind is presently (i.e. at once) filled with the clear light of it.

(Locke, 1961, IV. II. 1.)

Locke goes on to say that in demonstrative proofs the evidence is not so clear and bright 'nor the assent so ready, as in intuitive knowledge'.

In the case of the knowledge of the external world, which Locke says comes only through sensation, though it is not so certain as intuitive knowledge, it nevertheless deserves to be called knowledge. Among the several reasons that Locke gives for this is the following:

*Sometimes I find that I cannot avoid the having those* ideas *produced in my mind.* For though, when my eyes are shut, or windows fast, I can at pleasure recall to my mind the *ideas* of *light*, or the *sun*, which former sensations had lodged in my memory: so I can at pleasure lay by that *idea*, and take into my view that of the *smell* of a rose, or *taste* of sugar. But, if I turn my eyes at noon towards the sun, I cannot avoid the *ideas* which the light or sun then produces in me. So that there is a manifest difference between the *ideas* laid up in my memory (over which, if they were there only, I should have constantly the same power to dispose of them and lay them by at pleasure) and those which force themselves upon me and I cannot avoid having. And therefore it must needs be some exterior cause and the brisk acting of some objects without me, whose efficacy I cannot resist, that produces those *ideas* in my mind, whether I will or no.

(Locke, 1961, IV. IX. 1.)

Locke, it is true, does not regard such beliefs as self-authenticating, otherwise he would not feel the need to defend their reliability. Nevertheless, it is significant that an important strand in his defence of the reliability of sensory beliefs has to do with the undeniability or irresistibility of certain of them, irresistible in the sense that the sensory awareness of a properly functioning cogniser, together with minimal assent, is causally sufficient for their immediate production.

### AN ANALOGY

So far in this chapter it has been argued that it is plausible to suppose that there are evidence conditions which a person may possess which are causally sufficient, together with minimal assent, for the production of certain of his beliefs. If so then the will has a minimal role in such belief-formation, being restricted to the directing of attention to relevant data, and to giving assent.

These points can be underscored by the use of an analogy that has been used more than once in recent epistemology, the analogy of a properly working thermometer (Armstrong, 1973, pp. 116-19). The state of the thermometer will causally depend upon the temperature of the environment in which it is placed. In the analogy, the thermometer's being in good working order is like a person being in a proper intellectual and sensory condition. The state of the mercury in the thermometer represents beliefs caused by the environment to which a person's intellectual and sensory state is subject. As the environment changes, so the thermometer's state changes, just as some of a person's beliefs change with changing circumstances.

This analogy can be extended. Suppose that the thermometer is fixed to a thermostat. Then the changing environment will, let us say, cause the mercury to descend in the thermometer which in turn will trigger off the thermostat, thus firing the central heating, and in turn raising the level of the mercury. This is rather like, in one given set of circumstances, one belief being causally sufficient for the production of another belief, the sort of case that was discussed earlier.

The possibility of malfunction in the thermometer is a reminder that it is possible not only to believe upon evidence, but also to believe upon what a person takes to be evidence, but which is not really evidence. A person may take something to be evidence through misinformation, or because of sensory and intellectual malfunction due to such things as amnesia, deafness or hallucination.

In belief there is an added complication, which takes us beyond the simple thermometer. It is possible for human beings to come to believe things not only by means of personal evidence, or as a result of some sensory or intellectual malfunctioning, but also because they want to, perhaps in order to compensate themselves for certain needs or inadequacies. A beekeeper may convince himself that it is not his bees that have swarmed, but his neighbour's.

The idea of a non-evidentially motivated belief is essential to phenomena such as wishful thinking, for wishful thinking is wishful believing. Unless one is going to hold that all cases of wishful thinking involve self-deception, then what such thinking shows is that it is incorrect to attempt to *define* belief in terms of evidence. Belief may be motivated by beliefs about what will follow if one does not believe.

Further, at a more theoretical and systematic level, it is often said that people believe certain things about themselves, and about the world around them, not because there is much, if any, evidence for the truth of these beliefs, nor because they are malfunctioning in any straightforward sense, but because they are spiritually sick. This is an important strand in both Christian theology and Marxist ideology, for example. Marxists say that the moral and social beliefs of capitalism, and the religious beliefs of many in capitalist societies, are not the product of evidence but are projections to compensate the individuals in question for the present deficiencies of their lives.

What is the test of one belief's being causally responsible for producing another belief? At first sight, it might seem that if the believer is aware of the first belief, then this is sufficient under appropriate circumstances for the believer actually believing on that account. Yet this will not do, for there are many cases where beliefs are undoubtedly causes of other beliefs, but where the person in question is not aware of those beliefs, and many cases where the believer is aware of certain evidence, but where the believing is not caused by the evidence but by other factors. For example, Agnes may believe that she ought to wear gloves while handling her bees because she believes that the bees may sting, without consciously being aware, on this occasion, that she believes that bees sting. The belief may be habitual, highly dispositional in character. Nevertheless, it would be true to say that she believes she ought to put her gloves on because she believes that the bees sting.

It might be said that what reveals the relevance of a belief to the causing of another belief is whether or not the person in question, if asked 'Do you believe that $q$ because you believe that $p$?' would say yes. Though the belief may not have been consciously considered before, yet, it might be thought, the question could reveal the relationship, and would reveal it if the person believed in the relationship, or recognised it for the first time consciously, when questioned.

But a Marxist, or a Freudian would regard such an account as a blatant begging of the question. And how could wish-fulfilment be accounted for on such a view? The fact that the person would himself assent to the view that such a believing is caused by another belief, does not necessarily reveal what the real causal link is. This is not a solution, it is merely a restatement of the problem, according to the Marxist. For the Marxist has, he thinks, a better explanation of why the person believes, an explanation in terms of the Marxist view of society and of social change.

The above account is oversimplified in several respects. No allowance has been made for factors such as forgetfulness. A person may not be able to recall or avow any reasons, when asked to do so. Yet this would not invalidate their efficacy. So a further condition covering possible forgetfulness would have to be inserted. Further, nothing has been said to cover cases where beliefs are caused partly by evidence and partly by non-rational causal factors. Perhaps rationalisations involve such mixed causes. Finally, no account has been taken of beliefs adopted not on the evidence, nor as rationalisations, but for pragmatic reasons, as in the account of belief offered by Meiland (Meiland, 1980).

A range of cases, from Marxist explanations of certain beliefs through less theoretical cases of wish-fulfilment and rationalisation to pragmatism, has now been introduced. How do such cases affect the matter of belief and the will? They do not affect it at all. The thesis is that in A believes that *p* because she believes that *q* or A believes *p* because she sees B, the 'because' is causal, and that if the relationship between these beliefs is causal then A's believing that *p* cannot be due to her will in the strong sense, but must be due to the operation of other factors. It is no part of our thesis to argue that whatever A believes that is not a basic belief is causally due to other beliefs. This may or may not be true. If some beliefs are caused but are not caused by other beliefs that a person holds, then this also has negative implications for the view that one might will to believe in the strong sense.

So it is plausible to suppose that some beliefs about matters of fact are caused by what the believer takes to be evidence, or by other beliefs which are in turn caused by what is taken to be evidence, in a way which does not allow them to be subject to the will. In addition it has been seen that the fact that there are cases of belief arising through wish-fulfilment, or through projections of the sort Marx mentions, or through other mechanisms or policies, does not constitute a reason for thinking that belief is due to the will. It is only a reason for thinking that not all belief is due to personal evidence, but has other causal explanations. From this it can be concluded that the idea that no evidential beliefs about matters of fact are subject to the will has some plausibility. And, even if the occurrence of wish-fulfilment is evidence that some believing is due to the will, such cases are of marginal interest to the epistemologist whose concern lies in determining whether more central cases of believing may be subject to the will in the strong sense.

DECIDING TO BELIEVE

Is it not possible to believe that *p* by an act of the will, simply because one wants to, or because one finds *p* an interesting proposition? Is it not possible to believe by an act of will in the strong sense?

There is something of a philosophical consensus against such a position. Swinburne and Cohen, for example, distinguish between belief, which is not subject to the will, and acceptance, which is. And Swinburne distinguishes believing *p* from taking *p* for granted; his argument for this is that what distinguishes belief is that 'if my belief existed as a result of my decision, I would be aware of my belief coming into existence immediately following my decision to believe' (Swinburne, 1973, p. 183). This assumes that all such decisions are conscious, and that any taking *p* for granted must come about as a result of such a conscious decision. Swinburne also argues that there is a conceptual difference between 'A believes *p*' and 'A takes *p* for granted' (Swinburne, 1973, p. 183) in that one cannot instantly choose to believe *p*. But then one cannot always instantly choose to take *p* for granted.

But there are cases of taking for granted which do not come about as a result of a decision, and which are, by Swinburne's argument, indistinguishable from belief. A person can be shown by argument, for example, to have been gratuitously taking a particular proposition for granted. What Swinburne needs in order to distinguish belief from acceptance is a condition which all beliefs have which no acceptances have. But belief and acceptance are such multiform, not to say Protean, concepts, that this condition appears to be unlikely to be fulfilled. For it is obvious (I take it) that there are many things each of us takes for granted without having decided to. Hence there are cases of taking for granted that lack the mark that should, according to Swinburne, distinguish belief from taking for granted. Hence,

45

whatever the differences between taking for granted and belief, the voluntariness of the former and the non-voluntariness of the latter is not among them.

Cohen recognises, as Swinburne does not, that the same proposition may be both believed and accepted. But what seems entirely absent from his account of belief and acceptance is the thought that beliefs can be valued, endorsed, assessed, strengthened or supported, as a matter of conscious, deliberate policy; in other words, in Cohen's own terminology, that beliefs can be accepted. Such features of belief would be perfectly consistent with Cohen's account of the onset of belief as something that is involuntary or non-voluntary in character.

One of the most influential discussions of this issue in recent philosophy is Bernard Williams' 'Deciding to Believe' (Williams, 1973). Dealing with straightforward factual beliefs Williams argues that, in the main, to suppose that one can decide to believe, just like that, is to misunderstand certain of the logical features of the notion of belief.

In talking of belief 'just like that' Williams does not distinguish the case of a person's deciding to believe *p* when already believing not-*p* from the case of deciding to believe *p* while knowing that not-*p*, or from the case of deciding to believe *p* when believing neither *p* nor not-*p*. Perhaps he thinks that these distinctions are of no importance, but it will be suggested later that such a thought would be too hasty. And, even if Williams succeeds in demonstrating the impossibility of believing 'just like that', he has not thereby shown the impotence of the will. Breaking the smoking habit may involve the will, even though a person cannot break the habit 'just like that'.

Hume maintains a very similar view to Williams', though one that is expressed in causal and psychological, rather than in conceptual, terms.

It follows, therefore, that the difference between fiction and belief lies in some sentiment or feeling, which is annexed to the latter, not to the former, and which depends not on the will, nor can be commanded at pleasure. It must be excited by nature, like all other sentiments; and must arise from the particular situation, in which the mind is placed at any particular juncture. Whenever any object is presented to the memory or senses, it immediately, by the force of custom, carries the imagination to conceive to it; and this conception is attended with a feeling or sentiment, different from the loose reveries of the fancy. In this consists the whole nature of belief.

(Hume, 1975, V. II. 39)

This is in accordance with what Hume wrote in the *Treatise*.

We can never be induced to believe any matter of fact except where its cause or its effect is present to us . . . The mind has the command over all its ideas, and can separate, write, mix and vary them, as it pleases; so that, if belief consisted merely in a new idea annexed to the conception, it would be in a man's power to believe what he pleased.     (Hume, 1911, Appendix)

The significance of the fact that Hume can also write of having the intention of proportioning belief to the evidence, of refusing to believe, and of being commanded to believe (Hume, 1975, X. 1) will, I hope, emerge later on.

Williams allows that one obvious connection between belief and the will, is that it is often open to people to decide whether or not to express a belief, to decide 'to use words to express or not to express what they believe. This is, however, a decision with regard to what is said and done; it is not the decision to believe something' (Williams, 1973, p. 147). This is far from saying that belief itself is open to human decision or subject in a direct way to the will.

Williams provides a number of arguments to support the view that belief is not directly subject to the will. The first appeals to the close connection between belief and truth. According to Williams, beliefs aim at truth.

When somebody believes something then he believes something which can be assessed as true or false, and his belief, in terms of the content of what he believes, is true or false. If a man recognises that what he has been believing is false, he thereby abandons the belief that he had . . . to believe that *p* is to believe that *p* is true.     (Williams, 1973, p. 137)

To say 'I believe that *p*' itself carries, in general, a claim that *p* is true. This is what Williams means when he said that belief aims at truth.

Jane Heal has pointed out that 'truth by itself has no motivating power at all' and that Williams' idea that beliefs aim at truth presupposes that judging, like any other goal-directed action, is something we do at will. It is her view that concern for truth is not itself a concern of action, but is an intrinsic feature of actions with other concerns (Heal, 1988, p. 100).

For the present, this much of what Williams says can be assumed to be correct; for a person sincerely to say 'I believe *p* and I recognise that *p* is false' is either to speak deliberate nonsense or to fail to recognise part of the conceptual structure of belief. Recognition of its falsity is perhaps logically sufficient for the cancelling of a belief, even though the person concerned may still want to believe the proposition. Agnes may want her hive to produce a surplus of honey this year, while recognising that it won't. But it does not follow that while the absence of evidence is sufficient for Agnes to abandon the belief, she will in fact abandon it, or that she can only adopt beliefs upon evidence. Quite apart from the weakness of will issue, the connection between belief and falsehood is stronger or more direct than the connection between belief and truth. Even if recognised falsehood is logically sufficient for the abandonment of a belief, a proposition may be adopted, for example as a working hypothesis, for which there is at present little evidence for the person adopting it. There is some evidence for it, and so it counts as a belief, but that evidence may at present be outweighed by evidence against, without totally obliterating the evidence for.

The fact that belief has degrees is another reason for wondering whether the will is as impotent as Williams claims, and whether the distinction between belief and acceptance is as hard and fast as Swinburne and Cohen maintain. A weak belief has some of the features of acceptance.

The second, and perhaps chief, argument that Williams offers against deciding to believe is that believing is passive. His argument is that this passivity is a necessary and not a contingent feature of believing, a fact closely connected with the matter just discussed, that believing aims at truth.

It is not a contingent fact that I cannot bring it about, just like that, that I believe something, as it is a contingent fact that I cannot bring it about, just like that, that I'm blushing. Why is this? One reason is connected with the characteristic of beliefs that they aim at truth. If I could acquire a belief at will, I could acquire it whether it was true or not; moreover, I would know that I could acquire it whether it was true or not.     (Williams, 1973, p. 148)

This argument is a powerful one. What Williams is drawing our attention to here is that if a person could acquire a belief at will, that belief could be acquired without regard to the truth or otherwise of the proposition. If it were possible to believe just any proposition at will this would involve being able to control what was true by an act of the will, by willing away whatever supported the belief in the first place, whatever made it true. No doubt there are propositions the truth or falsity of which we have no attitude to, and which may for that reason be subject to the will. But these are at best very marginal cases. For example, there may be propositions the evidence for and against which is precisely evenly balanced. Or propositions which we have absolutely no reason to regard as more likely than not.

But, because the vast majority of our beliefs have some evidence in their favour, and have other beliefs with which they cohere, it is extremely implausible to think of choosing to believe the negations of such propositions, just like that. But the more peripheral the belief in relation to a person's other beliefs, and the less evidence for or against it that the proposition in question has, the more plausible it is to find a significant role for the will in the formation of belief. But then such propositions are, almost by definition, less interesting and important than those which we have overall evidence for or evidence against.

Perhaps it is plausible to suppose that beliefs can be chosen in inverse proportion to the evidence that the person believing them has, and to their coherence with other beliefs, and in direct proportion to the desire for the truth of the proposition (Potts, 1971). So the most plausible situation for believing a proposition $p$, 'just like that' is where

    (i) there is no more evidence for $p$ than against it
    (ii) the belief that $p$ is not believed to be required by other beliefs, and not ruled out by other beliefs

and

    (iii) where a person has a non-evidential motive for believing $p$.

Where a person has a non-evidential motive or reason for believing $p$, and if motives or reasons are causes, then the belief that $p$ will be caused. Even though this would not be a counter-example to the view that believings are caused, it would be a counter-example to the rule that all believings are evidentially caused. But even if this possibility is cogent it provides only a marginal qualification to Williams' contention about belief and the will.

## ROUND ABOUT BELIEFS

There are certain plausible ways in which a person might, over a longer period of time than is implied by the phrase 'just like that' bring it about that he believes *p* by adopting evidence-irrelevant methods. For example, a person can come to believe that a proposition is true by frequently repeating that proposition to himself as an incantation. In such a situation a person must want to believe the proposition, and the wanting must be unconnected with his recognition of certain evidence. There is no shortage of actual examples of such attempts to believe. Many will be strongly inclined to say that people ought not to want to believe under such circumstances and perhaps they are correct, but such verdicts presuppose that such believings are possible.

In addition to such crude attempts to believe there are cases that involve a person acting as if he already believed. In fact there is a whole spectrum of such cases, from incantation to behaving as people do who believe the proposition in the hope that belief will catch up with behaviour. A notable example of a thinker advocating such a course of action is Blaise Pascal. Following a statement of the Wager Argument for God's existence in the *Pensées*, Pascal considers the case of someone who says 'Something holds me back, for I am so made that I cannot believe. What would you have me do?' This is a situation, according to Pascal, in which a person is intellectually convinced of an argument, the wager, but cannot bring himself actually to believe it, actually to gamble. Pascal's advice is

> Endeavour, therefore, to gain conviction, not by an increase of divine proofs, but by the diminution of your passions. You wish to come to faith, but do not know the way. You wish to cure yourself of unbelief, and you ask for remedies. Learn from those who have been hampered like you, and who now stake all their possessions. These are the people who know the road that you wish to follow; they are cured of the disease of which you wish to be cured. Follow the way by which they began: by behaving as if they believed, by taking holy water, by having masses said etc. This will bring you to belief in the natural way, and soothe your mind.                  (Pascal, 1961, p. 158)

Pascal seems to be offering two sorts of advice. One sort concerns the diminution of the passions. We shall consider this shortly. The other is advice to behave like people who already believe. Pascal is not supposing that such behaviour will provide reasons not already possessed by the seeker, because he is supposing a situation in which

50

the person already has sufficient reason, the Wager Argument. Rather he believes that such a course of action will enable the person to appreciate that evidence in a fresh way.

In addition to such evidence-irrelevant ways of gaining belief there are, more importantly for our purposes, evidence-relevant ways. For example, though Agnes cannot at first believe that the queen bee lays unfertilised eggs which develop into drones, she may nevertheless come to believe this by listening to what beekeepers and bee-experts say or by looking at diagrams of bee anatomy. She may say that she wants very much to believe this, or that she would find having to believe such a thing objectionable. Agnes' wants in the matter are irrelevant. But by attending to relevant evidence over a period of time she may come to believe that drones are genetically identical to their mothers. Conversely, by neglecting to keep evidence in mind, or to assimilate fresh evidence, she may come not to believe what she formerly believed.

Finally, there is the case already mentioned when discussing Pascal, in which a person undergoes a regime designed to enable him to disregard irrational fears and desires, fears and desires that are not based upon reason or evidence. Pascal thought that the belief that there is no God is a belief that is irrational in this sense. A less momentous case would be that of someone who believed, against all the evidence, that bees invariably sting when they are handled and who for this reason was mortally afraid of them. Such a person might be persuaded over a period of time to observe and handle bees and so to come to see that such fears were irrational.

Many more cases could be given of people undergoing courses of action designed to produce belief. The activities involved, incanting, taking holy water, acting as if, considering evidence, are actions that involve the will, but which go beyond that minimal act that is involved in giving assent to a proposition for which a person already has sufficient evidence.

To say that the will is involved in such cases is not to say that one or more act of the will would be causally sufficient for the production of the belief. So if it is objected that such examples do not show that belief is due to the will in this strong sense then the point may be granted. It is being argued that the will is involved in a way that is causally necessary (though not causally sufficient) to such a degree that a person may, in such cases, be said to make themselves believe that *p*

– the will is involved to a greater degree than merely giving assent to evidence.

In his discussion of 'the application of decision to belief by more roundabout routes' (Williams, 1973, p.149) Williams discusses in the first place the case of someone who, by a course of action unconnected with truth, by an evidence-irrelevant way, gains the belief that *p*. He allows that such a case is possible. (Of course the two are not quite the same in that a person may seek to gain the truth because of a motive for the truth without being concerned about the evidence, or without being concerned about gaining the truth through evidence. Truth-centredness is not equivalent to evidence-centredness.) However, in the case of a person who has the conscious project of believing what he wants to believe, Williams holds that if such a person has a truth-centred motive then he could only bring himself to believe what he wanted to believe in a way that involved self-deception. This means, presumably, that he could only bring himself to believe what he wanted to believe with this motive if he deceived himself into thinking that what he wanted to be true and what was true inevitably coincided. But the issue is not quite as simple as Williams claims. He says

The man with this sort of motive [i.e. truth-centred] cannot conceivably consciously adopt this project (of getting a hypnotist to make him believe), and we can immediately see why the project for him is incoherent. For what he wants is something about the world, something about his son, namely, that he be alive, and he knows perfectly well that no amount of drugs, hypnotism and so on applied to himself is going to bring that about.
(Williams, 1973, p. 150)

There are at least two different things that such a person may do which may fairly be said to be an inducing of belief, neither of which is radically incoherent. A person may concentrate on the bare possibility that his son is alive to the exclusion of all else. For though the preponderance of the evidence is that his son is dead, his son may still be alive. For example, his son could have been mysteriously abducted, or be alive and be suffering from some breakdown, and so forth. A person may have a truth-centred motive, and while not resorting to a hypnotist may nevertheless, by concentrating on such bare possibilities, endeavour to bring it about that he believes that his son is alive, simply because he wants it to be true that he is alive and the evidence is consistent with the bare possibility that he is.

While the person with the truth-centred motive wants something about the world, namely that his son be alive, he may recognise that the most that he will get is some evidence for that proposition. While he may know that no amount of drugging and hypnotism is going to bring it about that his son is alive if his son is not alive, he may nevertheless hold the view that participating in certain causal regimes will bring it about that he has evidence for his son's being alive.

Even if what Williams says is granted in full, however, it only touches – as it was only intended to touch – the cases of evidence-relevant inducings of belief. The will can still be involved in a stronger sense than minimal assent in bringing it about that a person believes that *p*. This idea, that though one cannot decide to believe, just like that, nevertheless one may 'set oneself' to believe over a longer period, has been emphasised by several philosophers, notably by H. H. Price in his paper 'Belief and Will'.

Beliefs can be gradually cultivated, though they cannot be instantaneously produced, or abolished, at will. They can also be preserved when one is in danger of losing them. Doubts or inclinations to disbelieve, occasioned by adverse evidence, cannot be abolished instantaneously by a mere feat of will here and now. But we have it in our power to weaken our doubts little by little, until at last they fade away and are felt no longer.

(Price, 1954, p. 17; see also Price, 1969)

In an effort to get to like someone, a person may come to notice and emphasise their commendable features, and neglect or redescribe those that are less attractive. A person's interests may select or filter the evidence available. Someone who was previously regarded as a know-all may come to be regarded as an expert (Heil, 1983a;1983b). Whether this capacity to set oneself to believe is of wider philosophical significance is something to be examined later on.

There is an even more basic sense in which a person's beliefs are subject to the will. Each of us has, at any time, an epistemic endowment consisting of sets of beliefs and dispositions for acquiring more beliefs. The question can arise as to whether a person's particular endowment is appropriate. Perhaps it has been wrongly shaped or formed. Here we are focussing upon the place of the will in the modification of a person's belief-generating mechanisms.

It is reasonable to conclude that while believing that $p$ is not subject to the will, in a direct sense, it may be in a variety of indirect senses. In claiming in the *Meditations* that all error is due to the will Descartes was manifestly mistaken, but it is plausible to suppose that some error is due to the will, and perhaps even more plausible to suppose that some particular kinds of error are due to the will. These remarks will be developed in succeeding chapters.

### BELIEF AND ACTION

So there are circumstances in which believing may be subject to the will. Whether it has all the features of action is, however, another matter. Yet action itself may not be entirely voluntary, and for similar reasons to those which qualify the voluntariness of belief. Nevertheless, believing may be sufficiently voluntary to support the idea of there being epistemic acts or attitudes which fit into a wider voluntary framework.

Whether or not belief is itself an action, it certainly has many action-like features. For example, belief, like action, is subject to degrees of constraint and voluntariness. There are rational and irrational forms of each. Many desires to act are constrained or frustrated by what an agent is already doing, and likewise with belief. A person can decide to concentrate on particular kinds of activity, and favour acquiring certain beliefs. The carrying out of actions, as the acquiring of beliefs, can be goal-directed. As we shall see in chapter six, it is also possible to argue that believing, like action, is afflicted by weakness of will and self-deception.

If believing has some features in common with action, then it makes sense to raise the question: is believing subject to weakness of will as actions are? Can a person see that it is reasonable to assent to $p$, or that the preponderance of the evidence favours $p$, or that in some other sense $p$ ought to be believed, and yet not believe $p$ solely as a result of a failure of will (and not because, for example, it is suspected that there is other evidence which counterbalances the evidence he already possesses)? Surely the fact that this is an intelligible question is an additional argument for believing having action-like elements.

A person may believe that $p$ without having consciously and separately thought about $p$. It might be thought that such cases cast doubt on the account being offered, in that no occasion has occurred on which the individual has found not-*p* more acceptable than *p*. But this is based on a serious misunderstanding. The account of belief and the will being offered is not intended to be psychological, one in terms of the successive states of human consciousness, but in terms of truth-conditions, truth-conditions that may hold whether or not a person is aware that they hold.

If believing shares important features with action, are there other epistemic conditions which do the same? Two important ones are the act of withholding assent from *p*, or the act of suspending judgement with respect to *p* (Chisholm, 1982, p. 8). These can be defined in terms of the notion of belief just considered. A withholds belief from *p* if, having considered *p*, A neither believes *p* nor believes not-*p*. Then there is the epistemic act or attitude of displaying indifference with respect to either *p* or not-*p*, when neither *p* nor not-*p* is more reasonable than the other. How does displaying indifference with respect to *p* differ from withholding belief from *p*? In this, that withholding of belief with respect to *p* may be for other reasons than an equilibrium of evidence.

Deliberating with respect to *p*, entertaining *p*, and conjecturing that *p* are also action-like. But these are of less philosophical interest than those considered.

In addition to separate epistemic acts, as we noted earlier, there are degrees of belief. While the fact that belief has degrees has significant consequences for the concept of belief, the options that we shall be more concerned with in what follows are not over whether or not to believe, or how strongly to believe, but over choices between belief-policies. Though we shall not be stressing the fact, it ought to be borne in mind that two people may each believe the same proposition with different degrees of strength because they have different belief-policies.

SUMMARY

In this chapter two extreme positions have been considered. According to one, believings are caused by other beliefs or by sensations or other direct evidence, real or imagined. In such an account of believings, while people believe for reasons, the will has no place except in the minimal sense. It has been argued that there is a good deal of plausibility in this general view of believing, even though the standard arguments for it are not altogether compelling. We have recognised that the other extreme position, that a person might choose to believe *p* while knowing or believing that not-*p*, is unconvincing.

So, despite Descartes' views about error and the will, belief is not in any direct and straightforward way subject to the will and is in this respect not like many actions. It makes little sense to suppose that a person might decide to believe 'just like that' whatever came into his head to believe. For a person to decide to believe every third proposition is irrational in a way in which kicking every third stone is not. The second activity is arbitrary, and perhaps pointless, but it shows no conceptual misunderstanding, as would the proposal to believe every third proposition. Between these two extreme positions Price and others have argued for a further role for the will in the adoption of beliefs than mere assent to evidence. Because one cannot decide to believe that *p*, just like that, it does not follow that the will has no part to play in the directing of the attention, in neglecting and concentrating upon certain kinds of evidence and so forth.

But it would be radically to misconceive the role of the will to suppose that all it does is to provide a certain kind of slackness or arbitrariness, creating epistemic situations in which evidence together with minimal assent does not causally suffice to bring about belief. It is plausible to suppose that in those situations where a person believes upon insufficient evidence then the will plays a significant role in enabling that person to plump for one of a series of alternatives. Yet these cases of irrational belief, cases of rationalising and wish-fulfilment, for example, are of marginal interest to the epistemologist, who is primarily concerned with the nature of the justification of belief, not with its absence.

In what follows it will be argued that the will is involved in the formation of rational beliefs at a more important level than any so far discussed, in the selection of what I have called belief-policies. (On the idea of a belief-policy in a related sense see Brandt (1985), and Braithwaite (1950)).

Two sorts of general questions can be asked about our beliefs: What degree and kind of evidence ought a person to possess before believing *p* or withholding belief from *p*? And, are evidential considerations alone relevant to believing? When Hume said, famously, that the wise man proportions his belief to the evidence he was, in one brief *dictum*, offering answers to these two questions. He was saying that belief is proportional to evidence and that only evidence matters. And he was making a recommendation, the recommendation of a particular policy. He was not describing what in fact happens in every case of belief, nor what is a necessary truth about belief, but laying down what, in his view, a man ought to do if he would be wise. Hume is attributing some degree of power to the will despite his view that the will is passive in the formation of belief. It is to these questions of epistemic policy, and the ethics or economics of belief that they engender, that the next chapters are devoted.

# 3

# *The idea of a belief-policy*

In this chapter I wish to develop the idea of a belief-policy as the chief vehicle for choice in belief, and argue that belief-policies are inevitable – we all have them – and that replacement and modification of belief-policies in the interests of greater rationality is one of the chief focusses of the will in belief. Belief-policies are what epistemologists typically argue about in discussing epistemic rationality (as we shall see in more detail in the next chapter). As a consequence belief-policies are of far more significance than is the question of whether or not we can choose to believe, just like that, or choose to believe by more round about routes. We choose to believe by choosing, or choosing to retain, belief-policies for acquiring, retaining, or discarding our beliefs.

The idea of a belief-policy has been briefly foreshadowed in chapter two. As I shall use the expression a belief-policy is a strategy or project or programme for accepting, rejecting or suspending judgement as to the truth of propositions in accordance with a set of evidential norms. An evidential norm may include reference to both the presence and absence of evidence. Such a policy may be dispositional and tacit, or the result of an overt choice. The policy (or policies) each of us grows up with is an example of a tacitly held policy, though it may become explicit. The deliberate adoption of a belief-policy on the grounds that an earlier belief-policy was unsatisfactory in some respect, is an example of the second. What is crucial (as far as the issue of belief and the will is concerned) is that the acceptance of a belief-policy about a matter of fact cannot be a matter of evidence (or its absence) alone and therefore may be as voluntary and free as any human action (on a compatibilist view of freedom) is. A person's overall noetic structure may accommodate more than one belief-policy.

How does the idea of a belief-policy connect with rationality in believing? In two ways. Each person's belief-policy is the embodiment of a theory of rationality or of rational belief for that person, though, in view of the plasticity of the term 'rationality' this is not to say a great deal. Secondly, in view of the strongly if not wholly voluntaristic nature of belief-policies, while considerations can be adduced in favour or against each such policy, there can be no rationally compelling second-order argument for the superiority of one policy over all others, though there can be fairly compelling arguments for the superiority of one belief-policy over *some* others.

In order to establish the importance of a belief-policy it might be sufficient to point out, in a G. E. Moore-like way, that we all do form our beliefs in the light of such policies, which are continually being regulated by reference to factors such as acquaintance with new and different types of evidence, the recognition of cognitive limitations, and the detection of errors in reasoning. An attempt will be made to argue for such a conclusion, and to try to establish two other matters; that there are readily discernible limits to the belief-policies one may adopt, and that belief-policies may be classified into certain types. Finally I shall return to the question of the extent to which, since a belief-policy is not adopted or rejected on evidence, but rather contributes to determining what good evidence is for the person whose policy it is, it may for that reason be said to depend upon the will.

## PERSONAL JUSTIFICATION

Those grounds which actually evidentially justify a person in adopting or retaining a particular belief may be called the personal justification of that belief. In so far as believing can be regarded as an action, and assuming that the only factors relevant to the taking of the action are evidential factors, then this sense of justification justifies the taking of the action. So long as a person is not afflicted by weakness of will, a justified belief is one that will be adopted or retained by a rational person on those grounds. By contrast an ideal evidential justification is one that would justify a belief by evidential considerations that are not available to the person at the time the belief is adopted, and which perhaps only God or some other ideally placed observer would be in a position to verify. Roderick Firth characterises an ideal observer as one 'who is omniscient and impartial, influenced only by those features in a situation relevant for the justifying of a belief. Omniscience may entail impartiality' (Firth, 1956). Compare Feldman (1988). In ideal justification conditions of justification are required which are unfulfillable in a practical sense. No false proposition can ever be ideally justified, but many false propositions are personally justified. Ideal justification indicates that all the possible evidence regarding *p* would conclusively establish the truth-value of *p*, whereas in personal justification all the evidence is never available.

So one important distinction between these two kinds of justification is that personal justification is justification for a person at a time. Given a person's present stock of data, that person's own justification is that degree of evidence that justifies that person in believing certain propositions, rejecting others, and suspending judgement over the remainder. I shall argue that all personal justification is in fulfilment of one or more belief-policies, whether consciously adopted or recognised or not.

These two kinds of justification may in turn be contrasted with practical justification or practical cognitive decision-making. On these distinctions, see Goldman (1980) and Sosa (1980). Take as an example the case of a manager who has to decide what is likely to happen to the markets. She has to justify her belief that, say, the markets will fall, to her fellow-managers. In such a situation, her belief is constrained in all of the ways in which the person seeking a personal justification is constrained, and in addition by the 'costs' (not necessarily financial) and the differing importance of various alternative policies. The manager may need to act on the proposition even though the examination of the evidence is not as thorough as it would be in other circumstances.

The difference between the two might also be expressed in the following way. Suppose that the degree of belief in a proposition whose truth is unknown, but which will become known in the future is determined by the longest odds that a person would be prepared to take on the proposition. Then what crucially distinguishes practical cognitive decision-making from the personal justification of belief is that acceptable odds are a function not only of the likely truth of the proposition, but also of the desirability or otherwise of the outcome, including the consequences of coming to no decision by a certain time. A person may be prepared to take short odds on a proposition which is very unlikely to be true if its being true would be of great benefit, but long odds on an equally unlikely proposition whose truth would bring great evil. More will be said about importance in chapter five.

A rather similar distinction holds in ethical reasoning. There is ideal or objective ethical justification, the justification of an action that all things considered is the best of all alternatives. For a utilitarian this would be the action which is actually productive of the maximum happiness or satisfaction. For a deontologist it would be that action which in fact exemplifies some fundamental moral rule or principle. By contrast, a personal ethical justification is one that is made on the best estimates of the likely outcome of a series of alternatives, (or, for the deontologist, the best available judgement as to whether or not a proposed action exemplifies a basic moral principle). In addition there are ethical decisions made on incomplete data and constrained by time.

This distinction corresponds, in deontic ethics, to that between subjective and objective duty. A person may discharge his subjective duty, his conscience may be clear, and yet fail in his objective duty because there are factors which, objectively speaking, he ought to have taken into account and which he failed to do. We shall return to this issue when discussing the choice of belief-policies in chapter five.

### RECOMMENDING BELIEFS

In his paper 'Belief and Will' Price says

> If you are in a reasonable frame of mind (as we are assuming that you are in this case) you cannot help preferring the proposition which the evidence favours, much as you may wish you could, I mean, you cannot help preferring the proposition which *your* evidence favours, the evidence *you* are at the moment attending to, though the evidence which other people have may of course be different . . . It just is not in your power to avoid assenting to the proposition which the evidence (your evidence) favours, or to assent instead to some other proposition when the evidence (your evidence) is manifestly unfavourable to it.                          (Price, 1954, p. 16)

Let us abbreviate Price's claim to the following proposition: A reasonable person must believe what his evidence favours. What does Price mean here by 'his evidence'? He appears to mean what we have called personal evidence. So Price is claiming a strong connection between the belief that $p$ and the personal evidence for $p$.

Price says that one cannot help preferring the proposition which one's evidence favours. As he also says 'preferring' denotes something which involves an act of the will, the giving of assent, though this is a gift which he thinks, in the circumstances he describes, cannot be withheld. In saying that there are certain situations in which one cannot help assenting to a particular proposition, Price seems not to be allowing for the possibility of weakness of will, for situations in which though a person's evidence favours a particular proposition he cannot bring himself to believe it. Discussion of weakness of will in the accepting of certain propositions will be deferred until chapter six.

What sort of an expression is *A reasonable person must believe what his evidence favours*? It may seem, at first sight, as if Price is treating it as a contingent truth, claiming that, while reasonable people do in fact believe what their evidence favours, and cannot as a matter of psychological fact avoid doing so, it is logically possible to suppose them not doing so. He may also be suggesting that though a person cannot choose to believe against the evidence in the short term, it is possible to do so in the longer term. Price means by choosing to believe in the longer term a choice that follows a course of action as a result of which more and different evidence becomes available. To choose to believe *p* rather than *q* is to choose to gain evidence which will make believing *p* rather than *q* more likely or inevitable. Choosing to believe is not choosing to believe against the evidence, but choosing to gain other evidence, thus bringing about a different justified belief.

Another reason for thinking that the principle might express a contingent truth is that Price writes of preferences. It is often said that a person is not able to help preferring *x* to *y* when what is meant is that a person has a very great preference for *x* over *y*. Although Agnes could eat her bread with jam on it rather than honey, she so likes honey in preference to jam that she cannot help asking for honey. In any situation in which there is only jam and honey available, Agnes cannot envisage herself preferring jam. Nevertheless, it is conceivable that her preferences may change and she may come to like them about equally. Is Price saying that though the reasonable person's preferences are such that the proposition which the evidence favours must be preferred, nevertheless a time might come when this is not so? Hardly. For if he were saying this, then he would have to be prepared to say that there might, for all he knows, be some reasonable people who prefer propositions which their evidence does not favour, and this would go against the very thing that he is insisting upon. The same argument tells against the proposition being understood as a general truth about the actual preferrings of reasonable people.

The obvious alternative is to take the expression to be a necessary truth, as equivalent to *Necessarily, a reasonable person believes what the evidence favours*. Let us suppose that this is what Price intends. What reason is there to accept this and not, for example, *A reasonable person may sometimes believe a proposition that is not favoured by the evidence*? Or, *It is sometimes reasonable for a person to withhold assent from a proposition which the evidence favours*? Price might say that it is part of what it means to be reasonable that such a person cannot help preferring the proposition which the evidence favours. In fact Price stresses this: 'If you are in a reasonable frame of mind (as we are assuming that you are in this case) . . . '. Is this plausible? To start with, 'reasonable' is a notoriously slippery word, a philosopher's nose of wax, which prima facie is unlikely to yield any firm and generally acceptable conceptual truths. There are many examples of reasonableness which link it not to the inevitable acceptance of evidence, but to reflecting upon and reconsidering evidence, and so not accepting it inevitably. Thus Bernard Williams:

That there is such an activity (viz. withholding of the assent) is indisputable, and that there should be something like it is surely a precondition of there being any self-critical thought at all. Just to ask of some familiar pattern of thought, 'but does it follow?';not to jump to conclusions; and so forth – all these are examples of the 'withholding of assent'. (Williams, 1978, p.179)

For every philosopher who links reasonableness (conceptually) with the acceptance of evidence there is likely to be another one who, like Williams, links it also with self-criticism and intellectual and cognitive reflectiveness.

Alternatively, it might be argued that Price's proposition expresses a necessary truth because of what 'evidence' means. Then what Price is saying is that evidence for $p$ is whatever causes a reasonable person to assent to $p$ with that degree of strength that the evidence warrants. But is this any more plausible? In the first place Price leaves it unclear what is meant by evidence. Does he mean empirical evidence, the immediate evidence of the senses? Many reasonable people have adopted an attitude of distrust towards the immediate evidence of their senses, and have discounted it in favour of the testimony of other people or of their reason. Does he mean evidence in some other sense? If Price's proposition is to be more than a tautology then some independent meaning has to be given to 'evidence'. It cannot be defined in terms of what warrants reasonable belief. It would not do, for example, to say that what is meant by evidence here is 'total evidence', i.e. the evidence of senses, testimony, memory, reason etc., since no one disputes that reasonable people must believe only those propositions which their total evidence favours. The problem lies in deciding what (in cases of conflict, for example) is the actual evidence that warrants belief.

Perhaps – it might be argued – Price is here reminding us of a commonplace, namely that a reasonable person believes in accordance with what her total evidence favours. The problem with this suggestion is that any such commonplace is very unclear.

So what is to be made of Price's claim? Viewed as a contingent truth it is somewhat dubious, while regarded as a necessary truth it is likewise not obviously true. I suggest that Price is not stating a truth, either necessary or contingent, about reasonable people, but is in effect saying: only those who believe only upon evidence are in my view reasonable. Or, 'If you want to be reasonable, strive to bring it about that you only believe what the evidence favours.' In this respect what Price says is parallel to Hume's *dictum* 'A wise man proportions his belief to the evidence.' Hume is saying that any man who does not conform his belief to the evidence (and he implies that, as a matter of fact, many do not) is not a wise man. To be wise, a man ought so to order his epistemic affairs as to proportion his belief to the evidence.

Such proposals as Hume's and Price's are neither true nor false, though they may be acceptable or unacceptable. Furthermore, because they are neither true nor false, because they are pieces of advice rather than pieces of information, they are not, in any straightforward sense, matters of belief. Such recommendations are contributions to what might be called second-order epistemology; they are not beliefs, they are not even beliefs about beliefs, but each is the recommendation of a belief-policy.

Such belief-policies provide one important avenue along which the will enters into belief. It may be that what such philosophers as Price, Swinburne and Williams say about the passivity of all beliefs, is only true of some beliefs, and that with respect to many other propositions people may believe them, or not, in accordance with their belief-policies about them. While beliefs are not a matter of choice, belief-policies are. And even those propositions which are accepted passively could become subject to the will through the acceptance of a new belief-policy. While, having accepted a policy, the will may then have no independent role to play in accepting or rejecting propositions, other than giving assent to a proposition upon that mix of evidence required for such propositions by the policy, the exercise of the will in a stronger sense than merely giving assent upon evidence may be involved in the adoption of any belief-policy. If so then the will is involved in the warranting of belief at a much more fundamental level than has so far been discussed.

So I am arguing that passivists such as Price do operate and recognise belief-policies, and in doing so give tacit recognition to the place of the will in belief. More will be said about this in chapter four. If the existence of belief-policies is granted, then it is up to the passivist evidentialist to show that they are the result of evidence in precisely the same way that, according to them, beliefs are the product of evidence. If this is so, how is one to account for differences between people who have the same evidence? No doubt, in some cases, by the influence of prejudice and indifference. But if some of these differences are due to the working of different belief-policies then such policies are not merely summaries of evidence, they have a normative and controlling role. Belief is no different from other matters where normative considerations enter, when it is a commonplace that different people may have different policies embodying different norms.

It might be objected that what I am calling belief-policies are ways in which belief is related to evidence in the more round about ways mentioned by philosophers such as Williams and Price; techniques rather than norms. But this would be to confuse ways of attaining goals with ways of choosing goals.

I am arguing that reference to at least one belief-policy is a necessary ingredient in the justification of A's belief that *p*. What entitles A to believe (on the evidence that he possesses, and to the degree that he does) is a matter of policy.

We do adopt belief-policies, and it makes sense to suppose that we may consciously choose to do so, as we shall see in more detail later. But it is not necessary to consciously adopt a belief-policy in order to have one. For as inquisitive cognitive agents we may each be said to grow up possessing such policies, formed by nature and early nurture. These furnish the array of standards with which each of us at an early age unselfconsciously views the world. They involve policies regarding the trusting of the senses, about the reliability of testimony, and about much more, such as the reliability of fundamental beliefs about the reality of the past and of other minds. Such a native-born credulity is frequently modified in the light of costly mistakes, costly in terms either of bodily pain or intellectual error or both.

Such 'basic' (historically or causally speaking) beliefs as each of us grows up with are *de facto* expressions of belief-policies. Such beliefs can also be modified or even (according to one kind of sceptic) they can be totally abandoned in the light of a person's later-developed belief-policies, and such later belief-policies need not be the outcome of evidence alone. Coming to possess a belief-policy is not passive in the way in which, according to passivists, coming to possess any belief is.

## CHOOSING BELIEF-POLICIES

If the adoption of belief-policies is not a matter of evidence, but is necessarily, in part at least, a matter of decision or choice, choice about how evidence is to be regarded, on what principles, if any, should a person decide whether or not to change his belief-policy? Are such policies a matter of arbitrary decision, or are there rational considerations, though perhaps not evidential considerations, that operate? Put another way, are such belief-policies akin to ethical or other normative principles, and if so how akin are they? Is this another area in which it makes sense to speak of an ethics of belief?

In discussing Price's remarks about the inevitability of assent upon evidence we alluded to the fact that evidence is a matter of degree. (This fact, incidentally, makes Price's account look even more unrealistic, in that the evidence may favour a proposition, but only very slightly. In which case, though the evidence favours that proposition it would be unrealistic to suppose that the person in question cannot help preferring that proposition, except in the tautologous sense already discussed.) If evidence is relevant to belief, and if evidence is a matter of degree, the question can naturally arise –

what amount of evidence is appropriate for what degree of belief? Hume's *dictum* does not by itself tell us what degree of evidence warrants what degree of belief. How are the two to be calibrated?

The crucial difference between the two cases, recommendations of beliefs and recommendations of belief-policies, is that in the case of recommendations of beliefs evidence is directly relevant. In the case of recommendations of belief-policies, though there may be *grounds* for making a recommendation, these grounds cannot be wholly evidential. (If they were, then we should be involved in a regress of a familiar kind, for if all the relation between believing and evidence is a matter of policy, and if all policies are based wholly upon evidence, then . . . ). Among the grounds for accepting a belief-policy might be the limitation of error, or the achievement of a certain kind of predictive success, or the maximising of true beliefs, or a willingness to take risks over truth.

A TAXONOMY OF BELIEF-POLICIES

If there are limits to the belief-policies which it is rational to adopt, how is that range to be established? I shall begin by proposing a simple classification or taxonomy of belief-policies. This is purely for expository purposes. No philosophical issue hangs upon it, and no doubt alternative classifications can be imagined. But such a taxonomy serves to give initial plausibility to the idea of there being numerous belief-policies to choose from.

We have made the point that belief is a matter of degree, as evidence is. And therefore it is possible to envisage different calibrations between degrees of belief and degrees of evidence; and perhaps between beliefs which have a threshold relation to evidence, and beliefs which do not (Mavrodes, 1982). So one needs a basic distinction in understanding belief-policies, between questions of source and questions of standard. Belief-policies can be distinguished by the kinds of considerations which count as evidence – sense-experience, memory, testimony, expert authority – and by the differing standards that a proposition or set of propositions must meet in order to be considered belief-worthy.

Building upon this distinction I shall propose a further distinction between belief-policies which are permissive and those which are mandatory. A mandatory belief-policy is one formulated in terms of a criterion or a set of criteria which are necessary and sufficient for the adoption of a rational belief. So it might be held that A's beliefs ought to be formed in accordance with the following Cartesian belief-policy: *believe only what is self-evident or what can be suitably derived from what is self-evident*; or with the conservative policy: *believe only what coheres with the beliefs one already has.* Behind the adoption of the first policy is the further conviction that a certain type of foundationalism was satisfactory as a theory of epistemic justification; behind the second is the assumption of a coherence theory of epistemic justification.

These are instances of belief-policies which are central to epistemological controversy. But many more belief-policies of the same logical type can be supposed. Anyone who was resolved to believe only what his mother-in-law said, or only what all true democrats believe, or what the Party enunciates, would also be adopting a mandatory belief-policy.

By contrast, a permissive belief-policy has the form: one may believe what is not C, where C is some criterion or test of rationality. One might believe what is not self-evident to the senses (or derived from what is self-evident to the senses) or not known to be logically self-contradictory or incoherent, perhaps on the grounds that nothing is self-evident to the senses, or that what is self-evident to the senses is crushingly restrictive in scope. Or a person might adopt the belief-policy of believing whatever he finds himself believing which is not forbidden as a belief by his mother-in-law, or by what all true democrats believe, or by what the Party enunciates.

It is possible to propose a further division into those belief-policies which are falsificationist in character and those which are verificationist. It has frequently been observed that there is a logical asymmetry between verification and falsification in that it is possible to conclusively falsify a universal proposition, but not to conclusively verify one. This difference does not extend to singular propositions. To falsify that Agnes keeps bees it is necessary to verify that she does not. And many of our beliefs, perhaps all of our beliefs outside science and metaphysics, have to do with beliefs about individuals and about restricted classes of things as opposed to beliefs about unrestricted classes of things. Furthermore, to falsify some genuine universal proposition, say, *all bees hibernate*, is to verify the truth of some singular proposition, for example, that *this bee has failed to hibernate*. These points of logic hold irrespective of the mode of verification or falsification, whether it is by means of sense-experience, or what mother-in-law says, or whatever. Nevertheless, the gains from adopting a falsificationist belief-policy may be thought to be considerable, in that it is not necessary to verify a universal proposition in order to be warranted in believing one.

An example of a falsificationist (though not a Popperian) ethic of belief is: *any belief that p that is stronger than a mere conjecture ought to be proportional (or to bear some other similar direct relationship) to the number and seriousness of failed efforts to falsify p.* More will be said later about the distinction between mandatory and permissive policies, and also that between verificationist and falsificationist policies.

So it is possible to distinguish belief-policies into those that are permissive and those that are mandatory, and into those that are verificationist and those that are falsificationist. These distinctions may be systematically combined. Someone who adopted the belief-policy of mandatory verificationism may be influenced by a philosophical position of a familiar type, for *only* those propositions the truth of which was verified by means of the criterion of verification would be believable; sense-experience, or what mother-in-law says, or whatever. All other propositions he would either suspend judgement over, or reject, depending upon what further belief-policy he adopted with respect to those propositions. Similarly a mandatory falsificationist would adopt the policy of believing only those propositions which have so far survived the fires of attempted falsification, falsification by sense-experience or by some other mode. A permissive verificationist would adopt the belief-policy of allowing himself to believe some propositions whose truth was verified. And likewise with permissive falsificationism.

### THE RETREAT TO COMMITMENT

Sometimes a person may have a belief-policy without realising it or without realising its full implications. Most of us are in this position as we grow up, adopting by example and testimony the belief-policies of our parents and mentors without being aware of, or critically reflecting upon, the fact. This can happen even in the case of a developed philosophical defence of some position in the theory of knowledge.

It is possible to see an instance of the adoption of a belief-policy almost unawares in William Warren Bartley's *The Retreat to Commitment* (Bartley, 1984). Bartley defends the position which he calls 'comprehensively critical rationalism' against foundationalist epistemologies such as those of classical rationalism and empiricism. The trouble with any such foundationalism, according to Bartley, is that it involves a 'retreat to commitment'; it relies upon a person's non-reasoned commitment to certain foundational truths, and thus has no answer to any irrationalist, such as Bartley believes the Christian to be, who may make irrationalism a form of basic commitment. This is what Bartley dubs 'the dilemma of ultimate commitment' (Bartley, 1984, p.72).

According to Bartley the rationalist (and any foundationalist) and the irrationalist are in the same logical boat. Bartley calls this the *tu quoque* argument:

(1) for certain logical reasons, rationality is so limited that everyone must make a dogmatic irrational commitment; (2) therefore, the Christian has a right to make whatever commitment he pleases; and (3) therefore, no one has a right to criticize him (or anyone else) for making such a commitment.

(Bartley, 1984, p. 72)

Such an argument, Bartley thinks, leads to an ultimate relativism, the relativism of diverse ultimate starting points, and to the pointlessness of argument, since any challenge to a position will quickly be seen to become powerless in the face of the ultimate commitments which each of us has. It follows that each and any standard is a matter of irrational choice.

In terms of our earlier taxonomy Bartley offers a mandatory falsificationist belief-policy. According to it one must form one's beliefs in accordance with what he calls the four checks – of logic, sense–observation, scientific theory, and the check of the problem – and these checks are, logically speaking, falsificationist in character, 'critical' in Bartley's terminology. It is Bartley's aim to defeat this *tu quoque* argument 'by showing that it is possible to choose in a non-arbitrary way among competing, mutually exclusive theories' (Bartley, 1984, p. 83).

Take classical rationalism, for example, 'pan rationalism', as Bartley calls it. It comprises two theses. The first is that any position which can be justified or established by rational argument is to be accepted, and the second is that only positions which can be justified or established by rational argument are to be accepted. 'The pan rationalist accepts anything that can be rationally justified, and also is ready to justify rationally anything that he accepts' (Bartley, 1984, p. 93).

Bartley shows that it is impossible to hold these two requirements simultaneously, because the acceptance of the second requires that the first requirement be justified by rational argument, and this cannot be achieved. And even if it could be achieved such an argument would only be convincing to someone who already accepted the need for justification, which is precisely the point at issue (Bartley, 1984, pp. 93–4).

Which of (1) and (2) ought to be rejected, since they are requirements that cannot be held compatibly? Bartley's response to this question is interesting. He says

Now there are several good reasons for rejecting the second requirement rather than the first. Since we are searching for an adequate rationalist identity, we shall hardly want to abandon the demand that the rationalist accept any position that can be rationally justified. Moreover, the second requirement can be shown by argument to be self-contradictory . . . The second requirement is self-contradictory because it, too, cannot be justified by appeal to the rational criteria or authorities.　　　　(Bartley, 1984, p. 95)

Bartley is here appealing to certain 'reasons', particularly to the claim that a person must accept any position that can be rationally justified, because this is part of the 'rationalist identity'. Bartley has convictions about a form of rationalism which he regards as superior to other positions, and he regards himself as needing to rehabilitate it in the light of the *tu quoque* argument.

Bartley is convinced of the need for what he calls *critical* rationalism. It is not sufficient to acknowledge, as he thinks Ayer and Popper do, that some basic matters cannot, as a matter of logic, be justified, that what sets the standards cannot itself, as a matter of logic, be subject to those standards (Bartley, 1984, p. 104). These acknowledgements, salutary though they are, are not by themselves sufficient, since they simply underline the 'fideism' of traditional rationalism, a fideism which goes back, Bartley thinks, to the historical fact that it offered itself as a rival authority to theology.

71

So Bartley makes a radical proposal, that, following and building upon the epistemology of Sir Karl Popper, the whole idea of epistemic justification should be abandoned.

*Nothing gets justified.* Instead of following the critical rationalists in replacing philosophical *justification* by philosophical *description*, we may urge the philosophical *criticism* of standards as the main task of the philosopher. *Nothing gets justified; everything gets criticized.* Instead of positing infallible intellectual authorities to justify and guarantee positions, one may build a philosophical program for counteracting intellectual error.    (Bartley, 1984, pp. 112–13)

This is 'pancritical rationalism', a position which is willing to hold positions, including this position itself, open to criticism, never cutting off argument by resorting to faith or irrational commitment to justify some belief (Bartley, 1984, p.118).

I shall try to show that Bartley's way of dealing with this cluster of issues, together with some of the arguments which he uses, serve to mask, perhaps from Bartley himself, that either what he is proposing is a purely formal or semantic position, the substitution of 'criticism' for 'justification', or that it is a substantive thesis which is at odds with the intention behind 'pancritical rationalism'. It is not that what Bartley says is incorrect, but that he himself has misconstrued its true character. He is offering a proposal or set of proposals about the formation of responsible beliefs, whereas he thinks he is providing a general argument for the superiority of pancritical rationalism to the critical rationalism of Ayer or to the classical rationalism of Descartes, both of which, he thinks, are forms of fideism.

This can be seen by looking at how Bartley deals with some obvious objections to his position. One objection he considers is that the whole idea of criticism itself presupposes standards, that it is logically impossible to criticise unless one has certain criteria in terms of which one mounts the criticism.

Bartley offers two answers to this difficulty. One is to say that the premises which the pancritical rationalist uses for the purpose of criticism (Bartley, 1984, p. 122), are those which are unproblematic at the present time, not those which are regarded (by an irrational commitment) as unproblematic in some logically privileged sense.

When one belief is subjected to criticism, many others, of course, have to be taken for granted – including those with which the criticism is being carried out. The latter are used as the basis of criticism not because they are

themselves justified or beyond criticism, but because they are *unproblematical at present*. These are, *in that sense alone and during that time alone*, beyond criticism.
(Bartley, 1984, p. 122)

The much-vaunted criticism of rationalism turns out to be a temporary affair. But it is open to anyone to claim to be critical in this sense, criticising other positions in the light of present beliefs. Could these beliefs accepted for the time being themselves be overturned? Bartley must acknowledge that they could, but only by using arguments based upon premises which are themselves only temporally local.

One major aim of Bartley's book is to put paid to the *tu quoque* argument. There is nothing in the previous paragraph which has the slightest impact upon that argument. There is nothing to stop a deep-dyed irrationalist taking up the position corresponding to that which Bartley himself takes up as a 'critical rationalist'. Such a person would not be a classical fideist or irrationalist, but then Bartley is not a classical rationalist, he is a 'critical rationalist', a 'pancritical rationalist'. Why could there not, for all that Bartley has shown to the contrary, be a pancritical fideist, or a pancritical irrationalist?

This is impossible, Bartley would say, because of the standards of criticism which the pancritical rationalist appeals to which the pancritical irrationalist does not and cannot appeal to and still remain a pancritical rationalist. As we have seen, Bartley refers to these standards as the four checks, the check of logic, of sense-observation, of scientific theory, and the check of the problem (Bartley, 1984, p. 127). Where do these means of eliminating error come from, and what status do they have? If they have a merely temporary status, in the sense just discussed, then the pancritical irrationalist need have no qualms. They prevail at present in the mind of the pancritical rationalist, but they cannot be justified, and they are destined to pass away.

Bartley might retort that his pancritical rationalism is superior to the irrationalist equivalent because it avoids the *tu quoque* argument whereas the irrationalist equivalent does not.

Consequently, the *tu quoque* argument cannot be used at all against pancritical rationalism. Theologians have argued that not only to abandon allegiance to Christ, but even to subject that allegiance to criticism, is to forsake

Christianity. But for the pancritical rationalist, continued subjection to criticism of his allegiance to rationality is explicitly part of his rationalism.

(Bartley, 1984, p. 120)

To be sure, to abandon logic is to abandon rationality as surely as to abandon Christ is to abandon Christianity. The two positions differ, however, in that the rationalist can, from his own rationalist point of view, consider and be moved by criticisms of logic and rationalism, whereas the Christian cannot, from his own Christian point of view, consider and be moved by criticisms of his Christian commitment. (Bartley, 1984, p. 134)

To comment on what Bartley takes to be the Christian position would take us too far afield, but it is necessary to say something about the asymmetry that he supposes to exist between his own critical position and that of what he takes to be an irrationalist alternative. Briefly, Bartley is claiming that he can criticise whereas the irrationalist cannot.

Such asymmetries only appear to hold because of an equivocation over 'criticism'. Sometimes 'criticism' is used substantively, as the critical application of the standards listed above, the four checks. At other times it is used in a purely formal sense, as criticism in the light of some standard or other, not necessarily the four checks.

If we suppose for the sake of argument that Bartley is correct in his characterisation of Christianity then the Christian theologians are objecting, in the first quotation given above, to the use of the four checks critically, not the use of any checks critically. In a precisely parallel way, the pancritical rationalist accepts not any criticism, but criticism in terms of the four checks. And similarly, in the second quotation just given, the two positions only differ because Bartley is not comparing like with like. He says that the rationalist can consider and be moved by criticism of logic and rationalism. Yet the rationalist will not be moved by just *any* criticisms of logic and rationalism. Suppose that someone said that logic was to be criticised because it is at odds with the Word of God. Would the critical rationalist be moved by such a criticism? Presumably not. Again, Bartley says that the Christian cannot, from the Christian point of view, consider and be moved by criticisms of a Christian commitment. Why not? The Christian (as described by Bartley) cannot be moved by criticisms based upon the four checks, but then critical rationalism cannot be moved by criticism based upon Christianity. And if critical rationalism can be moved by criticism based upon the four checks then the

Christian theologian can be moved by criticism based upon the Word of God. Far from being asymmetrical, provided that like is compared with like, the two cases are fully symmetrical.

This shows that Bartley is mistaken in thinking that he has established by some objectively valid argument the superiority of pancritical rationalism over pancritical irrationalism. There may be such an argument, but he has not produced it. And this failure indicates that what Bartley has done (as distinct from what he thinks he has done) is to recommend forcefully and eloquently one type of belief-policy – pancritical rationalism. This is not to say that it is impossible to argue between different belief-policies, but the arguments are going to be much more tentative, subtle, and provisional than the arguments Bartley has produced for showing the superiority of pancritical rationalism over all other belief-policies.

Thus in the work of at least one philosopher the fact that there are various belief-policies, and that these necessarily take the form of rival, incompatible recommendations, is not clearly seen, as is witnessed by Bartley's vain efforts to prove the superiority of 'pancritical rationalism' over various versions of irrationalism. Nor is the existence of the dilemma of ultimate commitment (Bartley, 1984, p. 140) a compelling argument for a falsificationist ethic of belief, since that dilemma (supposing it to be a dilemma) reappears in a slightly different guise in various pancritical approaches, rationalist and irrationalist.

Yet Bartley only half sees these matters. He proposes a policy of overall rationality, not just of epistemic rationality. Nevertheless the various 'strategies of criticism' which he mentions are in effect a belief-policy. Bartley advocates the policy: *believe only those propositions which you are willing to criticise in terms of the four checks*. He aims to show that it is possible to choose in a non-arbitrary way among competing mutually exclusive theories. Perhaps this is possible, but not by providing a proof that one is superior to all others.

The ill-success of Bartley's argument shows, I believe, that his criteria of the four checks function for him as a belief-policy. There is nothing self-evidently and exclusively rational about these criteria, nor are they determined solely by the evidence as Bartley sees it. Rather, Bartley is seen to have *chosen* or *committed himself* to these criteria on grounds that are not exclusively evidential. Bartley's use of these criteria reveals him to be what he regards as a fideist, albeit a fideist of a sophisticated kind. His idea that fideism can be squeezed out by applying the criteria is ill-judged; the Christian fideist can use parallel criteria to develop a pancritical fideism. Each set of criteria can be used to adjudge evidence while not being based upon evidence.

## SWINBURNE ON BELIEF

As we have already noted in discussing the nature of belief, Richard Swinburne comes close to defining belief in terms of probability, if he does not actually do so. This leads him, naturally enough, to discuss inductive standards. His discussion is relevant for us in that he recognises the existence of different standards of belief, different inductive standards; and he acknowledges the part played by non-evidential factors in the formation of beliefs.

To begin with, Swinburne recognises two distinct senses in which a belief and probability may be related. First (as noted in chapter one) he holds that to believe that $p$ is to believe that $p$ is more probable than not-$p$ (Swinburne, 1981, p.4). Secondly, to believe that $p$ is probable is to believe that $p$, even where $p$ is only marginally more probable than not. Swinburne treats the question of whether believing that $p$ is marginally more probable than not-$p$ is a case of believing that $p$ as a linguistic or semantic matter, a question of what usage is 'tidier' (Swinburne, 1981, p.5). But these two positions are not merely semantically different; they are substantively different belief-policies as is shown by the fact that people operating the two different principles will end up with two non-coincident sets of beliefs. And *pace* Swinburne there may be an argument to show there is some point between $\frac{1}{2}$ and 1 where it is more reasonable to talk of belief. Someone may argue that if a proposition is marginally more probable than not it may be believed; if it is substantially more probable than not, it must be believed.

If one belief-policy is to believe what is more probable than not, then Bayes' theorem is one way of formalising this; a formal method of decision between hypotheses which states that the probability of some hypothesis on evidence E and background knowledge B is a function of the prior probability of the hypothesis and its explanatory power. The actual use of the theorem depends upon giving a value to the hypothesis and this may, in turn, depend upon judgements which are not wholly evidentially and arithmetically based (Putnam, 1981, pp.189–93).

Besides these central affirmations about inductive standards, and therefore standards of belief-worthiness, at various places Swinburne commits himself to other standards. For example, 'One ought to believe what other people. tell one' (Swinburne, 1981, p. 196). Swinburne maintains that we have a duty to take seriously what our friends tell us is of great importance.

If Swinburne is a reductionist on the epistemology of testimony then we ought to believe what other people tell us because we have good reason for believing that what they will tell us is more likely to be true than false. But he may not be a reductivist. Despite his commitment to the involuntariness of belief, Swinburne recognises here that there are matters which one ought to believe; hence, if ought implies can, one can believe them, presumably by employing the more roundabout ways referred to by Bernard Williams, and by Swinburne himself.

The point of drawing attention to these different standards in Swinburne is not to argue that belief is subject to the will. For Swinburne might retort that these standards can be observed by attempting to conform one's believing to them over a greater period of time, by round about methods, and the like. The differing standards are in effect belief-policies, and, unless Swinburne is going to argue that each of these different standards is a different way of encoding the view that belief is only of what is probable, they signal the existence of different norms for believing.

There are other evidential standards to which Swinburne draws attention. For example,

A man's basic propositions may include not merely ordinary reports of things perceived and remembered but 'hunches' and 'intuitions' which he thinks are justified by the experiences to which he has been subjected but cannot justify in terms of propositions.                    (Swinburne, 1981, p. 22)

Again, it is possible to envisage clashes between what a hunch indicates is the case, and what the inductions of evidence point to.

A final example. Swinburne claims that it is possible to believe that *p* is just probable and to gamble on its falsity (Swinburne, 1981, p. 29). Gambling on the falsity of *p* looks like believing that *p* is true to a degree, say less than $\frac{1}{2}$; but then this suggests the possibility that a person might believe what is less probable than some alternative.

Occasionally Swinburne seems to be maintaining a contrary thesis, that at any one time one's inductive standards are held involuntarily, that they are based upon evidence in the way that one's beliefs are, and are as involuntary for the same reason. Certainly if I chose to alter my inductive standards for no reasons, then this would render them suspect even in my own eyes; none the less I might have a reason for changing them which was not based on evidence, as we shall see in a moment.

The purpose of mentioning these examples is not to offer a critique of them, but to show that there are different epistemic standards, and that this fact may force choices to be made between them

A multiplicity of standards provides the potential for a clash between them. What if, judged on the evidence that I myself have obtained, not-$p$ is more probable than $p$, but that someone else tells me that $p$ is true. What course of action am I to follow? To suspend judgement perhaps? To seek a revision of my principles?

So far we have identified different standards of the relation between evidence and belief. But in addition Swinburne recognises certain principles not derived or derivable from evidence which, according to him, are important in the rational formation of belief.

At various places Swinburne commits himself to various formulations of what he calls the principle of credulity.

> I suggest that it is a principle of rationality that (in the absence of special considerations) if it seems (epistemically) to a subject that x is present, then probably it is present; what one seems to perceive is probably so.
>
> (Swinburne, 1979, p. 254)

This is a principle of rationality which commends itself to Swinburne. No doubt there is much to be said for it. But the principle is not based upon evidence or probability, nor is it self-evidently true; it is a plausible principle in terms of which certain kinds of evidence ought to be assessed.

A second principle for the assessment of evidence which Swinburne endorses is what he refers to as the principle of charity. It has various non-equivalent formulations. For example,

Other things being equal, we assume that other people have purposes of a kind which we also have ourselves, and come to acquire beliefs in ways similar to that in which we do.    (Swinburne, 1981, p. 13. See also p. 40)

Other things being equal if A tells us that *p*, then it is probable that *p*. Whether it is strictly speaking charitable to have such a policy may be questioned. It may be thought to be more charitable to think that others acquire beliefs differently from ourselves, or to have no a priori pre-conceptions about this. We can let this pass. To take it any further would require us to look into the question of whether the evidence of testimony is to be reduced to the evidence that supports its reliability, a line of inquiry we eschewed in the Introduction. The point is that Swinburne's principle of charity is not self-evident, nor is it a principle obviously derived from evidence, but may be one in terms of which we are to interpret and assess evidence, in this case evidence about people other than ourselves. For a contrasting view see Adams (1987c, pp. 13–4).

Finally, there is what Swinburne calls the principle of simplicity:

We attribute to men relatively stable purposes and beliefs. We assume that in general the beliefs and purposes manifested in a man's actions today and yesterday are similar; that different men have similar beliefs and purposes; and that people's beliefs change when presented with stimuli in regular and similar ways.                                    (Swinburne, 1981, p. 13)

Once again, such an assumption may be warranted. But some would regard adopting it as a *petitio principii*. And it is not self-evident, nor is it based upon evidence in the sense that it is warranted by past experience of people. For many people are very different from ourselves.

These different formulations of belief-policies or parts of such are all the more interesting coming from a philosopher who insists so strongly on the involuntariness of belief.

## VAN FRAASSEN ON AUGUSTINE

A final example of a belief-policy at work in the writings of a contemporary philosopher I take from a paper of Bas Van Fraassen's. Van Fraassen, expounding Augustine, argues that a belief that is not rational may none the less be justified, and that this is Augustine's response to scepticism. If scepticism is true, then the question of basing belief on the probabilities does not arise, and another principle of rationality must be sought.

Such a principle may be found in an epistemic attitude which claims that it is rational to go beyond the evidence:

Just as in practical decisions, the most prudent decision is not necessarily the moral one to make, so also in epistemic decisions, the most prudent policy of belief formation may not be the wisest. Rationality is at most bridled irrationality, and the process of rational inquiry does involve venture commitment, enterprise, willingness to take a chance. If our belief, and belief change, is by and large rational, then rationality *is* shot through and through with leaps of faith.(Van Fraassen, 1988 p. 151. See also Van Fraassen, 1984)

The sceptic is not to be refuted at the theoretical level, according to Van Fraassen, but is disarmed by the view that there is more to epistemic life than mere (or sheer) calculation; genuine epistemic engagement, for example.

In 'Belief and the Will' Van Fraassen argues for the rationality of a person committing himself now to the truth of his future beliefs, of the need to 'form as a matter of principle an exceptionally high of opinion of their (viz. one's own) epistemic judgements in our own case' (Van Fraassen, 1984, p. 243). In Van Fraassen's view it is rational to believe a proposition that is entailed neither by our previous beliefs nor by those beliefs together with new evidence.

## BELIEF-POLICY FORMATION

We saw earlier that belief-policies may be voluntary in a conscious and explicit way, but that not all belief-policies are like this, nor could they be. Some belief-policies are innate or practically so. For these belief-policies perhaps it is sufficient for having the belief that *p* that a person has a certain disposition (his innate belief-policy) and is confronted with a certain degree and kind of evidence. In the case of such policies there is no place for weakness of will, for having good reason for believing that *p*, but failing to think that *p*. It may be that such initial belief-policies can be given a causal explanation in terms of enabling agents to survive in an environment which, if not respected, is mortally hostile. In addition there are no doubt tacit or implicit belief-policies, policies which it is impossible to articulate precisely or to become aware of precisely. For examples of such, consider Oakeshott (1962), and Hayek (1967).

Other belief-policies are voluntary in a more self-conscious way. We are able, for a variety of reasons and motives, to take up one doxastic standard or another, even different doxastic standards for different matters, or for different occasions, in the light of considerations which are not solely evidential.

Consider a material object such as a chair, which each of us has to reckon with if we are going to travel painlessly or without serious injury through the physical environment. In addition to 'reckoning' with such an object, which involves identification at an unsophisticated level, a person may develop more or less sophisticated theories about such objects, their physical properties, social function, cultural history and the like. The contrast between a naive and a sophisticated attitude to a chair is rather like that between a belief-policy which a person unthinkingly inherits, perhaps as part of the very process of growing up, and one which he adopts as a result of a process of critical reflection.

John Heil has claimed (Heil, 1983a), in commenting upon the 'processes responsible for the generation of beliefs', that such processes represent dispositions or habits, intellectual and epistemic virtues and vices. He refers to the operation of such mechanisms in the formation of beliefs as 'automatic', while at the same time claiming that such mechanisms may be encouraged to develop or wither. It is not easy to see how such views are consistent, but perhaps they are if it is held that in the case of a fully formed disposition belief is automatic, while allowing that dispositions of this kind can be voluntarily reformed.

The question may be raised as to whether, as a result of the adoption of more sophisticated belief-policies, the rudimentary set which constitutes our innate stock may be repudiated, or whether sets of belief-policies have a hierarchical structure, each founded upon one or more elementary or basic or non-repudiatable belief-policies. This matter will be taken up later when we consider whether it is possible consistently to hold to scepticism as a belief-policy.

In considering belief-policy formation it is tempting to think that all defensible policies fall into a basic rationalist or evidentialist pattern, that they all relate to the adoption of logic and to the formation of belief due to the possession of empirical evidence or to the lack of counter-evidence. In order to see that this is not so we may consider the belief-policy of a follower of Kierkegaard who has the policy (with respect to at least some kinds of propositions) of believing because there is and must be a lack of evidence for the truth of such propositions. The very impossibility of providing evidence is a reason for believing without or against evidence.

Thus Kierkegaard has a twofold belief-policy, one covering empirically discoverable matters of fact, the other religion. So he is not arguing that, for just any proposition $p$, one may believe $p$ because, or although, there is more evidence against $p$ than for it. It is only in religion, where faith is a matter of total commitment, that one should not base one's faith on anything which may, for all we know, be false. The passionate nature of faith requires objective improbability, for the acceptance of risk is a measure of the intensity of the believer's passion (Adams, 1987a and 1987b).

Whatever may be thought about the wisdom of such a policy it would obviously be wrong to rule it out on conceptual grounds, as a matter of definition. Perhaps no one ought to adopt such a policy, though it is not easy to see how this could be argued. But in any case our concern at present is not with recommending belief-policies, or with seeing how they could be recommended, but with trying to understand them. We shall consider a fideistic belief-policy rather like Kierkegaard's in the final chapter.

In view of what has just been claimed about Kierkegaardian belief-policies, doxastic incontinence cannot be defined in terms of believing $p$ against the possession of overwhelming or preponderating evidence for $p$. If we were to define it in such a fashion then a Kierkegaardian would by definition be doxastically incontinent, and this seems implausible, just as it seems implausible, at the other extreme, to say that the belief that $p$ just is the apparent evidence there is for $p$. For a Kierkegaardian, presumably, what would count as doxastic incontinence in religion would be a species of worldliness – the policy of insisting upon standards of evidence for the truth of some proposition that were inappropriate for that kind of proposition.

John Heil calls the view that ties warranted beliefs to practical reasoning 'consequentialist' (Heil 1983a, p. 757), and the view that warranted belief is solely a matter of believing in accordance with certain epistemic norms non-consequentialist. But this classification confuses reasons with motives. It is possible to defend evidentialism on consequentialist grounds.

One can perhaps also envisage a mixed evidentialist – non-evidentialist belief-policy being adopted for non-consequentialist reasons, the developing of a certain kind of doxastic virtue or because of a paramount concern for truth for its own sake. So a person's motive for holding a certain belief-policy may be the comfort or psychological release or development of personal integrity that it brings with it. And the belief-policy for which that person has such motives for developing may or may not be one according to which beliefs are to be formed solely by evidence.

As a person develops belief-policies he adopts certain standards of belief-acceptance and rejects others. In so far as he internalises these standards he may be said to develop one or more epistemic virtue. Such an account of epistemic virtue is diachronic in character, and linked to internalist accounts of the justification of beliefs. It is to be contrasted with an account of epistemic virtue which functions as a criterion of epistemic justification on an externalist account of justification, the sort of account of virtue as developed by reliabilists such as Goldman and Nozick. Such an account of epistemic virtue has been sharply criticised by Jonathan Kvanvig, who suggests a more diachronic and social approach to epistemic virtue (Kvanvig, 1992).

## THE ROLE OF THE WILL

We began this chapter by claiming that in the adoption or retention of belief-policies the will must play a significant role. What is that role? Two issues need to be carefully separated, the place of the will in the adoption of one or other belief-policy, and the place of willing, wishing or wanting in accepting propositions. It has been argued that the will may be involved in forming some belief-policies *ab initio*, and in altering inherited belief-policies. It has also been argued that it is incorrect to assume that all rational evidential belief-policies advocate a straightforward proportioning of belief to evidence. What policy about evidence is to be adopted is a matter of decision, a decision which is not an irrational wish or whim, nor one determined solely by evidence.

Such a view of belief-policies provides part of an account of epistemic rationality. Assuming a truth–centred motivation we may say, initially, that a belief is epistemically rational for A if it is in accordance with A's evidential belief-policy. Otherwise it is epistemically irrational for A. Epistemic rationality is therefore not a property of belief as such, but of A's belief or believing. There is no way of introducing rationality which transcends or overarches such person-relative rationalities. However, this does not imply relativism, except in a trivial sense. Relativism is trivial when it simply records the fact that different people believe different things. It is more serious when it claims that no way of finally settling such differences exists. Interminable and systematic disagreements, though a fact of life, welcome or unwelcome according to your point of view, do not imply serious relativism, but rather the reverse.

# 4

## Belief-policies: some alternatives

It should be re-emphasised that the belief-policies to be considered are all policies regarding the formation of beliefs about matters of fact either wholly or partly on evidence. So policies about metaphysical truths and ends other than the acquisition of true beliefs and the elimination of error by reference to evidential considerations fall outside the scope of this chapter.

### LOCKE ON BELIEF

J. A. Passmore has shown that for John Locke belief is voluntary at least to this extent, that according to him a person may choose whether to examine the evidence, or expose himself to the evidence, or not, but that once the choice is made then the resulting belief will be determined by that evidence (Passmore, 1978). That is, candidly choosing to examine the evidence is being committed to giving minimal assent to whatever proposition the evidence favours.

As Knowledge, is no more arbitrary than perception, so, I think, Assent is no more in our Power than Knowledge. When the Agreement of any two *Ideas* appears to our minds, whether immediately, or by the Assistance of Reason, I can no more refuse to perceive, no more avoid knowing it, than I can avoid seeing those Objects, which I turn my Eyes to, and look on in day-light: And what upon full Examination I find the most probable, I cannot deny my Assent to . . . *Yet we can hinder both knowledge and assent, by stopping our Enquiry,* and not employing our Faculties in the search of any truth. If it were not so, Ignorance, Error or Infidelity could not in any Case be a Fault. Thus in some Cases, we can prevent or suspend our Assent: But can a Man, versed in modern or ancient History, doubt whether there be such a Place as *Rome,* or whether there was such a Man as *Julius Caesar.* (Locke, 1961, IV. XX. 16)

For any belief attention is necessary and the consent of the will is in turn necessary for the giving of attention. Once attention is given belief necessarily follows, causally necessarily from the evidence presented to it by the senses and by testimony. Ignorance and error are blameworthy when they arise from a failure to carry through inquiry as it should be carried through. But who is to decide when such a failure occurs?

On the one hand it seems that Locke wants to say that assent is involuntary, while on the other hand he wishes to condemn certain beliefs, particularly those of the enthusiasts and fanatics of his day. How is he able to do both?

Passmore interprets Locke's attempt to reconcile the passivity of assent with responsibility for believing as in the last resort implying some radical view of freedom with respect to assent. Locke believes that people can voluntarily suspend their beliefs not merely in those situations in which they discover that their beliefs rest on unexamined grounds, but also, in a more radical manner, they can suspend belief when they suspect that there is evidence against the belief. On this view, Locke assimilates his account of belief to his account of desire (Passmore, 1978, p. 197).

I suggest that what Locke is saying is that the belief that some proposition *p* might, through a reconsideration of evidence, or the awareness of new evidence, come to be governed differently by one's overriding belief-policy. Given that a person has the policy of (say) only believing *p* when there is no evidence against *p* he might, upon seeing that there is evidence against *p*, suspend belief. Suppose that Joe has the policy of never giving money to vagrants who call at his door. On answering the door, and seeing that there is a vagrant there, Joe refuses to yield to an appeal for money. But suppose that the man shows Joe a badge, claiming that he is a *bona fide* (though ill-clad) collector for Joe's favourite charity. Then Joe might either change his belief, and give a donation, or continue to believe that the man is a vagrant, though a cunning one. His decision about this will not be based upon the evidence alone, but on his policy with regard to the evidence.

Is this a plausible reconstruction of Locke's view? At first sight it may seem not to be. For Locke says that probability leaves us as little liberty as demonstration, (Locke, 1961, IV. XVI. 9), at least in the case of those propositions the evidence for which is what Locke calls 'concurrent', i.e. where there is no clash of evidence. So that it appears that the will has no more or less of a role with matters of probability than with trains of deductive reasoning. And Locke implies, though he does not expressly claim, that in the cases where there is a conflict of evidence then the will has a more proper role to play in the adjudication of it.

Locke allows for the suspension of belief as part of his general conception of rationality. But it would be a mistake to construe him as holding that the minds of all men have a natural inclination to suspend belief. He allows that many people as a matter of fact never suspend belief or see the need to do so. Yet I suggest that the difference is not that certain people have powers which others lack, but that people differ in their belief-policies; some policies call for, or allow, the suspension of belief, while others do not.

It is possible to see Locke's own belief-policy in the process of being developed in the chapter 'Of Degrees of Assent'. When he deals with what he called 'concurrent reports' (Locke, 1961, IV. XVI. 6), then the mind is determined, the will plays little or no part, 'and we reason and act thereupon with as little doubt as if it were perfect demonstration'. Locke writes as if this is not a matter of policy, but of straightforward fact, and we shall look at the significance of this later.

Then there are those matters in which one's direct experience and the testimony of others concur. Thirdly, there are the cases of which one has no direct experience and in which the testimony of others concurs. In all such cases

the matter goes easily enough. Probability upon such grounds carries so much evidence with it that it naturally determines the judgment and leaves us as little liberty to believe or disbelieve, as a demonstration does, whether we will know or be ignorant. (Locke, 1961, IV. XVI. 9)

But what of cases where 'testimonies contradict common experience, and the reports of history and witnesses clash with the ordinary course of nature or with one another'? It is here that Locke introduces a significant difference. He speaks of certain standards of investigation as being required. He writes that 'there it is where diligence, attention, and exactness are *required* [emphasis added], to form a right judgement and to proportion the assent to the different evidence and probability of the thing' (Locke, 1961, IV. XVI. 10). In other words, Locke here is beginning self-consciously to formulate a

87

*policy* about belief, one we might provisionally express as: *One ought only to believe a proposition p rather than q if the real probabilities favour p over q*. One ought to adopt this policy rather than, say, *Whenever there is a clash of evidence one ought to suspend belief*. And then Locke adds some remarks on what he takes to be proper judgements of real probability. For example, there is the interesting section on inverted probability in which Locke says that nothing can be more probable now than it was to the original observer of it (Locke, 1961, IV. XVI. 10). So, as regards matters of fact, Locke's policy appears to be: *When there is a clash of evidence one ought to proportion belief to the real probabilities, taking steps to ascertain what those probabilities are.*

Locke adds one important qualification to this, about miracles, 'one case wherein the strangeness of the fact lessens not the assent to a fair testimony given of it' (Locke, 1961, IV. XVI. 13). So Locke's further amended proposal for believing matters of fact might be expressed as *Except in the case of well-attested miracle stories, when there is a clash of evidence belief ought to be proportioned to the real probabilities.*

According to Locke one final modification is needed, to cover those matters of fact that are made known by revelation (Locke, 1961 IV. XVI. 14). Such propositions are to be believed upon the testimony of 'such a one as cannot deceive or be deceived, and that is, of God himself'. Where God reveals *p* then *p* ought to be believed. Locke makes two important provisos. The revelation must be properly attested, and the sentences of which it is composed must be understood 'else we shall expose ourselves to all the extravagancy of enthusiasm and all the error of wrong principles, if we have faith and assurance in what is not divine revelation' (Locke, 1961, IV. XVI. 14). So Locke's final belief-policy might be expressed as: *when there is a clash of evidence then except in the case of well-attested and properly understood divine revelation belief regarding matters of fact ought to be proportioned to the real probabilities.*

In drawing up such a principle, Locke is not describing what people do, but making a recommendation about what they ought to do, and in so doing he is rejecting all other policies, such as: *whatever seems probable at first glance ought to be believed* or *whatever has customarily been believed ought to be believed* or *whatever is said by a teacher who claims to be inspired ought to be believed.*

The development of Locke's belief-policy about matters of fact throws further light on what David Hume is doing in his famous section on miracles in the first *Inquiry*. No doubt with writers such as Locke in mind Hume proposes a rival belief-policy about miracles, one in which no exception is to be allowed for historical testimony about miracles. Hume does not dispute that there is evidence for miracles, only that such evidence could ever be sufficiently strong to make the miracles credible as the foundation of a religion.

So that, as Locke sees it, people differ in the beliefs they hold not only because they differ in their experience, and hence in the evidence which they come to possess, but also because they adopt different standards for assessing such evidence. Passmore says, in closing his discussion of Locke's ethics of belief, that Locke at first does what he can to reconcile his theories with his experience by suggesting that, from the point of view of better-informed observers, the irrational beliefs have a rational foundation, that they rest upon errors of fact rather than errors of judgement – errors of fact arising either out of ignorance or the assignment of wrong measures of probability. If only people could bring themselves to inquire, they would cease to hold irrational beliefs. Even if this is so there is still a residue of cases, as Passmore acknowledges, in which people have all the evidence before them which they could possibly need, and yet still believe irrationally. 'In the end Locke is led to conclude that men can believe falsely, not as the result of having inadequate evidence, but as a result of being dominated by powerful inclinations' (Passmore, 1978, p. 208).

Passmore is only half-correct in this verdict. He is correct in his view of what Locke's own policy about belief is, namely to regulate the degree of assurance in a proposition so that it accords with the evidence (together with the provisos about miracles and revelation which Passmore does not mention here), but he is mistaken in representing Locke as holding that all those who dissent from such a belief-policy do so 'as a result of being dominated by powerful inclinations'.

Locke holds that those who dissent from him are forming their beliefs in accordance with different belief-policies. To say that according to Locke the rational person is one who is dominated by passion for truth, as distinct from party passions, is not accurate, for the sectaries, also, as they see it, are dominated by a passion for truth. To deny this would be to beg the question against them.

Locke's view is that the will is operative in belief partly in being able to reconsider data, but chiefly in the part it plays in the adoption of a policy regarding belief. Here the will is not determined by evidence, but by interests of various kinds, such as the desire to conform the pattern of all human belief to that of certain beliefs, for example, scientific beliefs.

In his belief-policy Locke hovers somewhat inconsistently between what R. M. Chisholm has called 'particularism' and 'methodism'. Regarding judgements of immediate perception Locke is a particularist, or comes near to being so, as when he says that our awareness of particular things amounts almost to knowledge. Locke backs up his particularism with the judgement that 'if we persuade ourselves that our faculties act and inform us right concerning the existence of those objects that affect them . . .' (Locke, 1961, IV. XI. 3), and this looks methodistical, as does his general ethic of belief.

### W. K. CLIFFORD AND THE ETHICS OF BELIEF

W. K. Clifford's position is much more explicit than Locke's. It is through Clifford's work that the phrase 'the ethics of belief' has entered the philosophical vocabulary. Clifford claims that 'It is wrong always, everywhere, and for anyone, to believe anything upon insufficient evidence' (Clifford, 1970, p. 179).

It would be a mistake to construe Clifford as holding that every belief requires the same degree of evidence, for he extends his treatment to those beliefs that he calls 'trifling and fragmentary'.

But forasmuch as no belief held by one man, however seemingly trivial the belief, and however obscure the believer is ever actually insignificant or without its effect on the fate of mankind, we have no choice but to extend our judgement to all cases of belief whatever.     (Clifford, 1970, p. 166)

While it is noteworthy that Clifford never says what degree of evidence constitutes sufficient evidence, it is perhaps plausible to interpret him as Mavrodes does, (Mavrodes, 1982), as claiming that sufficiency operates as a kind of threshold which every proposition must cross if it is to be believable, and the crossing of which is sufficient for the believing of any proposition.

It would seem to follow from such a position that anyone whose belief is justified knows what counts as sufficient evidence for the belief. This has to follow, because on Clifford's view people act on insufficient evidence when there is more evidence either for or against the belief which they could obtain without much effort, and when they know this. In the case of one example, Clifford says 'Not only had they been accused on insufficient evidence but the evidence of their innocence was such as the agitators might easily have obtained, if they had attempted a fair enquiry' (Clifford, 1970, p. 154). In addition, Clifford mentions the suppression of doubts and the avoidance of investigation as factors which are signs that a belief is held on insufficient evidence. So for Clifford the acquisition of sufficient evidence for a belief is a fairly self-conscious affair, a case of internalism in justification.

The threshold interpretation of Clifford would also allow him to find room for degrees of belief. Sufficient evidence is then what justifies believing a proposition to the lowest degree, enabling one to cross the threshold of belief. To believe without such sufficiency would be epistemically irresponsible. The greater the amount of evidence beyond this sufficiency, the greater the degree of reliance that is warranted. Yet the threshold interpretation may be said to take away much of what is distinctive about Clifford's position, unless the threshold is set at a fairly high level.

Clifford's position (and to a less explicit degree, Locke's) might be seen as attempts to extend the justificatory aspect in knowledge to belief. Knowledge, on the orthodox position, is justified true belief. Clifford (and Locke) are proposing policies which extend justification to all belief, not as a matter of definition, but as a matter of policy. So that no one ought to believe unless there is sufficient evidence to justify the belief. But in fact many people believe unjustifiably, either irrationally or on a different belief-policy; hence Clifford's stern recommendation.

Quite naturally Clifford's vehement ethic of belief is based upon a strong voluntarism, but one of a rather curious kind. Beliefs, even the very strongest, do not causally necessitate some particular action, rather they 'suggest' one action rather than another. So beliefs cannot themselves be actions in a straightforward sense for all actions are suggested by beliefs. And it is possible, in any situation in which a belief suggests an action, to perform some alternative action. With regard to any action suggested, one has a duty to investigate whether or not one ought to perform that action. From this it follows that, although a person is not able, in the first instance, to choose what to believe, a person has the opportunity to reconsider the belief upon considering whether or not the action suggested by the belief ought to be performed. This, at least, seems to be what Clifford means by the following

Even when a man's belief is so fixed that he cannot think otherwise, he still has a choice in regard to the action suggested by it, and so cannot escape the duty of investigating on the ground of the strength of his convictions.

(Clifford, 1970, p. 155)

Clifford's chief argument is that every belief has consequences.

If a belief is not realised immediately in open deeds, it is stored up for the guidance of the future. It goes to make a part of that aggregate of beliefs which is the link between sensation and action at every moment of all our lives, and which is so organised and compacted together that no part of it can be isolated from the rest, but every new addition modifies the structure of the whole. No real belief, however trifling and fragmentary it may seem, is ever truly insignificant. (Clifford, 1970, p. 155)

In addition, not only does every belief have consequences, every belief has public consequences.

Our words, our phrases, our forms and processes and modes of thought, are common property, fashioned and perfected from age to age; an heirloom which every succeeding generation inherits as a precious deposit and a sacred trust to be handed on to the next one, not unchanged but enlarged and purified, with some clear marks of its proper handiwork.

(Clifford, 1970, p. 156)

The argument seems to be:

(1) All beliefs have public consequences.
(2) All well-founded beliefs, even if false, have good public consequences.

For example, they bind men together, they strengthen the intellect, and they prevent credulity, and these are necessary for the maintenance and growth of civilisation.

(3) Only well-founded beliefs have good public consequences.

Therefore

(4) All beliefs ought to be well-founded.

Clifford links well-foundedness to truth, but does not emphasise this connection. He certainly does not hold that well-foundedness is necessary for true belief. He says

> If I let myself believe anything on insufficient evidence, there may be no harm done by the mere belief; it may be true after all, or I may never have occasion to exhibit it in outward acts. But I cannot help doing this great wrong towards Man, that I make myself credulous. (Clifford, 1970, p. 158)

The argument here is reminiscent of that of some utilitarians in ethics, who argue that though a particular action may not have any bad consequences, performing such an action may weaken the resolve of a person not to perform similar actions which do have bad consequences. Clifford's position is that a well-founded belief is more likely to be true than not. If Agnes manipulates her bees without wearing a veil she may not be stung. But this is a dangerous practice, and will lead in the long run to more bee-stings rather than less. Therefore, it ought never to be risked. Similarly, ill-founded propositions ought not to be believed.

Clifford's argument has several glaring weaknesses. All three premises of his argument are contingent propositions which may well be false. Not believing *p* could also have good public consequences. Clifford needs to show that nothing besides believing has good consequences. Furthermore, his belief-policy may be viciously regressive. For according to him I must not believe *p* unless I have sufficient evidence for *p*. But having sufficient evidence for *p* just is believing a proposition *p* (the proposition that I have sufficient evidence for *p*), and so on *ad infinitum*. The objection confuses an equivalence with a definition, and the regress is only objectionable if what Clifford is proposing is a definition of belief. See Swinburne (1981, p. 6).

Earlier it was said that though belief-policies control what a person who adopts them counts as evidence, they are not based upon evidence. Clifford's argument may appear to contradict this in that he is founding the acceptance of a belief-policy on consequences. However, the consequences in question are not straightforward empirical consequences, but desirable, perhaps even morally desirable, states of affairs. Clifford is saying that his policy about belief ought to be adopted because of the generally beneficial consequences for the individual and for civilisation of developing habits of mind tending to maximise the number of credible beliefs, and not because it results in more credible beliefs than any of its rivals.

Despite Clifford's eloquence it is not obviously true that all beliefs have the public consequences he claims for them, or that they all have public consequences of a non-trivial kind. Perhaps Clifford would reject any counter-examples as not being cases of belief, as not 'real beliefs' ('No real belief, however trifling and fragmentary it may seem, is ever truly insignificant'). But this looks implausible, for well-founded beliefs have often produced dissension and persecution. And mythical beliefs and noble lies have often unified societies.

It has sometimes been argued that the best safeguard for truth is not to suppress and warn against ill-founded beliefs, but to encourage the maximum expression of belief of whatever kind, with the perhaps naive expectation that in competition with false belief truth will always prevail. Thus John Milton:

Since therefore the knowledge and survey of vice is in this world so necessary to the constituting of human virtue, and the scanning of error to the confirmation of truth, how can we more safely, and with less danger, scout into the regions of sin and falsity, than by reading all manner of tractates, and hearing all manner of reason? (Milton, 1834, p. 19)

It could be claimed that a society united in such an attitude is a more unified society than one which is not.

Critics of utilitarianism such as D. H. Hodgson (1967) and G. J. Warnock (1971) have argued that there is an incongruity, if not an incoherence, in a situation in which each individual acts with the intention of maximising utility. So to act will be productive of disutility. At least some forms of utilitarianism require that some individuals are not utilitarians.

Towards the betterment of the human predicament, the simple recipe of general beneficence must be, while admirably intentioned, very minimally efficacious. If this were everyone's sole criterion of right and wrong action, it may reasonably be supposed that comparatively little direct harm would be done, but also very remarkably little good. For how much good can we do, if we cannot even usefully communicate? (Warnock, 1971, p. 34)

A similar objection can be advanced against Clifford's adequate evidence ethic of belief. While it cannot be demonstrated a priori that a world in which each individual adopts the Cliffordian ethic is one in which there is more ignorance or is in other ways less civilised than one in which at least some individuals do not, it is plausible to suppose that this is at the least an open question, to be investigated empirically, and that it might turn out that, other things being equal, a world in which at least some people were not Cliffordian would be a better world (however 'better' is to be understood) than a monochrome Cliffordian world.

Clifford seems to be arguing that only if his ethic is adopted will maximum beneficial consequences follow. His observations about credulity suggest another possible argument, however, one that stresses the desirability of achieving certain intellectual virtues, and not the importance of consequences. As there are arguments in ethics stressing the importance of the cultivation of certain virtues for their own sake, so there may be parallel arguments for intellectual virtue. It is even possible to construct an argument of a deontological kind for the same ethic of belief, though Clifford himself does not favour this. To argue for instance, that truth is of paramount or overriding importance, that the best way of attaining truth is by adopting an adequate evidence ethic, and that therefore one ought to adopt this ethic, even if doing so created social disorder or had other unfortunate consequences.

If evidential sufficiency is not interpreted as a threshold for responsible believing, then Clifford's ethic of belief is a very tough one. It would exclude, for example, reliance upon hunches. A detective may not have sufficient evidence, (if by this is meant evidence that justifies belief in some proposition rather than any alternative) that Pete stole Joe's beehive, and there may be evidence which points to the conclusion that Pete did not steal the hive. But the detective may have the feeling that despite current evidence Pete did take the hive and she may not only believe this, but also act upon her belief. In doing so she is not obviously acting irrationally or immorally, for she may be acting upon her past experience. Alternatively her hunch may not be an unarticulated, but strong, belief, but a weak belief. In believing that Pete took the hive the detective may have little evidence for this proposition, but she may have evidence for the general proposition about the nature of such hunches. It would be tough to say that she did not have sufficient evidence to believe to any degree that Peter stole the hive.

There are even more serious consequences of Clifford's ethic of belief. Clifford would say that in most situations in which human beings find themselves they ought to withhold assent from most propositions. For example, although a person may have sufficient evidence that the bees are swarming now, and therefore ought, according to Clifford, to believe that the bees are swarming now, he does not have sufficient evidence that the bees will swarm in a week's time, and so according to Clifford he ought not to believe that they will be swarming then. (This is not the same as advocating that the person ought to believe that they will not be swarming in a week's time. To believe that, he would need to have evidence that they will not be swarming in a week's time, which is also something that he does not have.) Surely, though it is implausible to maintain that a person ought to believe that the bees will be swarming in a week's time, nevertheless may it not be reasonable to believe that they will be?

Clifford is in effect arguing that only if there is sufficient evidence for a proposition $p$ ought $p$ to be believed, that the onus is on the provision of evidence. Otherwise the only rational course is to suspend judgement with respect to $p$. But why is it fitting to adopt this ethic and not the ethic that $p$ may be believed unless there is sufficient evidence against $p$? While I have no evidence against the proposition 'You will wear plastic gloves tomorrow' nor against the proposition 'You will wear leather gloves tomorrow', am I not free to believe either?

Clifford's guilty-until-proved-innocent approach to the relation between evidence and belief means that he offers a single criterion to cover all cases of belief, a necessary and sufficient condition of belief-worthiness. He does not, unlike the particularist, start from the position of what people actually believe, and say that what they believe is a good guide to what they ought to believe, and that they ought to go on believing what they do believe unless there is good reason not to.

There are other problems in employing Clifford's ethic of belief which lend further implausibility to his account. Consider a situation in which there is insufficient evidence for $p$ and also insufficient evidence for not-$p$. Then, on Clifford's ethic of belief, a person ought to believe neither $p$ nor not-$p$. This seems straightforward, and acceptable. It is what Clifford means when he says that if a person has no time to obtain sufficient evidence for a proposition then he has no right to believe. But there is a further sense of epistemic indifference (Chisholm, 1966, p. 19), a situation in which one can, rationally, either believe *p* or believe not-*p*. Here what is rational is not suspension of belief, but the indiscriminate believing of either *p* or not-*p*. In the first sense of indifference, according to which the rational policy is to suspend judgement, the sceptic is indifferent with respect to all propositions or (depending on the kind of scepticism) with respect to all contingent propositions. For according to the sceptic, since no proposition is epistemically justified, no proposition ought to be believed and the rational thing is to suspend judgement about all propositions.

In the second sense of indifference, Clifford would deny that any proposition whatsoever is epistemically indifferent, for either a person has sufficient evidence for a proposition *p*, in which case it ought to be believed, or insufficient evidence for *p*, in which case it ought not to be believed, because the bad public consequences of so believing will outweigh any good consequences. An objection to this is that it appears to be simply false that all propositions for which a person has insufficient evidence are such that believing them brings about more evil than good.

Finally there may be propositions which are epistemically justified, but which there is no point in believing, because they are more complex hypotheses accounting for certain facts for which there exists an equally justifiable but simpler hypothesis. Clifford would say that any such gratuitous proposition is unjustified, and therefore ought not to be believed. For Clifford's ethic is such that if we need not believe *p* the more complex hypothesis, then we ought not to believe *p*. A gentler ethic would allow that though *p* need not be believed, yet it may be.

## WILLIAM JAMES AND THE WILL TO BELIEVE

Clifford's ethic of belief was opposed by William James in his essay 'The Will to Believe' (1970). James does not flatly contradict Clifford. While he does not deny that adequate evidence is sufficient for justifying belief, he challenges Clifford on its necessity, and in effect argues that there are cases where one may, and perhaps must, believe upon insufficient evidence.

When one turns to the magnificent edifice of the physical sciences, and sees how it was reared; what thousands of disinterested moral lives of men lie buried in its mere foundations; what patience and postponement, what choking down of preference, what submission to the icy laws of outer fact are wrought into its very stones and mortar; how absolutely impersonal it stands in its vast augustness – then how besotted and contemptible seems every little sentimentalist who comes blowing his voluntary smoke wreaths, and pretending to decide things from out of his private dream.

(James, 1970, p. 165)

Again,

wherever the option between losing truth and gaining it is not momentous, we can throw the chance of *gaining truth* away, and at any rate save ourselves from any chance of *believing falsehood*, by not making up our minds at all till objective evidence has come. In scientific questions, this is almost always the case. (James, 1970, p. 175)

These statements significantly limit the area of disagreement between Clifford and James. Nevertheless James proceeds to argue that wherever there is a situation in which belief cannot be established on purely evidential grounds then a person must decide what to believe and what to leave open. To decide to leave the question open is for James as much a decision of the will as is the decision to believe. Decisions to believe include decisions not to believe. This is so, provided that the belief in question is, in James' terminology, live, forced, and momentous.

By a live option James means one that represents a real possibility for someone, given what is already believed. For most who read this page, to believe that a neighbour is a witch, or that a cracked mirror will bring misfortune, or that the sun is at the centre of the universe, are not live options. In saying that an option is forced James is making a logical point. If a person is presented with two alternatives, and enjoined to believe one of them, it may be that the injunction can be avoided because the alternatives presented are not logically exhaustive of the possibilities. If a person is invited to choose the honey or jam, the fate of taking either can be avoided by refusing to choose at all, by deciding to have neither. Similarly if a person is enjoined to believe either that $p$ is true or that it is false, she can avoid the choice by remaining agnostic. But if the choice is limited either to choosing honey or not choosing it, or to believing that *p* or not believing *p*, then the option in each case is forced. To neglect the issue, or to dither, is in these circumstances to make a choice.

By a momentous option James means one that has important or significant consequences for the chooser, either because a unique opportunity is presented, or because the stake involved is large, or because having made a decision one way, there is no prospect of reversing it.

So James aims to identify situations which Clifford's account cannot cover. Clifford assumes by his claim that it is more rational to suspend belief where there is insufficient evidence rather than believe that it is possible in all circumstances to do this. James claims that there are situations in which belief of some sort is logically unavoidable. By saying that there must be a choice to believe where the option is momentous James is denying that all options have momentous consequences, whereas Clifford is in effect claiming that all options are equally momentous since no belief, no matter how seemingly trivial, can be isolated from the habits of mind it exemplifies and causes, and from the consequences that it can have for society at large.

Clifford's ethic of belief is based upon the policy of avoiding error at all costs, whereas James's position is that the better policy is to believe the truth. The two injunctions 'Avoid error' and 'Believe the truth' are not materially equivalent, for unlike the policy of maximising truth the policy of minimising error is compatible with believing nothing at all.

Are there any options which are live, momentous, and forced? In his essay 'The Will to Believe' James offers three sorts of cases which he believes that Clifford's ethic of belief cannot cover, and elsewhere he offers one other. One of these, which concerns moral issues, falls outside the scope of this study.

By momentousness no doubt James has in mind religious matters. He need not have had. Let us call a proposition which does not refer to God in any way, or imply his existence, a secular proposition. There are innumerable true secular propositions, but it would be rash to say that they are all equal in importance. Epistemic importance and its place in deciding between belief-policies are taken up in the next chapter.

In the course of discussing the religious case James expresses and defends a wider principle, that '*a rule of thinking which would absolutely prevent me from acknowledging certain kinds of truth if those kinds of truth were really there, would be an irrational rule'* (James, 1970, p. 181). There may be situations in which it is a logically necessary condition of discovering whether or not *p* is true that one believes that proposition upon insufficient evidence. James offers as an illustration the case of personal relations.

*Do you like me or not?* – for example. Whether you do or not depends, in countless instances, on whether I meet you half-way, am willing to assume that you must like me, and show you trust and expectation. The previous faith on my part in your liking's existence is in such cases what makes your liking come. (James, 1970, pp. 177-8)

So James holds that there are states of affairs that one cannot realise except by believing certain propositions upon insufficient evidence. Since it is better to realise these states of affairs than not, it is better to hold certain propositions upon insufficient evidence than not. We might express this by saying that according to James there are propositions that we have good grounds for believing but not sufficient evidence for believing. Yet James' example is not very clear because it is not clear whether taking someone to be your friend is a case of believing what is true upon insufficient evidence or whether the unsupported belief is judged to be merely causally necessary for establishing the friendship

Though perhaps one person cannot have another person as a friend unless he believes him to be trustworthy without sufficient evidence, it by no means follows that one cannot have sufficient evidence for the proposition: *Friends cannot be made unless one first believes them to be trustworthy upon insufficient evidence.* As a result of generalising from experience there can be evidence for *this* proposition.

Further light may be thrown on this by a consideration of a position that is even stronger than James', one which holds that there are occasions when it is correct to believe against the evidence. Jack Meiland gives an example of a wife who has grounds for suspecting that her husband is unfaithful

However, the wife believes that their marriage is basically sound and can weather this storm . . . she knows that she cannot conceal her suspicions and hence decides to believe that her husband is not being unfaithful to her.

(Meiland, 1980, p. 16).

In these circumstances, Meiland is arguing, the wife is justified by certain rational considerations, though not by evidence, in believing that her husband is faithful, when there is evidence that he is not. The reason for believing is the wife's desire to maintain the marriage.

It might be argued that Meiland's argument is mistaken. For what the wife believes is not *My husband is faithful* but *If I succeed in believing that my husband is faithful then it is more likely than not that my marriage will be preserved*. The fact that there is no evidence for the first proposition does not mean that there is no evidence for the second, conditional proposition. There may be no evidence that Joe's bees have swarmed, but plenty of evidence that if Joe's bees have swarmed their honey production will fall.

Only if there were no evidence for the more complex proposition would Meiland's counter-example be effective against what he calls an adequate evidence ethic. Is it likely that the wife has no evidence for the appropriate conditional? If, as Meiland maintains, the wife believes that her marriage is sound when there is more evidence against this proposition than for it, how is what Meiland calls choosing to believe different from desiring? One answer may be: believing (falsely) that the husband is faithful helps to bring it about that he will be faithful. But how is this known? If there is evidence for it then it would appear that Meiland's position is a species of evidence ethic after all. If there is no evidence for it then why is believing her husband to be faithful a more rational choice than believing that he is unfaithful? Why is it more likely to achieve the desired end of keeping the marriage intact? If the fact that there is, or is not, evidence is irrelevant, then the one hypothesis may be equally as rational as the other. But according to Meiland 'the wife believes that their marriage is basically sound and can weather this storm' (Meiland, 1980, p. 16), and there is no suggestion that she has no evidence for *this*.

Is there any plausibility in the view that a person can adopt a belief-policy in which the belief that $p$ is brought about not by evidence for $p$ but by the desire for $p$ to be true? Such a position might be called a no-evidence belief policy. It is not a case of believing at will unless desires are (implausibly) thought to be within immediate control. Two versions of such a policy can be envisaged:

(a) When the balance of evidence is against *p*, but it is desired that *p* is true, then a person may believe *p* in order to make it true, if there is reason to think that believing *p* will make it true.

(b) When the balance of evidence is against *p*, but it is desired that *p* is true, then a person must believe *p* in order to make it true.

The problem with either version of such a policy is that it appears to involve the believer in a contradiction. For if I believe *p* in order to make *p* true then I must believe both that *p* *is* true and also necessarily have the belief that not-*p*. Such a difficulty would appear to afflict all policies of the form 'X believes *p* in order to make *p* true'.

An objection of a different kind to the James/Meiland position, is that it is immoral to self-induce an epistemically unjustified belief because to do so violates an individual's personhood. Richard M. Gale holds that 'It is always wrong to bring it about that a person becomes less than or less of a person or that a potential person becomes something less than a person' (Gale, 1980, p. 6). And he holds that to self-induce an epistemically unjustified belief violates this notion of personhood. But Gale's highly moralistic account of personhood is questionable. Even if it is granted, however, it is not obvious that someone who, given equal evidence for *p* and against *p*, holds that one may believe *p* if there are non-evidential reasons for doing so, violates their personhood. And in any case, do considerations of personhood have an absolute standing, as Gale suggests? Could it not be retorted that in the James/Meiland sort of case there is a balance of moral considerations, of considerations about personhood to be weighed against the considerations of benefit to be derived from a belief that is evidentially unjustified? There does not seem to be anything in what Gale says that forbids anyone adopting the James/Meiland position on balance.

James and Clifford are usually thought of as holding opposed views. Clifford advocates an evidentialist belief-policy, while James is (for certain situations at least) the advocate of a non-evidentialist belief-policy. But, if Clifford is interpreted in the threshold way discussed earlier, there may be a way of combining their views, as follows:

It may be that the following belief-policy could be held: *evidence of amount E is necessary for any responsible belief of degree D but not sufficient.* A further condition is required to warrant responsible believing to that degree, if (that is) one interprets Clifford as holding: one must believe *p* only when there is sufficient evidence for *p* (and not, one may believe *p* only where there is sufficient evidence for *p*). It may be that (adapting James) if *p* is of sufficient epistemic importance one is justified in believing *p* to degree D.

## THE MANDATORY AND THE PERMISSIVE

What unites the belief-policies so far considered, despite their noteworthy differences, is that they are all what were earlier called mandatory belief-policies: that is, they lay down conditions for when belief is required or obligatory.

The basic distinction between mandatory and permissive belief-policies is between circumstances in which it is obligatory to believe, and circumstances in which it is not.

These circumstances may have differing degrees of strength or stringency. For example, one belief-policy, a pure or uniform belief-policy as it might be called, is where, for any proposition, if and only if that proposition meets a condition C ought one to believe it. Alternatively an impure belief-policy would be one where one ought to believe if C. This allows that there might be a mixed overall policy. In one field of inquiry, belief may be governed by C, and if C then one is obliged to believe. In other fields belief may be governed by a different condition D. Thus a person might hold that one is only required to believe propositions of a certain kind if they are justified by sense-experience to a certain degree, but with respect to contingent propositions of some other kind one is required to believe them only if they are warranted by some authority or expert. Think of the hybrid belief-policies that can readily be found in attempts to handle alleged conflicts between religion and science.

An extreme and possibly incoherent version of such a hybrid belief-policy are theories of so-called 'twofold' truth, the claim that the same proposition can express a theological truth and a philosophical false-hood, or vice versa. For an interesting discussion of such themes, see Brown (1989).

In addition to this distinction, *within* each belief-policy it is possible to hold, or to deny, that there is a class of permissible beliefs. Thus a person may hold a permissive belief-policy, say that one may believe *p* unless *p* is falsified, and also hold that given that *p* is falsified one is obliged to believe not–*p*. Or it may be held that, on the falsification of *p* one may either believe not–*p* or suspend judgement..

In other words, each belief-policy, permissive or mandatory, may (or may not) hold that any proposition considered is either obligatory (by the terms of the belief-policy) or forbidden. If this is not a feature of the belief-policy, then it follows that there is a class of propositions which may or may not be believed.

So it would in theory be possible to hold a hybrid policy one element of which (whatever its other features) had no place for propositions neither forbidden nor obligatory, the other element of which did. So there might be a belief-policy which about scientific matters of fact (say) which had no place for propositions which one may believe, and a policy about religious matters of fact which did provide for propositions one may believe. Perhaps such an overall belief-policy would require that no matters of fact of any positive religious significance implied any matters of fact of scientific significance, and *vice versa*.

A falsificationist epistemology might be considered as a permissive ethic of belief, as follows: *One ought to believe only those propositions or sets of propositions which, having the greatest achievable content and explanatory power, have so far resisted the most strenuous attempts to falsify them.* Two things are worth noting about this position. The first is that, unlike all belief-policies so far discussed in this chapter, the belief of a proposition does not require justification, but the absence of falsification does. What is believed is a proposition which is uncertain. It is also worth noting that, in view of what we shall shortly discuss, the considerations which make for the falsification of a proposition are considerations which ought to appeal to every rational person. So if *p* is falsified by considerations C then those considerations should falsify *p* for any rational person.

Such a view clearly has a place for the will in the belief of a proposition. For a person can believe all sorts of hypotheses, but ought not to. In this situation a person's estimate of what is belief-worthy cannot be constrained by evidence, because the whole debate between falsificationists and others is about what is to count as evidence, and about scepticism concerning total evidence. In addition some falsificationists are suspicious of appealing to evidence in a theory-free way. So on this belief-policy experience or evidence exerts a negative control over the belief of propositions.

In accepting such a belief-policy, the will may enter, in two ways, in *accepting* such a policy in the first place, and then in *operating* it. In what way is the will involved in arbitrating between the falsificationist policy, and some rival? It is not suggested that the will is involved in exercising choice in some purely irrational way, by the operation of a whimsical volition. Such a view would be indefensible. The point is that what constrains choice (or causes choice, on a compatibilist view) are considerations which are not and cannot be wholly evidential in character.

One of the reasons that John Watkins, for example, rejects any view of rational belief based upon confirmation is because he is sceptical about probability judgements. So he has a reason for accepting falsificationism, and (if reasons are causes) he is caused to accept falsificationism by that reason. Falsificationism is therefore not, in Watkins' case, subject to the will in a libertarian sense. Nevertheless given falsificationism the belief of some propositions cannot be evidentially necessitated since falsificationism itself is not evidentially necessitated.

The will also operates in a not wholly evidentially constrained way in the *operation* of a falsificationist belief-policy. Suppose that two incompatible hypotheses each pass the negative test. Two incompatible propositions (or sets of propositions) are then both equally belief-worthy. Which is to be preferred? Watkins holds that

the negativist conception of the role of experience in science needs to be accompanied by a methodological theory that entitles us to judge, in cases where two or more rival hypotheses have all so far passed the test of experience, which of them is best. But if such a methodological theory is not to have an arbitrary or dogmatic or *ad hoc* character, it must be governed by some overall aim for science; moreover, this aim should itself be non-arbitrary. (Watkins, 1984, p. 118)

Accepting what Watkins says here, it is clear that if what arbitrates between two epistemically equivalent propositions or sets of propositions is the acceptance of a methodological theory about the overall aims of science, then such acceptance is not based upon experience or evidence alone, not even negative evidence.

There may be falsificationist belief-policies of varying degrees of sophistication. For example, in some cases the provision of negative evidence might be sufficient for the abandonment of belief.

Alternatively, it might not be sufficient in the absence of some alternative hypothesis, and negative evidence might lead to the adjustment rather than to the overthrow of a theory. For further discussion of this see Watkins (1984, pp. 156ff ).

A negative evidence or falsificationist approach is meant, in Watkins' hands, to provide a belief-policy for science. It is not plausible to extend it to cover everyday beliefs, for it is not plausible to suppose that the reason I have for believing that there are bees in the hive is that there is no evidence or experience against that hypothesis. This is because a belief that there are bees in the hive is not usually a hypothesis, but has direct evidence in its favour; the bees are clearly visible.

This being so, it is plausible to suppose that a person attracted to falsificationism as a belief-policy might hold it as part of an overall belief-policy, falsificationism providing the policy for science, while some other policy is held for beliefs about everyday matters of fact.


PLANTINGA'S PERMISSIVE POLICY

Alvin Plantinga develops his permissive belief-policy explicitly in the context of the ethics of belief. His claim is that it is not unreasonable or irrational to accept theistic belief (or, for that matter, beliefs of any other kind) in the absence of evidence or reasons. In making this claim Plantinga sees himself as explicitly opposing rival normative views of the grounds on which a person ought, or ought not, to believe a proposition of a particular epistemic kind. Epistemic permissibility is a sufficient condition of rationality in the formation of beliefs, because there is no logically compelling reason to accept the sufficiency of epistemic obligatoriness grounded in some form of what he calls strong foundationalism.

So Plantinga recognises that 'there do seem to be duties and obligations with respect to belief, or at any rate in the general *neighbourhood* of belief' (Plantinga, 1983, p. 30). And he proceeds to deny that to believe in the existence of God without evidence is violating some intellectual duty.

So Plantinga holds that one *may* believe certain propositions without having a rational (in the sense of evidentially self-evident) justification for them, a position clearly in contrast with that which claims that one ought to believe only if A, where A is the fulfilment of some general epistemic requirement which holds of all people in virtue of their rationality. Such permissiveness is not tied either to a process of justification or of falsification, even though Plantinga somewhat misleadingly, as we shall see, uses the term 'justification' in connection with this permissive ethic of belief.

So one may believe propositions which are not justifiable in strong foundationalist fashion. But are there then any limits to what propositions one may believe? May one believe anything, say, the first thing that comes into one's head each morning? Plantinga, reasonably enough, wishes to say 'No' to such a suggestion. And he supports this claim in two ways. He provides powerful arguments against what he calls classical foundationalism, the view, roughly, that a person is only entitled to believe *p* if the evidence for *p* is such that any rational man would accept it. So one reason for holding this permissive ethic of belief is because the most serious rival to it, classical foundationalism, is intellectually flawed. For this reason there is a logical inevitability about such a permissive ethic, in Plantinga's eyes. But, given that there must be this permissiveness, what prevents the choice of a belief on purely whimsical grounds? Plantinga's answer involves drawing a distinction between *grounds* and *evidence*.

This distinction can be explained as follows. While someone may be entitled to hold a belief that *p* such a person may nevertheless not be entitled to hold that belief in all circumstances. In certain circumstances, a person is entitled to believe, without evidence, that God exists, but it does not follow from this that there is an entitlement to believe in any circumstances that just anything exists.

So the way in which criteria for justified belief are developed is not a priori but in terms of actual cases. Plantinga is a particularist; each of us has, as a matter of brute fact, propositions which we regard as self-evident or at least unquestioned. It would be wrong, epistemically unwarranted, in these circumstances, for any of us to deny these self-evident beliefs in the interests of trying to develop or conform to some a priori epistemology. Failing the fact that some general criterion of justification is self-evident to everyone – and so far no such criterion has been unearthed, and Plantinga offers a general argument which claims to show that no such criterion can be unearthed – there is no alternative but for each of us to start from our own individual situation, from what we ourselves find to be self-evident, and to build upon that. This is a version of foundationalism; we might call it *personal foundationalism.*

Criteria for proper basicality must be reached from below rather than from above; they should not be presented *ex cathedra* but argued to and tested by a relevant set of examples. But there is no reason to assume, in advance, that everyone will agree on the examples. The Christian will of course suppose that belief in God is entirely proper and rational; if he does not accept this belief on the basis of other propositions he will conclude that it is basic for him and quite properly so. Followers of Bertrand Russell and Madelyn Murray O'Hare may disagree; but how is that relevant?

(Plantinga, 1983, p. 77)

This still does not quite meet the objection that was voiced earlier. Granted that in establishing criteria for epistemic justification it is necessary to proceed inductively, what counts as a proposition that we are to take note of? Granted that no proposition that was incoherent could be regarded as justified, is anything and everything else permitted?

It is here that Plantinga's distinction between *evidence* and *grounds* becomes important. Only if a belief is groundless is it permissible to disregard it from an epistemic point of view. Basic beliefs, beliefs which are held, but not on the basis of other beliefs, are nevertheless not groundless.

Upon having experience of a certain sort, I believe that I am perceiving a tree. In the typical case I do not hold this belief on the basis of other beliefs; it is nonetheless not groundless. My having that characteristic sort of experience . . . plays a crucial role in the formation of that belief. It also plays a crucial role in its justification. Let us say that a belief is justified for a person at a time if (a) he is violating no epistemic duties and is within his epistemic rights in accepting it then and (b) his noetic structure is not defective by virtue of his then accepting it. (Plantinga, 1983, p. 79)

A number of things now need to be noted. Plantinga does talk of *justification*, but it is what we earlier called *personal justification*, the justification of a person at a time; it is not the justification of a belief or a proposition on evidence acceptable to any rational man. Furthermore such a justification is basic to the extent that it is not founded upon other propositions. Nevertheless it is not groundless, but is derived from a person's own experience, one which may or may not be matched by the experience of others. That experience may justify that belief to that person, in which case the person is entitled to that belief. So this thesis in epistemology, while it is propounded in terms of the example of theistic belief, is of wider application. It concerns the general epistemic structure and grounds of belief, not the peculiarities of theistic belief.

We began our account by saying that Plantinga's is an example of a *permissive* ethic of belief. But it is only such from a certain point of view. If it is compared with any epistemology which construes epistemic duties in terms of sets of general necessary and sufficient conditions applicable to any rational person, then Plantinga's ethic of belief is permissive, for from that point of view those who do not meet those conditions are nevertheless entitled to believe certain propositions with no loss of rationality. But since Plantinga holds that the failure of classical foundationalism is a root-and-branch failure, a failure of principle, it is not as if the permissiveness is a special case. Given this general failure, there is nothing for it but for everyone who wishes to order beliefs in a rational fashion, and to justify them, to proceed on the basis of the grounds that each has for the beliefs held. But since, from the point of view of the various ethics of belief discussed earlier, Plantinga's is a theory of belief *permission* rather than belief *obligation* we shall continue to refer to it as a 'permissive' ethic.

What, then, is Plantinga's belief-policy? Can we speak of a belief-policy here? Why not? The policy that Plantinga is advocating, the only rational policy that he thinks it possible to advocate (and here he agrees with some whose views we have discussed earlier, and disagrees with others), is that one has a prima facie duty to believe any proposition for which one has grounds which are not defeated by other considerations.

> We may say that a condition that overrides my *prima facie* justification for *p* is [a?] *defeating condition* or *defeater* for *p* (for me). Defeaters, of course, are themselves *prima facie* defeaters, for the defeater can be defeated. Perhaps I spot a fallacy in the initially convincing argument; perhaps I discover a convincing argument for the denial of one of its premises; perhaps I learn on reliable authority that someone else has done one of those things. Then the defeater is defeated, and I am once again within my rights in accepting *p*
>
> (Plantinga, 1983, p.84)

If a belief-policy is permissive, and can be established to be such, then presumably no belief-policy can be mandatory. Yet if 'belief' is treated in a person-relative sense, as being something that can only be true of a person at a time, then it may follow that A's belief-policy may be mandatory while B's is permissive. And there is nothing in logic to stop a person adopting a mandatory belief-policy in another cognitive area or areas. I discuss this point more fully in the final chapter when considering the relation between Plantinga's belief-policy and fideism.

Summing up, Plantinga might be represented as holding that in opting for classical foundationalism philosophers have made the wrong epistemic choice. The argument for this conclusion is twofold: the inadequacies of classical foundationalism, particularly its appeal to the self-evident, and the plain facts of experience, the fact that each of us does have beliefs which for us are properly basic even though not self-evidently basic to any rational person. These beliefs are the result of our evidence and perhaps, epistemically speaking, that should be the end of the argument. But it is not. We are seduced by the siren-call of classical foundationalism; we adopt some version of it as our belief-policy, and in choosing this alternative ethic of belief we are forced into denying, or at the least suspending belief in what we know to be true. Plantinga is aiming to reverse this position.

TAKING STOCK

This is perhaps a convenient place to pause and take stock of the line of argument that has been pursued in this and the previous chapter.

In discussing the general question of the relation of belief and the will an attempt has been made to formulate the following general position: that our beliefs about matters of fact are invariably governed by belief-policies, invariably if we would be rational about our beliefs. There may be a possible world in which a person is a complete or perfect passivist regarding his beliefs, an epistemic robot. But such a world would hardly commend itself as a paradigm of epistemic rationality.

Such belief-policies cannot be determined by evidence alone. Other non-evidential considerations are needed, considerations such as the desire to maximise truth or to minimise falsehood generally or in areas of particular significance or importance, or where truth can be attained only by overcoming certain kinds of difficulty.

All those policies that we have considered as evidentialist policies are united by is the conviction that the only considerations that ought to weigh in the adoption of factual beliefs are about evidence. In contrast a case can be made out for there being a variety of non-evidentialist belief-policies, such as those propounded by James and Meiland, according to which some believings are justified by other than solely evidential considerations. But a permissive belief-policy does not entail the relevance or importance of non-evidential factors in rational believing, since Plantinga argues for a permissive ethic of belief which is solely evidential, unless evidence is going to be question-beggingly defined in terms of only what meets the stringent (and Plantinga would say incoherent) standards of classical foundationalism. Nevertheless, while there is no entailment between permissiveness and non-evidentialism the two are certainly consistent.

It is necessary to distinguish clearly between reasons for adopting belief-policies and reasons for adopting beliefs. There is a contingent relation both between the adoption of belief-policies and evidence and the adoption of beliefs and evidence. One might have a situation in which a person adopts a rigid evidentialist policy for non-epistemic reasons. Clifford seems to be a striking case of this, for the reasons that he gives for adopting his rigid ethic of belief have to do with the desirability of social cohesion and the preservation and fostering of civilisation, rather than with the gaining of any epistemic goals. On the other hand, it is possible that someone should hold a non-evidentialist belief policy, at least with respect to some propositions, for epistemic reasons, that is because he thinks that adopting a non-evidentialist policy regarding belief is the best way of attaining certain sorts of knowledge about the world. Perhaps William James is an example of this, bearing in mind his assertion that a rule of thinking which would absolutely prevent me from acknowledging certain kinds of truth, if these kinds of truth were really there, would be an irrational rule.

To say that there are these two broad types of belief-policy is not to say that if one adopts one policy one adopts it for all one's beliefs. It has been shown that, on one interpretation, James restricts his non-evidentialist belief-policy to a certain range of options, and is an evidentialist with regard to scientific propositions.

Further, as we noted earlier, it may be argued, or at least allowed, that there are many propositions about matters of fact, or about ostensible matters of fact, that it is implausible to suppose are the subject of any belief-policy whatever. Let us call these fundamental beliefs about matters of fact. These are fundamental beliefs in the sense that directing attention is logically sufficient to gain the beliefs in question. For example, if one pays attention to what one's fingers are touching one feels certain sensations, feelings of pressure, resistance, smoothness, and so forth. In paying attention under these circumstances one cannot fail to have these sensations, and certain beliefs about these sensations. One does not choose this evidence except in the minimal sense that one chooses to direct one's attention to it.

These sensations may or may not be good evidence for the further belief that one is touching and depressing the keys of a word processor, and they may or may not be good evidence that there is an external world of mind-independent objects of which a word processor is one. There are certain propositions that an alert person placed in a situation will inevitably believe about that situation.

Furthermore, it is not merely that there is a set of propositions which one finds oneself believing, but that belief-policies logically depend upon there being such sets of propositions, in that such policies can only make sense given that there are beliefs which at that time are not subject to any belief-policy. These matters will be considered further in the next chapter.

So, in provisional conclusion, it is possible to suggest a further classification of belief-policies into beliefs about matters of fact which people find themselves holding, evidential belief-policies, and non-evidential belief-policies.

# 5

# *Which belief-policy?*

It has been argued that a person's epistemological theory about factual propositions can be expressed as a belief-policy covering the degree and kind of evidence for such propositions, and the importance that he attaches to both. There are different possible belief-policies embodying differing (though no doubt overlapping) standards of rationality.

As I shall use the expressions, to *justify* a belief involves providing grounds for that belief which are not person-relative, but which are generally acceptable and convincing to anyone no matter what his belief-policy; a strong requirement. To render a belief *rational* to a person it is sufficient to show that it is consistent with the belief-policies held by that person at a time, and that the belief-policy or policies in question do not violate certain necessary conditions for rationality as such. It is not necessary that the belief be consciously derived from the belief-policy, since a belief may, as a matter of fact, antedate the formulation of any policy. In this chapter we shall be pursuing the question of which belief-policy or policies it is rational to accept.

In chapter four a number of broad classifications of belief-policies was suggested. Restricting our attention to beliefs about contingent matters of fact it was claimed that it is possible to classify belief-policies into three broad categories: belief-policies which people find themselves holding at an early age, evidential belief-policies, and non-evidential belief-policies. In addition a distinction was drawn between permissive and mandatory policies, and between verifica- tionist and falsificationist policies. Each class of policy is not exclusive of each of the others, and so various combinations are possible. For example, it is in principle possible to have a belief-policy which is not wholly evidentialist, and is permissive; or a belief-policy part of which is evidentialist, the remainder of which sanctions non-evidential criteria; or one in which the first part is mandatory, the second part permissive, and so on.

The fact that there are many possible belief-policies raises the question of how one may, and perhaps must, choose between them. There are rival ways of considering rationality in the forming of beliefs. It may be held that what is rational in belief is what is required. Or, alternatively, what is required or permitted. It is not clear that one can make a rational choice between such broad differences. Each can seem plausible. Justifying non-arbitrary choice is difficult, and, if the justification of standards of rationality is a necessary condition for the justification of a belief, then doubt may be cast upon whether it is ever possible to justify a belief.

In considering the choice of a belief-policy we shall not be concerned with what Gilbert Harman has called 'maxims of reflection' (Harman, 1986, p. 2) in belief-formation, the need to be careful, to avoid inattention, and the like. We shall take it for granted that the observance of such practical procedures is common to the formation of belief-policies of whatever kind. The aim will be to provide some observations and arguments about how the question of choice between belief-policies is best approached; not to offer an optimal belief-policy, but to offer rational discussion about the very idea of such a policy, and of ways in which a satisfactory policy might be chosen.

## OVERARCHING PRINCIPLES OF RATIONALITY

In the first place we shall discuss what have been called overarching principles of rationality, necessary conditions for any rational belief-policy to fulfil. Such conditions will include logical consistency; that is, as far as the holder of any belief-policy knows or is aware, the beliefs warranted by it must be consistent. Further, a belief-policy should be subjectively closed under deducibility and conjunction. That is, as far as the believer is concerned, if a belief-policy commits such a person to believing $p$, and $p$ entails $q$, then the believer is committed to believing $q$. And likewise with conjunction.

In proposing a sharp and philosophically significant distinction between belief and acceptance Cohen argues that belief is not subjectively closed under either deduction or conjunction, but that acceptance is subjectively closed under each (Cohen, 1992, pp. 27ff.)

Belief-policies are beliefs, beliefs about what a person ought to believe. So Cohen's claim, if substantiated, would be serious, for it would have the effect of demonstrating that a belief-policy had few rational features. It might be possible to parry the force of his argument by conceding that some belief-policies are not subjectively closed under either deducibility or conjunction, while others are. So it might be that the belief-policies we grow up with, being primitive and well entrenched, are not closed, while those that are avowedly voluntary, are.

In any case Cohen's arguments for the distinction are not compelling. Cohen claims

The fact is that you are not intellectually pledged by a set of *beliefs*, however strong, to each deductive consequence of that set of beliefs, even if you recognize it to be such. That is because belief that *p* is a disposition to feel that *p*, and feelings that arise in you, or grow on you, or come over you, through involuntary processes of which you may be wholly or partly unconscious, no more impose their logical consequences on you than do the electoral campaign posters that people stick on your walls without your consent. Beliefs carry no commitments. They are neither intentional nor unintentional. So the statement that you believe that *p* does not necessarily imply that you believe that *q*, even where *q* is quite a close and well-recognized logical, conceptual, or mathematical consequence of *p*. If your logical, conceptual, or mathematical perception is rather limited, active, incoherent, or uninfluential, you may well feel it true that *p* and that if *p* then *q*, without feeling it true that *q*. (*Ibid*, p. 27f.)

It is surely taking the involuntariness of belief too far to suggest one is not intellectually pledged by a set of beliefs to each deductive consequence of that set of beliefs, even if one recognises that the deduction holds. In the case of acceptance, Cohen understands subjective closure under deducibility as follows

Acceptance is *subjectively* closed under deducibility if and only if necessarily for any *p1, p2* . . . and *pn* and for any *q*, anyone who accepts both the conjunction of *p1, p2* . . . and *pn* and the deducibility of *q* from that conjunction, also accepts *q*. (*Ibid*, p. 29).

If Cohen grants subjective closure under deducibility to acceptance, and denies it to belief, this may be because he is not comparing like with like. For the parallel in the case of belief should be

115

Belief is subjectively closed under deducibility if and only if necessarily for any
*pl*, *p2* . . . and *pn* and for any *q*, anyone who believes both the conjunction of
*pl*, *p2* . . . *pn* and that *q* is deducible from that conjunction, also believes *q*.

This surely seems plausible. If a person is limited in understanding and
does not understand what deduction is or involves, then clearly this
will impair an awareness of deducibility and *a fortiori* of closure under
deducibility. But then the same applies to acceptance.

In fact if in Cohen's words one *recognises* the deductive consequence
of a set of beliefs one presumably believes it, though he denies this. If
he is correct in this denial then his references to limitations of logical
perception are beside the point. If they are not beside the point then
they apply equally as much to acceptance as they do to belief.

A person might, through lassitude, fail to draw the conclusions of
the logical operations in which he believes. But the question is not
what steps he actually takes, but what steps he is committed to taking
by his beliefs. The fact that paralysis or weakness of will intervene is
neither here nor there.

## IMPORTANCE

It is obvious that what a putative believer regards as important affects
what is believed, and this is not confined merely to the point that
importance determines or influences topics of attention. As Jane Heal
has shown (Heal, 1988), the disinterested search for the truth is
conditioned by what the searcher regards as being worthwhile; not
just any possible truth claims the attention of the would-be
disinterested searcher. Swinburne has put the same point rather
differently:

The more important is something which I seek, the more important it is that I
should have a true belief about how to get it. Hence . . . the more important
it is, if I am to be rational, that I should investigate and investigate for longer
how something is to be attained.          (Swinburne, 1981, p. 75)

Keeping to our overriding concern, in this book, with beliefs for
which evidence is relevant, it might be thought that this point could
be met if an account of epistemic importance could be given in purely
cognitive terms. But it is unlikely that this can be done, as I will try to
show.

Perhaps epistemic importance could be characterised along the following lines:

A's belief that $p$ is of more epistemic importance to A than the belief that $q$ if the truth or falsity of $p$ affects the truth or falsity of more of A's beliefs than does the truth or falsity of $q$.

This cannot be a definition of epistemic importance, however, since a belief that $p$ may affect many trivial beliefs, but a belief that $q$ only one important belief. A better characterisation may be:

A's belief that $p$ is of more epistemic importance to A than the belief that $q$ if the truth of $p$ and $q$ both affect the truth of $r$ but $p$ affects the truth of at least one more proposition than does $q$.

Difficulties remain, however, since every belief which the truth of $p$ affects may be trivial and every belief not affected by either $p$ or $q$ may be important. Perhaps a fuller account of epistemic importance can only be provided in terms of a person's overall noetic structure, foundationalist or coherentist.

Because of the difficulty of establishing a clear sense of pure epistemic importance it will from now on be assumed that there is no such thing as a pure cogniser, and that one cannot give an account of pure cognitive worth such that the only 'utility' is acquired truth.

If it is going to be impossible to establish a formal sense of importance, then importance must be related to a person's goals or ends. These goals or ends may be alethic and cognitive; it is a mistake to think that a person's ends must all be psychological or ethical in character, as Heil has shown in an interesting discussion of the relative places of epistemic and non-epistemic ends in believing (Heil, 1992). But it is hard to imagine that the will is not involved in the choice of alethic ends. For the will is involved in any comparable choices about non-alethic ends, whether intermediate or final ends. By a choice I do not mean an unreasoned choice; it may be that the choice is formed and executed through argument and reflection as well as through desire, but such factors are not purely evidential in character.

This can be shown as follows. Swinburne makes the point that knowledge is valuable in itself, and especially knowledge of things which concern the nature, origin, and purpose of our particular human community; and the nature, origin and purpose of the Universe itself (Swinburne, 1981, p. 75). And he goes on to consider whether gaining knowledge is, for some people at least, a matter of duty.

But it seems obvious that, while many would agree with Swinburne, many would not; and that the disagreement between them is not solely a disagreement about evidence, or one that evidence could settle. There is a duty to investigate, say, the age of the earth for its own sake only if it is objectively good to do this and if I can be persuaded of that objective good. But I may not be persuaded. Any belief-policy is going to be influenced by whether or not such ends are judged important enough to be adopted.

Yet this is not the most important sense of importance as regards the formation of belief-policies. I wish to argue that there are two other senses of importance which have a greater right to claim our attention in that they enter more intimately into the choice of a belief-policy.

In this study we are concentrating our attention almost exclusively on evidential considerations entering into beliefs about matters of fact. In pursuit of beliefs soundly based upon evidence, not only is there the question of what epistemic ends or goals a person has, what sorts of truths are believed to be right or beneficial or whatever to pursue, there is also the question of the duties and responsibilities to oneself and others which affect the rigour and extensiveness of one's evidential enquiries. Such duties are not determined by belief-policies, but are determinants of them.

If I have responsibilities to others the discharge of which turns on conveying truths to them (as a teacher or professional engineer, for example), then I have a corresponding duty to investigate and assemble such truths to the best of my ability. Is the will involved here? It may or may not be. If such responsibilities are contractual, say, as in the case of employment as a researcher or investigator, yes. The belief-policy which I adopt will depend upon my will; if the responsibilities are not contractual (as with responsibilities of children to parents, for example) then the will may be less prominent in first establishing what is regarded as important, but more significant in sustaining it over time.

Importance in this sense is a motive for truth-seeking or error-avoiding. So it may be that the importance of a proposition is due to the fact that much hangs on it for human good or ill, perhaps because the policy-formulator has a special responsibility for others (Quinn, 1991). This sense of importance must be contrasted with those further senses in which importance is *at the expense of* truth. It may be that what is of supreme importance is to come to a quick decision, or to achieve happiness and peace of mind. In which case considerations of truth and falsity may be conscientiously sacrificed to them.

If importance does enter in this way, then it is clear that judgements of importance will vary, and that in such judgements the will may be involved. There may be non-evidence-based differences of opinion as to the relative importance of different responsibilities; belief-policies with differing degrees of slackness or stringency will result. It may also be that what forces a decision is merely a factor outside the agent's control; the passage of time to the hour of decision, say. In which case, though a person may have a purely truth-seeking intention in contrast with those situations in which non-truth-centred considerations apply, nevertheless the hour of decision may force a belief.

It is sometimes averred that the only truth-centred considerations are evidence-seeking or evidence-providing methods. But this is false. A person may by his lights pursue truth by pursuing happiness. This may be misguided, but it is not incoherent. Whatever its merits such a policy is to be distinguished from that of someone who abandons all concern for truth and believes what is comforting simply because it is.

Are we straying away from solely evidential considerations at this point? Not necessarily. A distinction needs to be drawn between non-evidential *reasons* and non-evidential *interests*. A person may adopt a belief-policy in which only evidential considerations figure, but he may have non-evidential reasons for attaching more importance to certain kinds of propositions than to others. Non-evidential interests may only be satisfied at the expense of truth.

Not only that; despite a person's best efforts to keep evidential belief-policies to the forefront, a permissive belief-policy inevitably allows the intrusion of non-evidential factors. For, granted that a person's belief-policy permits belief in a certain proposition, the person must nevertheless have a reason for doing so and for not believing some alternative. And unless a mandatory belief-policy is adopted at this point these reasons must be of a non-evidential nature.

A permissive policy is not a policy that a person is permitted to adopt, or not. It is a policy whose criteria permit (rather than require) the adoption of certain beliefs. Given that in the case of one or more propositions it is accepted that there is an onus to establish them by reference to evidence, and the standard of evidence is agreed, the question can arise about whether that standard is applied in the falsifying of a proposition, or in its verifying. Establishing a proposition by evidence could mean either attempting to falsify it by devising and conducting relevant experiments, or by establishing a preponderance of evidence in its favour. If the former, one is permitted to believe *p* unless and until *p* is conclusively falsified; if the latter, one may not believe *p* unless *p* is verified, or to the degree that it is verified.

The existence of these senses of importance, affecting the choice of a belief-policy, and in turn matters in which the will is involved, also connect with degrees of belief.

It is clear that beliefs have degrees whether belief is understood dispositionally, as dispositions to behave or feel, or more occurrently. A measure of the strength of at least some beliefs may be strength of feeling, or behaviour or the odds that a believer would choose to gamble on the truth of a proposition.

Lying behind the thought of degrees of belief may be another general principle about belief. On a dispositional account of belief a person at any one time has myriads of beliefs. What form do these have? Do they have the form: A believes *p* more than *q*, where *q* is some alternative to *p* (i.e. where *p* and *q* could not, logically be true together)? Or do they have the form: A believes *p* and therefore does not believe *q* to any degree, given that each is logically exclusive of the other?

Which answer we give has some consequences for the logic of belief. If the first view is taken, then to believe *p* is not necessarily to believe not-*q*; it is to believe *p* more than *q*. So that what a person believes is what a person, with respect to any set of propositions, overall believes about members of that set. Alternatively, one might take the view that to believe that *p* to any positive degree is to believe that *q* not at all. Belief to any degree that *p* is incompatible with belief to any degree in the logical alternatives to *p*.

As we noted earlier it seems that Swinburne adopts the latter position in his account of belief. For he says that to believe that *p* is to believe that *p* is more probable than not: 'The normal alternative with which belief is contrasted is its negation' (Swinburne, 1981, p. 4).

The normality of this seems doubtful. Swinburne is making a recommendation. But the recommendation has the effect of making belief an all-or-nothing affair. On this view, a person may have an array of beliefs, some of which are believed more strongly than others.

Whatever are the propositions believed to some degree, no proposition that is known to be incompatible with those propositions is believed to any degree. If the person is not aware of the incompatibility then the two incompatible propositions may both be believed to the strongest degree.

Any developed account of a belief-policy would have to cover the degree to which a belief that $p$ is required or permitted by the policy. And also, no doubt, the way in which a change in the degree of belief that $p$ which takes place in accordance with the policy affects the degree to which other beliefs are held.

It is possible to have different conceptions of the way in which considerations governing degrees of belief or partial belief may figure in an overall belief-policy. For example, one might take the view that, in Humean style, the degree of a belief ought to be proportioned to the evidence, presupposing, somewhat sanguinely, that not only may degrees of belief and degrees of evidence be calibrated, but that the two may be correlated satisfactorily.

Alternatively there can be beliefs which have little or no evidence in their favour which are not irrational and *a fortiori* belief-policies which engender them which are not irrational. And so in certain circumstances a belief can be determined not solely by evidential considerations, but by desires as well. An instance of this is that of a scientist who follows a hunch even though he has no evidence that his hunch is correct, or not correct. On this point, see Cohen (1992, pp. 89–90).

A more radical type of case where non evidence-centred concerns predominate is in *second-order beliefs*. A person may have good reason for believing something for no good reason. That is, there may be good reason for adopting belief-policies which warrant belief beyond, or even against, the evidence. Such reasons may be, broadly, of two kinds. There may be general reasons against having reasons for beliefs. The most notable case is scepticism. Scepticism may warrant a fideistic belief-policy, one that warrants belief in the absence of evidence, or beyond the evidence. Or one may have good inductive reasons for thinking that a leap of faith will be epistemically successful without having good reason to know what the epistemic success of the next leap will be, just as one may have good reason to think that a surprise is coming without having good reason for believing what the surprise is (otherwise it would not be a surprise). Alternatively, there may be reasons grounded in a particular view of human nature; for example, the basic belief that epistemic fulfilment is to be found in the minimisation of risk; or alternatively, in risk-taking. Different views of human nature are crucial to a comprehension and evaluation of different political philosophies; why not to different epistemologies?

## BELIEF-POLICY CONSTRUCTION

These are some of the ways in which non-evidential importance may enter into the *selection* of a belief-policy. But none of the matters so far discussed enter into the *construction* of such a policy. Can non-evidential matters of importance enter into the construction of a belief-policy? I argue that in certain circumstances they can, without falling into flagrant irrationalism.

Suppose there is no evidence for either $p$ or not-$p$, where $p$ is some contingent truth; or where evidence for $p$ and not-$p$ is as equal as can be. In such circumstances, a person may believe that $p$ or that not-$p$.

There may be many propositions which are not regarded as being of sufficient epistemic importance to settle on evidential grounds alone, which one may none the less be inclined to believe. Alternatively there may be other propositions which a thorough search leaves the evidence more or less the same as for the alternative proposition, in which case one might opt for the truth of $p$ or the truth of $q$. Neither of these cases corresponds to *forced* belief in James' sense. To see this it is necessary to distinguish between rational or logical forcedness, and temporal forcedness. A choice is logically forced, forced in James' sense, when a decision not to make a choice is in effect a choice. A choice is temporally forced when, though the choice offered is not logically exhaustive, a time limit is placed upon it; we shall assume that no such time limits exist.

Some may argue that in the case of evidential equilibrium we are required to suspend judgement. But on what evidential grounds could this be argued? How could it be argued that there is evidence to show that a person may *not* choose to believe to some positive degree that $p$ rather than $q$ is true where the evidence for $p$ is the same as the evidence for $q$, or where there is no evidence for either $p$ or $q$? It is hard to see what the answer to this question might be.

But, if a person is permitted to hold the belief that $p$ to a degree, even though there is no evidence for $p$, or only as much evidence for $p$

as for $q$, what positive reason could he give for such a belief? Well, why could not someone in this predicament justify his belief that $p$ on non-evidential grounds; on the grounds say, of pleasure, or epistemic coherence, or simplicity, or whatever? Or because of the dread of epistemic disequilibrium, agnosticism or doubt, and satisfaction in the the resolution of these epistemic situations, in a situation of overall evidential equilibrium.

## SOME ASSUMPTIONS ABOUT EVIDENCE-GATHERING

Throughout this study we have made the distinction between belief where the aim is to acquire truths and lose falsehoods – a truth-centred concern – and belief where other concerns prompt and influence belief about matters of fact. And we have assumed the prime importance of evidence to the prosecution of such truth-centred concerns. But we have not so far spelt out the assumption on which such concerns rest. We shall assume that a person has properly functioning noetic equipment and that he does not suffer from malfunctions in his reason or his senses. This does not mean that such a person is infallible, much less omniscient, but that the resources are there to make true judgements and to identify and rectify many mistakes. Secondly, we shall assume that the inquirer has indefinite though finite supplies of time and effort. He does not fail through fatigue or through pressure of time. Thirdly, we shall assume that in forming a belief a person is moved primarily by evidential considerations and that personal or other interests which could only be satisfied at the expense of evidence are ruled out.

A further assumption can be expressed in the words of John Locke:

He that makes use of the light and faculties GOD has given him, and seeks sincerely to discover truth by those helps and abilities he has, may have this satisfaction in doing his duty as a rational creature; that, though he should miss truth, he will not miss the reward of it.     (Locke, 1961, IV. XVII. 24)

Locke certainly regarded a person, considered as a rational creature, to have duties, and, it would seem, moral duties to the truth. In this passage at least he makes epistemology a branch of ethics, and carries the parallel between acting and believing as far as it could reasonably be taken. I shall not defend such a bold thesis, but shall borrow a part of it after a word or two more on epistemology and ethics.

Significant parallels between ethics and epistemology have also been suggested. But the existence of such parallels does not inspire great confidence in the ability of a philosopher to say anything sensible about policy choice. One only has to appreciate the long-standing controversy between consequentialists and deontologists in ethics, for example, as a difference about ethical policies, to see that the prospect of rationally adjudicating between these two schools of thought, of showing the ethical superiority of one of them to all the others, are dim.

Yet the history of controversy in ethics does prompt the observation that, while a definitive solution to the question 'Which policy?' may be impossible, nevertheless the fact of that impossibility does not provide a *reductio ad absurdum* of the idea of a belief-policy. Few argue that because there is a long-standing and irresoluble conflict between different schools of ethics there is therefore no integrity about any of the schools, nor is it usually argued that such endemic conflict is proof that ethics is all eyewash and make-believe. More to the point, the fact of irresolubility does not diminish the reality of the choice. Even non-cognitivists recognise the reality of ethical conflict, even if they do dismiss the idea of ethical disagreement.

Locke, as we saw, envisaged someone who asks what is required to function as a good cognitive agent as, in effect, asking what his moral duty is. I shall borrow from this the thought that each rational being has a positive engagement with the truth; either because he holds, with Locke, that it is a moral duty to 'govern his assent . . . as reason directs him' or because rational agents have a natural appetite or inclination for the acquisition of the truth, or for some other reason.

Belief-formation about contingent matters of fact is a practical matter and so, in some sense, an exercise in 'practical reason'. My use of that phrase is similar to Harman's 'reasoned revision of intentions', a review of the policy about what one is warranted in believing and intends to believe (Harman, 1986, p. 77).

By a positive engagement with the truth is meant a policy of maximising true and important propositions, and of minimising false and important propositions; of maximising true and unimportant propositions and of minimising false and unimportant propositions. Such an engagement is not equivocal, however, since two people may equally fulfil it who placed a different value on maximising truth and minimising falsehood. Nevertheless, such an engagement rules out cognitive quietism and agnosticism.

In *Theory of Knowledge* R. M. Chisholm refers to the responsibility of an intellectual being as that of trying his best to bring it about that, for every proposition *p* he considers, he believes *p* if and only if *p* is true (Chisholm, 1976, p. 14). This is all well and good, but as it stands it does not commit the intellectual being to the consideration of any proposition whatsoever. One way to answer this objection is to regard the responsibilities as resting on knowers, not intellectual beings. Or as being expressible as hypothetical imperatives, such as: if one wishes to acquire beliefs responsibly, one ought to try one's best to believe *p* if and only if *p* is true. That is, if one wishes to be a rational believer, one ought to do one's best to believe only what is true. It is thus not a satisfactory belief-policy to have no beliefs, (and so to have no false beliefs), any more than it is a satisfactory way to live never to say anything, and so never to tell a lie. I have no argument for this repudiation, other than a reiteration of the presumption that anyone who is interested in which belief-policy to hold is also concerned to acquire beliefs.

Before each of us reaches the stage of consciously forming and modifying belief-policies we grow up with such a policy or policies which develop as, through trial and error, we reckon with the world around us. It is perfectly possible, philosophically speaking, to reject any such initial and involuntary belief-policy in peremptory fashion, as Descartes, for example, did. It is characteristic of the philosophical methodist to do precisely this.

Anyone who does not reject initial beliefs in this fashion, and who wishes to be rational, accords some initial rational presumption to those beliefs. Such beliefs form for such a person a necessary feature of his overall belief-policy. Following Jonathan Kvanvig, I shall call this general approach to belief-policy construction, 'conservatism' (Kvanvig, 1989). Conservatism, itself the name of a family of positions, one of which is particularism, is not a self-evidently true doctrine. Nevertheless, it has this in its favour, that any alternative to it appears to be arbitrary. Suppose I peremptorily reject my initial beliefs about the truth of matters of fact. What do I put in their place? Presumably what takes their place is some general criterion or set of criteria in terms of which I will in future admit or shun particular

125

beliefs. But which criterion or criteria? On what non-arbitrary, non-whimsical basis, am I to choose?

There may be a satisfactory answer to these questions, but I do not know what it is. The conservative does have a non-arbitrary answer, which is that one ought to start from the position of accepting those beliefs which are at present serving one tolerably well; and that one ought to work outwards from where one is at any time, modifying and improving one's position by developing and applying sets of criteria for belief acceptance and rejection (Kvanvig, 1989, pp. 150–1).

A non-conservative might retort that the issue of arbitrariness is settled by the intrinsic rationality or appeal or convincingness of the general criteria in terms of which propositions about factual matters are to be accepted or rejected. The problem with this suggestion is that such general criteria do not spring fully-formed from heaven. And it will often be found that a rational consideration of the criteria itself logically depends upon beliefs about matters of fact which a person already holds. This would not be so bad were there not, in addition, conflicting sets of such criteria.

A non-conservative might also retort that conservatism is naive in that it endows with rationality beliefs which any person happens to have. Nor will the position be helped by building in conditions about what else a person must believe, or suspect, since if the person is irrational there is no reason why such irrationality should be restricted to one belief.

As a matter of fact initial stocks of beliefs do not typically reflect naivety or credulity, for each is the outcome of the need to cope with the world at a practical level. In addition to this constraint on any person's initial stock of beliefs, groups of people hold many initial beliefs in common. So naivety and credulity are in practice going to be further modified by the fact of common consent. For often, in similar physical circumstances, and perhaps other kinds of circumstances as well, we believe the same or similar things. This is not surprising, given the biological similarity between people and their inhabitation of a common physical and social environment. So it is not surprising that beehive makers and beehive users have important beliefs in common. One could also argue that, though the presumptive rationality of a conservative belief is not very great, nevertheless it is greater than that of any general criterion of rationality.

Alan Millar reinforces this conservatism in suggesting that standards with respect to propositions already believed (in our terminology, the particular propositions of a particularist) differ from those for propositions which one does not already believe. 'If a proposition *p* which you do not already believe comes up for your consideration do not believe it unless you have adequate grounds for doing so' (Millar, 1991, p. 190). What one already believes carries some presumption of truth. And similarly 'If a proposition *p* presents a view on some issue and there are plausible alternatives to *p* on that issue then do not accept *p* unless you have reason to prefer it to the alternatives.' I assume that 'accept' and 'believe' in these passages are being used interchangeably.

So the first issue that a policy constructor has to face is the arbitrariness of any starting-point. And, because there does not seem to be a satisfactory non-conservative response to that issue, and also partly for the sake of the argument, I shall henceforth in this chapter take some version of conservatism for granted.

But which version of conservatism? It is implausible to suppose that *p* is more belief-worthy than not-*p* simply because it is believed. What is required is a more self-conscious, reflective form of conservatism in which reference is made to beliefs about beliefs, to the believer's own valuation of beliefs, to the sorts of things that the believer wants (at the deepest level) to believe. So, in broad terms, that brand of conservatism is to be favoured which makes provision for the believer having a belief-policy about first-order beliefs which implies their presumptive acceptability. More will be said about the importance of the distinction between first-order and second-order beliefs in the last chapter, on fideism.

The aim of a belief-policy is not merely, or even, to provide a means of justifying the particular beliefs held by us in common, but to establish a method of sorting through those beliefs already held, and those likely to be held; a method of discarding some, if necessary, and one which will enable the number of acceptable beliefs to be added to.

Isaac Levi has likened the need to revise beliefs in the light of new evidence to a change in a consumer's income. Given that consumer's utility function, if some prices change, the marginalist theory of consumer demand specifies what the new equilibrium demand would be on the new prices. Obtaining new evidence is analogous to a change in prices, and a theory of rational probability revision determines the new position of rational equilibrium without making predictions or recommendations as to how equilibrium is to be achieved (Levi, 1970 pp. 137–8).

Furthermore the standards of belief called for may differ. The standard of belief of research programmes may be different from that of everyday propositions. Nicholas Nathan has shown (Nathan, 1987) that in epistemology it is important to have in mind the purpose for which evidence is sought. He distinguishes three such purposes: local uncertainty, stability of belief, and global suspicion. Put in our terms what Nathan is saying is that the determination of any belief-policy is partly a function of the epistemic purposes to which any successful policy is to be put. This is another area in which questions of epistemic importance may arise. We shall continue to assume that it is not necessary for any acceptable belief-policy to provide an answer to scepticism about matters of fact.

So there is no one answer to the question, what kind of justification is it reasonable to want? Any answer must make reference to purposes for which the beliefs are being held, and these purposes will differ either along the lines suggested by Nathan, or along other lines. We shall follow Nathan at least to the extent of assuming that the purpose for which an adequate belief-policy is being sought is not the defeat of global scepticism i.e. philosophical scepticism, but something like Nathan's stability of belief, which is to reinforce beliefs against the charge of wishful thinking or illusion, or to test them by such charges.

Besides the assumption of conservatism it will also be assumed that any version of 'pluralism', the doctrine that a variety of prima facie conflicting theories of knowledge about the same matters is warranted, is too facile to provide a satisfactory answer to our question. Pluralism, in its various kinds and intensities, is no doubt an interesting phenomenon, capable of being investigated sociologically and psychologically. But to suppose that it is philosophically satisfactory to state that there are many equally valid, though conflicting, responses to the problems of epistemology is to quell or repudiate that craving for generality which is characteristically philosophical. And to say that the difficulty of answering the question makes pluralism a plausible or attractive position is not much better as an answer. Both answers in effect even if not in intention substitute sociology for philosophy.

This stricture applies, though more controversially, to what is sometimes known as 'Wittgensteinian pluralism', the thesis that various language-games each have their own rules of intelligibility and their own epistemic rules and standards. As we have already seen when considering types of belief-policies, the idea that there might be more than one warranted belief-policy, one to cover one area of human enquiry, another to cover another, cannot be ruled out a priori. Wittgensteinian pluralism is to be distinguished from such an approach. It is unsatisfactory because firstly the claim that there are different language-games suggests the existence of a common standard or standards against which they are to be measured. How otherwise would the differences among the different forms of life be detected? But if there is such a common standard then the characteristic thesis of such pluralism must be false. Alternatively one could go on asserting the existence of a pluralism of forms of life, but only so long as one provides no reason for doing so.

Secondly a problem arises over the idea of justification being internal to a form of life or language-game. The proponents of such a notion must hold out against the idea that rival forms of life, and their justifications, could ever be compared. But in fact they are compared, and judgements are made as to their relative merits.

The reason why they are compared is that despite the emphasis on pluralism there is sufficient common interest and belief among all human beings to make comparisons possible and inevitable. Each form of life, because it is a form of human life, has at least part of its content shared with each other form of life. Granted, this shared content is minimal, and basic; but it suffices to make the thesis of Wittgensteinian pluralism, and the radical autonomy of each form of life, implausible. This point has been developed by John Kekes (Kekes, 1988).

The final assumption to be made is that Quine's naturalised epistemology, (Quine, 1969), and all similar pragmatist, evolutionary approaches to epistemology, are unsatisfactory. Quine bids us understand the link between observation and science in causal terms. Epistemology studies a natural subject, the human person, in terms of inputs of light and sound, say, and the output of descriptions of the 'three-dimensional world and its history'. The psychological puzzles are those that arise from the disparity of the meagre input to the 'torrential output'.

Such a proposal is unsatisfactory from our point of view because it provides a principled denial of all norms in epistemology. It assumes that what is, ought to be. This has its attractions, for it goes a good deal of the way to making epistemology 'scientific', a branch of psychology, perhaps, if psychology is scientific. It also does justice to the idea that our beliefs have a tradition through the aeons of which they have been honed and moulded; their very survival attests the fact that such policies cannot be completely ill-conceived. But it finds no place for reasoned normative reflection upon epistemic beliefs. For further criticism along these lines, see Stroud (1984).

Yet it may seem that Quine acknowledges a place for choice, and hence for the will, even in this starkly naturalistic landscape. For a corner-stone of his view is the indeterminacy of translation from one observer's language to another's. For Quine, sentences only have their meaning as a body; one cannot pair off the sentences in the two languages sentence by sentence. This is unlike verificationism, for example, according to which each sentence has a discrete meaning. Most sentences, not just the sentences in science, are in Quine's book theoretical. It may seem, therefore, that it is in principle possible to choose between rival theories which are not causally determined by the evidence, but which necessarily go beyond it.

No wonder there is indeterminacy of translation – for of course only a small fraction of our utterances report concurrent external stimulation.

(Quine, 1969, p. 81)

Translations are possible only by making arbitrary choices, arbitrary in the sense that in so far as empirical checking is possible the two theories would behave in exactly the same ways. There would, therefore, be choice, but it would range over those matters which are not determined by the data and hence which are extra-scientific. So there is no place for the will at the level of the formation of observation-sentences, only at the level of their incorporation into theories. The choices exercised at this level are of no account, since they concern matters which necessarily go beyond empirical checking.

### TESTING BELIEF-POLICIES

Earlier it was argued that just as in morals we would brush to one side the claim that someone who has never told a lie (because he has never uttered any assertion) is especially virtuous, so in epistemology a person who never believed anything and who on that account never had any false beliefs would hardly be imitable.

As we have also noted, there is much agreement in beliefs about mattters of fact at the common-sense level; and this has the following advantage, that the existence of a common stock of beliefs, however meagre, provides a foothold for testing, or beginning to test, rival belief-policies against each other. For if one possible belief-policy had as a consequence the wholesale repudiation of those beliefs which people hold at the common-sense level, then such a consequence would be a presumption against the acceptability of such a policy, to say the least. But the common acceptance of the beliefs precludes them from playing a distinctive role in adjudicating between belief-policies. They play the role of buttressing necessary conditions for the acceptance of any belief-policy, rather than that of providing clues for sufficient conditions.

Put another way, the existence of a common stock of beliefs makes the idea of the incommensurability of belief-policies from person to person rather remote. It prevents, or at least renders much less likely, the establishment of a criterionless choice between rival belief-policies, since any choice is going to have to provide an account of those logically primitive beliefs that most of us have in common when faced with common stimuli. It prevents the development in the ethics of belief of a theory like that of Hare's in ethics, according to which

If the enquirer still goes on asking 'But why should I live like that?' then there is no further answer to give him, because we have already *ex hypothesi* said everything that could be included in the further answer.

(Hare, 1952, p. 69)

For Hare, the end of the justificatory process is always a criterionless choice, an expression of individual preference. In the face of some overlap in the moral judgements of many people, that looks implausible. In epistemic matters, where, not without reason, a greater degree of overlap is being presumed, a Hare-type response can be ruled out.

So the methods of epistemology, and in particular the development of the idea of a belief-policy, ought to be seen as a further intensification or determination of reactions which, at an unreflective, everyday level, each of us has, and many of which we have in common.

Rival belief-policies may recognise each other as such by virtue of the fact that each is partly concerned with that common stock of beliefs to which we have been referring. They may have other reasons for recognising each other, as Alasdair MacIntyre suggests for the parallel case of rival moral traditions. For example it may be possible for a rival belief-policy to reveal features of one's own belief-policy previously hidden or unattended to (MacIntyre, 1981, pp. 276-7). Furthermore, the recognition of one belief-policy by another is necessary for establishing, or attempting to establish, its superiority over the other.

It is only through such mutual recognition that it can be established that one belief-policy is superior to its rivals. It is through such recognition that the rivals' weaknesses and strengths can be identified and the favoured belief-policy supported. It is only through such comparisons that commitment to one belief-policy can be reaffirmed in the face of perceived weakness, and that the conviction that it offers a more cogent account of certain features be strengthened. It is through such comparisons, and what is learned by them, that the superiority of one position over another is established. How else?

## THE DEVELOPMENT OF A BELIEF-POLICY.

The chief questions that now arise in the development of any belief-policy are those of *onus, standards, importance,* and *permissiveness.*

To take these in turn; is the putative belief in question to carry the burden of proof, or the burden of disproof? Can a proposition be believed in advance of a demonstration that the standards of belief-acceptance have been met, or must a person establish that the proposition meets certain criteria before it can be believed? The conservative and particularistic assumptions of this chapter would support the first view, since according to particularism each of us starts not from the acceptance of some epistemological theory, but from the belief that certain particular propositions are true. And if we start from this position, then the onus is on disproof. There is no logical or conceptual connection between particularism and the onus lying on disproof, since a methodist might hold that the onus was not on the need to establish methodism, but on others to cast doubt upon it.

Though given the spectre of arbitrariness it would be difficult to argue this convincingly.

With regards to the question of standards, the issues here revolve around slackness and stringency. As indicated when discussing Nathan's distinctions, we need not be concerned with the most stringent of standards, that which would satisfy the demands of the global sceptic, always supposing that such standards exist. Even if global scepticism is ignored, questions of stringency in criteria arise. Given that there must be some evidence on which to base a belief, how much evidence ought there to be? How credulous ought one to be?

If we are not considering any issues raised by 'cost' (which is to be distinguished from personal importance, as we have seen), then it might be argued that, as a minimum, standards of evidence ought to be those that make $p$ more probable than not-$p$, whatever the degree of belief. Belief must therefore be supported by some overall positive evidence for. This leaves open the question of whether one might approach the issue of evidential sufficiency in terms of a threshold of evidence.

Standards and onus may be linked. For if one starts from a particularistic position, it would seem to follow that the particular beliefs are an acceptable starting-point in formulating a belief-policy, because they are deemed to be based upon a certain degree of evidence which could be reconstructed even if it is unnecessary for the proposition in question to be justifiably believed. The primitive stock of beliefs is externally, if not internally, justified. The standards which are acceptable for the particular beliefs, those on which there is no onus of proof, should be acceptable for other beliefs, for which proof is called. The initial stock of beliefs sets the standards, though that stock of beliefs is compatible with many different standards. And the standards set by the initial stock of beliefs may lead in time to the disbelief in members of that stock, as more evidence becomes available.

In admitting propositions about factual matters into the stock of beliefs, not only do logical constraints (such as the overarching constraints discussed earlier) enter, but also others of a rather different kind, constraints having to do with simplicity, coherence and explanatory power. A person might prefer to believe a proposition about Joe because, though it is not favoured by the available evidence, in the narrow sense of eyewitness reports, it explains more of Joe's other behaviour than propositions which are better grounded in the evidence, but which leave Joe's other behaviour unexplained. To believe that Joe took the bees may explain why he had bee stings on his forearm, and why he has suddenly acquired an extra hive, even though only Smith was seen near the hives at the time of the theft.

Theories can be adopted or retained for their simplicity, economy, and power, and this is especially true of scientific theories. But the relation between a theory and the evidence that could provide a prima facie confirmation or refutation of it is not a mathematical or mechanical one. Theory retention is often a matter of convention, a decision; often theories are retained against the evidence in the absence of an alternative theory. When does an anomaly become a piece of crucial evidence overturning a theory? In a situation of Kuhnian 'normal science' a decision may be made not to permit the refutation of a theory by evidence (because, perhaps, it is the best theory available, all things considered), but to address the counter-evidence by devising ingenious auxiliary hypotheses. Any theory can be saved by the introduction of such hypotheses, which may be entirely *ad hoc*, and which may eventually prove to be so unsatisfactory, creaking under the weight of their own arbitrariness and complexity, as to call for novel theorising, or for the resuscitation of a hitherto-rejected theory. All such manœuvres betoken the place of the will in theory acceptance and rejection.

The point of logic holds if one is dealing either with low-level theories and explanations, those which are no doubt continuous with grand scientific theories, but which concern matters much nearer to an observer's own vicinity, or with the grand scientific theories themselves. Considerations of simplicity and explanatory power are matters on which an individual, in forming a belief-policy either about such low-level or high-level theories, must take a view. Which is not to say that considerations of simplicity and explanatory power go all one way; the more powerful explanation may be the less simple one. Simplicity may need to be weighed against power, and a judgement made.

Earlier a distinction was drawn between verificationist and falsificationist belief-policies. We can now see that it is possible to distinguish between at least two variants of each; one in which the truth-value of a proposition is verified or falsified by the evidence in a straightforward fashion; the other in which verification or falsification is partly a matter of convention, or decision. It is thus logically possible to be committed to a theory (and adapt the evidence against it by the use of auxiliary hypotheses) or to be committed to the evidence (and adapt the theory). One cannot, as a matter of logic, be committed to both, since there is only a contingent connection between any theory and the evidence. Nor can it be a matter of 'the evidence', since the issue concerns how evidence is to be handled in the first place. It might be held that none of these matters on which a decision has to be taken, or which is affected by convention, is a belief; but such a claim has a look of desperation about it (Lakatos, 1965).

Earlier epistemic importance was stressed, and an unsuccessful attempt was made to define it. Suppose that a person adopts the aim, in any belief-policy, of maximising true beliefs and minimising false beliefs. Without introducing considerations of relative importance, either purely epistemic importance or importance in some wider sense that includes epistemic importance, such a policy would be thoroughly lacking in direction. Are those beliefs to be acquired which are about one's own immediate vicinity? About one's body? Is fairly effortless belief in a trivial truth to be preferred to belief in truths which are more important but on which more effort must be expended?

As we saw, a measure of epistemic importance might be degree of entrenchment. This ties epistemic importance to logical and explanatory impact. Considerations of this kind introduce a measure of economy, if not of ethics, into proposals for the formation of beliefs. One ought to maximise the truth and minimise the falsehood of those propositions which, in one's judgement, have the greater logical and explanatory impact on other propositions. One might place a premium on generality; but on occasion the premium might be on particularity, the search for the negative, falsifying instance.

If the propositions which, for the particularist, form the initial stock of his beliefs are regarded by him as hypotheses open to refutation, then such a position is a version of falsificationism in rational belief-formation. But if, on the other hand, the propositions which form the initial stock are regarded as paradigm-cases of rationally accepted contingent truths, as in effect setting the standard for the acceptance or rejection of any further contingent truths, then there is a distinction to be drawn between the onus of proof and falsification. This is the sort of position that has been defended by, for example, G. E. Moore and Norman Malcolm.

In this position two stages are envisaged; a stage represented by the initial stock of contingent truths which, because of their paradigmatic role, are neither falsifiable nor verifiable, and a further stage, represented by those propositions for which evidence is relevant. The question can then arise: is this evidence to function by a process of falsification, or by verification?

Furthermore, there must be a presumption that, with respect to the stock of beliefs that is held in common by many people, both including and going beyond the initial stock of beliefs, there is a similar belief-policy at work. This is a presumption, and certainly not a logical implication, since, while given our other assumption about the purpose of belief-policies, we are not countenancing insatiable scepticism, none the less important epistemic mistakes on a large scale about matters of fact can be made, as the abandonment of the belief that the earth is flat, or of heliocentrism, or in the existence of phlogiston, testify.

So there is the effective, but still fallible, check of experience. One way in which a belief-policy is developed is by checking the initial stock of beliefs both against an individual's own experience, and the corporate experience and also by adding to the stock of factual beliefs both by the use of formal, logical rules, and more importantly by gaining further evidence.

There are two clear policy alternatives for the use of experience. One may adopt the policy of accepting only those additional propositions which have been justified in some sense, and to some degree. Alternatively one may adopt a falsificationist belief-policy. A decision about which of these policy alternatives to choose cannot be based upon evidence, since each is concerned with the rational assessment of evidence. One might base a decision upon logic; for example, on the logical asymmetry between falsificationism and verificationism. Or one might be moved by the counter-claim that the truth of the counter-instance to which the falsificationist makes appeal must itself be verified. Once again, this is not the place to adjudicate between such long-standing disagreements, but only to insist that they are disagreements about policy, and that, since the positions are exclusive (and exhaustive), anyone bent upon developing a belief-policy must take a view.

In the case of verificationism and falsificationism, as with other epistemological theses, a person may have good reasons, as he sees it, for combining the two in some way. He may argue that for certain types of case verificationism is rationally appropriate, while falsification is to be preferred for other types of case.

Having decided upon either verificationism or falsificationism, or upon some combination of the two, the policy-developer is faced with another choice. Supposing that verification and falsification are wholly and only concerned with propositions for the rational acceptance of which sense-evidence alone is relevant (and not with intuition or a sixth-sense, for example), then a decision has to be made whether the belief-policy so far adopted, verificationist or falsificationist, is intended to deal with all factual propositions, or only with some, and, if only with some, then with which.

In earlier discussion it was noted that 'science' is among the checks that W. W. Bartley proposes. One obvious problem in using such a check concerns its scope. A definition of 'science' would not appear to hold out the prospect of a solution to this problem. Perhaps it could be argued that any acceptable belief-policy ought to contain within it, as a sub belief-policy, acceptance of a plausible theory of scientific method. The belief-policy would then have the form: *I must believe those propositions which are presented as a result of the application of acceptable scientific methods, and I may believe any propositions which are consistent with those propositions and which are not excluded by other parts of my overall belief-policy.*

It is characteristic of verificationism to argue that science is an exclusive criterion for belief acceptance, and that all else is either a matter of logic, or is cognitively meaningless. In the absence of compelling arguments to sustain this position this is unacceptable. There may be other compelling arguments for the exclusiveness of science, but until they are produced the criterion of science can only be, at best, a sufficient condition for an acceptable belief-policy, and not necessary.

More generally, to extend the belief-policy beyond science requires the prior conviction that some ethical or religious expressions, say, are cognitive. It also requires the conviction that science itself is cognitive and not merely instrumental in character. It can be no part of a belief-policy *per se* to enter into such debates, but only to live with the fruits of them.

For any domain of human enquiry that is cognitive and not merely expressive or instrumental it would hardly be rational to exclude that domain from possible belief. After all, 'cognitive' merely means, having to do with cognition. So if it is judged that ethical or theological expressions are cognitive propositions then such expressions, either affirmed or denied, may form, and even must form, part of any belief-policy.

This is only to say that religion, for example, is a domain into which belief-policies enter; it is not to say what those policies are to be with respect to religion. And it is perfectly possible, (as is shown by its being commonplace), for a person to adopt a policy which extends to religion in arguing that the propositions of theism, say, are unacceptable because, it is judged, they conflict with science, just as it has been argued that science and religion cannot conflict, and so propositions of each may together be acceptable.

The problem with science functioning as a criterion for an acceptable belief-policy lies in defining or otherwise delimiting the range of what science renders acceptable. Acceptable, perhaps, to the cultural circle of scientists? In a pluralistic culture it might not be so easy to discover exactly who are the members of this circle and who are not.

There is an important interplay here between the standards of acceptance for a belief-policy which a person might offer, and other philosophical issues and concerns. Suppose that a person held that whatever criteria apply to the acceptance of propositions about science apply in every other case. This has the virtue of being a clear and perhaps straightforwardly applicable belief-policy. But it carries the philosophical consequence that it must be accompanied by, or have presupposed, a convincing argument showing that the propositions of religion, say, or ethics, are susceptible of empirical confirmation and disconfirmation. A position which went the other way, which held that there is a class of metaphysical propositions about God, or about moral rightness, would have as its consequence that there must be a different ethic of belief i.e. different criteria, for belief-acceptance in science and belief-acceptance in religion or ethics.

So it is impossible intelligently to discuss the criteria or 'checks' for belief-policies in isolation from other philosophical considerations, simply because considerations about generality and particularity arise, and these questions are philosophical questions. More will be said about belief-policies in connection with religion in the final chapter.

In the previous chapter we noted William James' belief-policy; he developed a mixed policy in the case of live, momentous, and forced options. If for a Jamesian such options coincided with propositions with a certain content, for example, theological propositions, then a twofold belief-policy would be being developed; one according to which a proposition was believable if there was not (for the falsificationist) sufficient evidence against it or, if it were a theological proposition, there was insufficient evidence against it, but it was live, momentous, and forced.

The following would be a mixed policy of a different kind. Suppose one held that the epistemic value of testimony was not reducible to that of sense experience. One might take the view, for example, that much of our knowledge must necessarily come through testimony, either the oral testimony of living experts and others, or through books. Such a position would hold that Hume, for example, was mistaken in subsuming the worth of testimony to general considerations about our experience of causes and effects. It would still apply standards to the evaluation of testimony, and so have an ethic of belief with respect to it. But since testimony is not reducible to sense-experience, an overall ethic of belief would necessarily be a hybrid.

So, given that there are beliefs that one may have or ought to have, or even must have, that are based upon testimony alone (and supposing a non-reductivist view of the worth of testimony) (Anscombe, 1979; Coady, 1992), one ought to adopt a twofold belief-policy, one governing matters for which direct sensory experience is relevant, another governing matters for which testimony alone is relevant, with arguments about the basis of the distinction, and a view on how any propositions which may be hybrid are to be dealt with.

In sketching how one might proceed in developing a belief-policy, I have chosen for convenience to consider the justification–falsification issue before the issue of whether belief-policies must be pure, or may be hybrid. However, this does not mean that there are no issues of logical priority in forming a belief-policy. Consideration of whether a belief-policy is permissive or mandatory must await the settling of the two sorts of issue just discussed. The reason for this is that the permissive–mandatory issue arises only in connection with fully developed policies. Given that, say, a pure falsificationist or a hybrid verificationist policy has been established, then (and only then) does it make sense to ask whether the policy also requires its holder to believe all propositions which meet the criteria of the policy, or whether it merely permits belief, or whether the policy requires the belief of some and permits the belief of others. Perhaps, for example, one is required to believe all verifiable (to some acceptable degree) propositions, and permitted to believe any proposition for which a non-evidential belief-policy is appropriate.

It is interesting that this last option would not be open to William James, since for him a non-evidential belief-policy is appropriate only where the belief is forced i.e. where a decision to believe or not to believe has to be taken. In such circumstances there can be no place for a permissive policy.

The fact that any such account might employ concepts of a theoretical character, i.e. those which go beyond what is, strictly speaking, experienced, is not an important objection bearing in mind that we are attempting to set forth necessary conditions for an acceptable belief-policy. For while theoretical concepts go beyond direct experience, they do not necessarily conflict with it, or with the other theoretical beliefs which may be held.

### A PROPOSAL

My chief purpose in this chapter has been to open up in a general and discursive way some of the factors which are involved in the choice of a belief-policy or belief-policies covering matters of fact employing evidential criteria. However, in the light of this discussion I shall tentatively propose one belief-policy for the acquisition of true beliefs about matters of fact, and briefly defend it. However, in view of what has been argued, the considerations on which such a policy is based can, at the best, only incline and never necessitate its adoption by anyone.

In this spirit we may say that the satisfaction of the following conditions is necessary for the adoption by a person of a belief-policy. Such a policy must be one that such a person is satisfied

(1) that the field in which a putative belief exists is a true cognitive field (Cf. non-cognitivism in ethics and religion).

So global scepticism is excluded.

(2) that the putative belief or set of beliefs contains no logical incoherence, and that standard inductive procedures are employed in generalising from experience where such generalisations are appropriate.

(3) that closure under deducibility holds.

(4) that the putative belief is such that either there is, on balance, more evidence for it than for its negation or there is a justifiable second-order belief which permits belief in a proposition for which there is no more evidence than for its negation.

(5) that the putative belief is either consistent with a stock of initial unreflective beliefs about matters of fact, and is an addition to the stock through personal verification and testimony, or is such that there is good reason, on the grounds of the counter-evidence provided by the putative belief, or explanatory power or convenience, or falsification, to overturn members of that initial stock of beliefs.

(6) that given one's responsibilities and duties to others the putative belief is of more cognitive importance than any rival proposition offering itself for belief with the same credentials.

The formation of such a policy in the light of such factors cannot, as a matter of logic, be wholly governed by evidential considerations. What governs it are matters in which the will plays a part, and hence the acceptance or rejection of single beliefs in accordance with whatever policy is adopted are also governed by considerations which are partly voluntary and so not wholly evidential.

# 6

# *Belief, weakness of will and self-deception*

It is necessary, at the outset, to distinguish between a cognitivist account of weakness of will, and weakness of will as applied to human cognitive activities. A cognitivist account of weakness of will would account for the phenomenon purely in terms of a conflict between beliefs or judgements. Whether it is plausible to account for weakness of will in such terms is not clear. In this chapter an attempt is made to confirm a significant parallel between action and the implementing of belief-policies by establishing the significant part played in the success or failure of implementation by weakness of will, whatever the correct account of weakness of will turns out to be.

In contemporary discussion, and from time immemorial, weakness of will has been discussed in connection with certain types of *failure to act*. The classical debate, as initiated by Plato, was the problem of how we could fail to act in accordance with what we know to be in our best interests. How can a person knowingly pursue evil as evil? How can we fail to do (*ceteris paribus*) what we know to be right? In contemporary debate, much of it initiated by the position taken up by R. M. Hare in *Freedom and Reason* (Hare, 1963), the issue (at least for Hare) is how a person can sincerely assent to the moral injunction 'I ought to do X' and not do X. Hare's view is that a person must, as a matter of logic, do X unless psychologically compelled to do otherwise, or unless 'ought' is being used not in its full moral sense, but in what Hare calls an 'off-colour' sense, as simply recording what other people, or society at large, thinks the individual ought to do, and not what he himself thinks he ought to do. These claims of Hare's, which have the appearance of being pieces of verbal legislation, have been widely challenged (Mortimore, 1971). None of the challenges, however, questions the fact of weakness of will.

## BELIEF AND PRACTICAL REASON

If believing is, on occasion, a human achievement, if it is a means of fulfilling obligations or of gaining a certain goal or objective, the goal of acquiring truths or of avoiding falsehoods, then it is plausible to suppose that it can be treated as a species of practical reason. (Compare Roy Edgeley's *Reason in Theory and Practice*, which aims to treat logic as a species of practical reason (Edgeley, 1969)). The practice of believing may be considered a means of gaining a chosen end, the possession of the truth. Believing upon evidence may be considered a means of gaining the truth evidentially. This is so even though all of us have many beliefs which have not been chosen, and those we have chosen we may not have set ourselves self-consciously to acquire. Furthermore, if possession of the truth is a good it is not the only good, but one which competes with others (Heil, 1983a).

The practical syllogism which explicitly expresses a typical piece of practical reasoning about belief might be as follows:

1. I want to gain the truth.
2. If I assent to *p* upon evidence E I'll gain the truth that *p*.
3. Therefore, I'll assent to *p* upon E.

The assent referred to in (2) can, of course, be held with varying degrees of strength, which ought to affect the strength of the concluding assent. None of us ever goes through such an argument, but then we rarely do so in connection with any directly practical matter, as Anthony Kenny points out (Kenny, 1975, p. 22). This fact must not count as an objection to the task of recasting our implicit reasoning about belief in explicit form.

On this view assenting to *p* upon evidence E is a means of gaining the truth. Presumably it is not the only grounds that anyone who assents to *p* would assent to it on, since the truth that *p* could be gained by being authoritatively told that *p*; perhaps evidence E obtains and *p* is false; perhaps there are instances of *p* which require, or have, no evidence to make them credible; perhaps someone holds the belief that the best way of gaining the truth is to go *against* the evidence.

Acquiring evidence for *p*, or having acquired evidence for *p*, are activities in furtherance of one of many possible evidential belief-policies, policies for gaining the truth. (2) expresses an individual's doxastic purposes, or the doxastic aspects of the person's overall

143

purposes. Since there are a number of controversial and incompatible methods – represented by the various belief-policies – of gaining the truth, there is need for the reasoner not only to settle upon doxastic purposes, but also to settle upon the best way, all things considered, of achieving those purposes, the best belief-policy to adopt.

John Heil has proposed (Heil, 1983a, 1984) that wherever a prospective believer consults his interests the beliefs which follow thereupon are always a matter of practical determination. 'Reasonable belief, like reasonable action, is most naturally regarded as the result of agent's practical reasoning' (Heil, 1983a, p. 753). If a person wishes to believe that which will give peace of mind or reassurance, then believing in accordance with such interests is a matter of practical reason. But, according to Heil, purely theoretical reason, which is concerned solely with the evidence for the truth of the proposition under discussion, is not a matter of practical reason.

This proposal, while interesting so far as it goes, does not go far enough. For a would-be purely truth-centred believer also has interests, in particular the interest of arriving at the truth about some matter and of avoiding falsity about it. It is that person's paramount interest to acquire such truths and to both devise and follow those methods which will lead to the truth, and to avoid falsehood whatever the cost. If this is so, then the formation of a belief upon purely evidential grounds may equally be regarded as a species of practical reasoning.

Kenny has suggested (Kenny, 1975, ch. 5) that practical inference aims at preserving not *truth* (as it does in deductive inference), but *satisfactoriness*. Granted that an individual has some goal, then his practical inference is valid or sound if it ensures a satisfactory outcome. If possession of the truth expresses a satisfactory goal for me, and if I believe that: if I assent to $p$ upon evidence E I will gain the truth that $p$ is true, then I must assent to $p$ upon evidence E, and the inference is valid as a piece of practical reasoning.

As we have stressed, the will is exercised in belief in a way which is not only influenced by purely evidential concerns. Concern for belief upon evidence may be conditioned by the believer's cognitive projects and also by non-cognitive goals. It is the inclusion of other goods, even other ways of acquiring true beliefs, besides the goodness of acquiring truth on no matter what evidence, which accounts for what Kenny calls the defeasibility of practical inference. Deciding between and among such goods, is one of the ways in which the will is exercised with respect to belief, and provides one of the reasons why there is more than one possible belief-policy.

So one way in which weakness of will can be expressed is as a failure to act upon the conclusion of a practical syllogism, 'I ought to do X'. The truth may be thought of as a good to be desired, evidence which a person possesses may constitute good grounds for believing that *p* is true, and that person may draw the conclusion 'I ought to believe *p*'. And yet such a person may fail to believe *p* because of pressure created by other cognitive or non-cognitive achievements or goals.

To gain a fuller and clearer picture of the failure of the will in believing it is necessary to reaffirm the distinction between cognitive and non-cognitive projects and goals, and evidential and non-evidential means of gaining cognitive goals. In keeping with the overall scope of this study our chief concern here is with self-deception arising from evidential issues alone, with clashes between different evidential means of gaining a cognitive goal. These are the central and interesting cases. But it must not be forgotten that there may be clashes between evidential and non-evidential means of gaining a cognitive goal, and between the respective attractions of cognitive and non-cognitive goals.

## BELIEF AND EVIDENCE

In focussing on the possible connections between belief and action (or failure to act) on the one hand, and evidence and belief (or failure to believe) on the other, we are not concerned with the question of responsibility for beliefs (much less with claiming that believing is always of moral value or importance), but with drawing attention to the phenomenon of weakness of will as regards believing, and exploring some of the features it has in common with action, as well as some of its distinctive characteristics. Further, the focus of the discussion will be on belief-formation upon actual evidence or its lack, and not with what might be called ideal belief-formation, the formation of belief given ideal data, data available only to an ideal observer.

What, then, is the relation between believing and evidence? In considering an answer to this thorny question we encounter an immediate difficulty. If our concern is not ideal evidence, but rather that set of data, propositions or whatever, that a person takes to be evidence, does this not generate a vicious regress? Or does it not reveal a significant lack of parallelism between belief and action on the one hand and evidence and belief on the other? The evidence in question is the evidence that the person in question takes to be evidence. It is personal evidence, not because it is made up, but because it is taken to be evidence. And 'taken to be' here is a synonym for 'believes'. So it might be objected that the relationship between a person's evidence and what is believed upon that evidence is the relationship between two beliefs. If so, how can the parallel between evidence and belief, and belief and action, be a significant one, since the relationship between evidence and belief is in effect the relationship between one belief and another? If the evidence is meant to explain the belief, what explains the belief that it is evidence for the belief?

Though the regress is real it is not infinite or vicious; it comes to an end (in rather the way in which the regress of justification comes to an end) by regarding certain data as needing no further justification, either because they are self-evident, or for some other reason. The difficulty can be met by noting that the belief in the first case is the *belief that p*, while in the second case it is the *belief that A, B, C, etc. are grounds for believing that p*. We might express the problem of weakness of will in evidential belief as: how can it be that a person can believe that, say, A, B, and C are good evidence for the truth of *p*, that such grounds outweigh any counter-evidence, and yet fail to believe *p*?

An immediate objection to this question is: perhaps there is no such failure. Behind this lies the problem of identifying success and failure in belief. If it is necessary to be able to identify failure of belief, it is necessary first to be able to identify belief. Attempts at identifying belief are plagued by the fact that first-person avowals of belief, even granting sincerity in avowal, often introduce an element of distortion. The very fact that the avowal is called for may cause a misperception of the situation. First-person avowals do not embrace those cases of belief which are unconscious or semi-conscious – deeply dispositional cases.

It is obviously impossible to meet this objection by covering the whole spectrum of belief. We shall attempt to isolate one central and interesting class of cases and to discuss the problems of the relationship of evidence to belief in connection with this class.

In concentrating upon a central case there are two extremes to be avoided. Circumstances such as shortness of time may force a person to act and such action may be taken to be a sign of belief. A beekeeper, say, may be forced by circumstances to inspect hives for disease when that action is not the outcome of a belief that the hives may be diseased, but is carried out at the behest of the authorities. The other extreme is the case of a highly theoretical or trivial belief which does not require any overt behaviour. For example, a trivial belief about some remote period in the past.

Between these two extremes is the sort of case where there is a connection between belief and behaviour of an established and regular kind. The belief is naturally expressed in the behaviour, though there is no necessary connection between the two. There are hosts of such cases; cases where the behaviour is a reliable though fallible sign of a belief. For instance, it is generally true that if a person, on hearing a characteristic sound in the house, goes to the front door, this is because of the belief that there is someone at the door as well as certain desires, for example, the desire to see who it is. It is generally true that if a person, on receiving a sealed addressed envelope, proceeds to open it, this is because of a belief that the envelope is addressed to him. There may be factors present which inhibit the behaviour, for example, the belief that a joke is being played. And there may be factors which call forth the behaviour in the absence of belief. But generally in such cases behaviour is a reliable guide of belief.

So we can often know through a person's actions, including his speech, when and what that person believes. Sometimes we may expect a person to believe, either to come to believe or to sustain a belief, and, as reliably evidenced by behaviour, there is no such belief. There may be obvious reasons for this. A person's sensory apparatus may be malfunctioning. Some vital data may not have been heard due to deafness, or because they were out of earshot. But among the reasons that a person does not believe when belief might have been expected may be the fact that the person cannot will to believe.

Here the matter gets a little more complicated, and the pattern of weakness of will comes to differ in the case of belief from that of action. Standardly in the case of action weakness of will is evidenced by a person's failing to act while believing that action is required. In the case of belief, weakness of will may take several forms. One form

147

would be a failure to give assent to a proposition while being aware that one ought, given one's belief-policy, to assent to it. Another would be a failure to believe *p* out of an unreasonable desire for more evidence against *p* to turn up.

A further case is where there is assent to a proposition in accordance with a belief-policy, but where believing does not carry with it the expulsion of, or rejection of, those other beliefs, already held, which are inconsistent with the newly held belief. Here by belief is meant assent upon evidence, and not merely the acceptance of an hypothesis, which may well have no evidence in its support. In the case of such acceptance there is no difficulty in supposing that a person might knowingly accept two conditional propositions with identical antecedents, but incompatible consequents. Given full belief, normal understanding and so forth, a person may come to believe *p* and yet continue to believe *q* and *r* where *q* and *r* are consistent with each other, but where each is inconsistent with *p*. A person may knowingly hold onto prima facie inconsistent beliefs, and fail to disbelieve either of them. This failure to disbelieve a proposition may also be a case of weakness of will, though it need not be, if a person's belief-policy allowed for such an eventuality, as it conceivably might do.

## WEAKNESS OF WILL

So far we have identified a class of cases where a person's belief is normally evidenced by his behaviour, and have noted that weakness of will may occur when a person does not believe when there is good reason to believe. It is possible to provide the following counter-argument; that, since a person did not behave as expected, there cannot have been a good reason to hold the belief which normally would give rise to the behaviour. But, as it is manifestly sophistical to argue thus in the central case of weakness of will – since cases of weakness of will do exist – it is equally sophistical, though perhaps not manifestly so, to argue in this way in the case of weakness of will with respect to belief.

Whether the person is able to, and actually does, detect weakness of will bears on the question of self-deception, which is one explanation of weakness of will, but by no means the only one. In the first place we shall be concerned with diagnoses of weakness of will which fall short of self-deception.

A person sincerely believes when a belief is formed in accordance with that person's belief-policy. If the policy is to form beliefs only upon sufficient evidence, then that person sincerely believes that *p* when sufficient evidence is possessed for *p* and when *p* is believed upon that evidence. There are many such factors which account for deviation from a belief-policy. For example, a person may fail to believe in accordance with a belief-policy because the proposition otherwise believed clashes with a previously held and evidentially well-grounded belief. Or, a person may fail to believe in accordance with a belief-policy because such a belief would clash with those advocated by an eminent authority.

Philosophers disagree over the character of such failures in the will. Some say that, because of the presence of passion, a person's cognitive faculties become temporarily 'bound up' (Charlton, 1988, p. 143), and as a result that person continues to believe unjustifiably. On another interpretation the person sees clearly what ought to be believed, but fails (by an act of will or the adoption of some technique) to believe it (clear-eyed *akrasia*, so called). On a still further view the fact of failure to believe means that the person has judged that it is better to fail.

All these are cases where a person knowingly fails to believe, so they do not involve full self-deception, though there may be elements of self-deception in the adoption of techniques of evasion. The person knows what the data are, and something of what they imply, but resists believing them. Nor does it follow that in such cases there is some intellectual or sensory defect in the individual in question. The person fails to believe, we are supposing, in full awareness of what the data are, and of their appropriateness to belief (as determined by the canons of the relevant belief-policy). In the same way, factors such as carelessness and inattention are disregarded except where these follow, logically and in time, the rejection of the data.

There are at least two senses in which philosophers and others have talked of incontinence, two models. According to the first of these, incontinence is a matter of a conflict of wants in which one's stronger or more stable and longer-lasting wants are suddenly overpowered by a temporary need or desire. This is the analysis offered by Kenny, for example, in *Will, Freedom and Power*. Charlton offers a similar analysis. He refers to a spectrum of cases covered by the phrase 'weakness of will' (Charlton, 1988, p. 178). In his account Charlton, following Davidson, attaches a great deal of importance to the prima facie character of practical beliefs (*ibid*., pp. 115). Incontinence, on this view, is simply the result of competing goals.

A second type of account of incontinence invokes wishful thinking and self-deception, cases where the agent does not recognise the wrongness of his failure to adopt or follow a belief-policy. Cohen distinguishes between self-deception, where a person is mistaken through his own fault, with no intention to deceive, and self-deceit, where a desire to deceive has unconsciously motivated that person (Cohen, 1992, pp. 134-5). No doubt incontinence can be explained in each of these ways, but it is self-deceit that creates the paradoxes. I shall continue to use 'self-deception' to cover this sort of case.

## MODES OF SELF-DECEPTION

Just as a failure to believe upon evidence or upon the stronger evidence may be due to self-deception, so self-deception may be explained in different ways. David Pears sketches various strategies of self-deception (Pears, 1984, pp. 59–63). Two broad approaches to the question of resolving the paradox of someone believing something he does not believe have been developed. Let us call these the *one-minded* and *two-minded* approaches.

An example of a two-minded approach is Donald Davidson's account of irrationality, including self-deception. Davidson (1982) supposes that irrationality is best explained by the idea that the mind can develop various semi-independent structures.

The way could be cleared for explanation if we were to suppose two semi-autonomous departments of the mind, one that finds a certain course of action to be, all things considered, best, and another that prompts another course of action. On each side, the side of sober judgment and the side of incontinent intent and action, there is a supporting structure of reasons, of interlocking beliefs, expectations, assumptions, attitudes and desires.

(Also consider Audi, 1979, and Mele, 1983b. A similar account can also be found in Pears, 1984. Two-minded accounts are criticised by, among others, Johnston (1988) and Van Fraassen (1988)).

Davidson suggests that it is not possible to account for action that is performed in the face of what a person believes is the best thing to do merely on the weakness of will principle. Weakness of will may be too irrational, due to the intrusion of some alien force, whereas certain kinds of irrationality, such as self-deception, have the character of actions done for reasons. So self-deception and the kind of irrationality associated with it is not simply action due to blind force (this is too irrational) nor action for a reason all things considered (this is too rational). It is an intentional act done against the agent's best judgement.

According to Davidson, whereas in the normal case it is what the particular beliefs and desires are beliefs about and desires for that cause the action in question (the intentional content of the proposition believed, given certain beliefs and desires, functions as a cause), in the case of irrational action the beliefs and desires cause the action, but not via the propositional content of the belief or desire. In self-deception the desire to retain a certain goal causes the person to believe that the goal will be more efficiently achieved. This pattern of explanation might be applied to epistemic incontinence as follows.

If M1 and M2 are two semi-autonomous structures, M1 may be supposed to have a certain belief-policy for believing *p* given evidence E. The recognition of the imminence of that believing and the anticipation of its consequences (the imposition of certain epistemic costs, say) causes M2 to adopt another policy, or to fail to abandon an existing policy. The belief-policy held at one level causes the belief that it is possible to integrate a new or desired belief with it, but not because the belief-policy acts as a reason. Self-deception imposes a spurious or artificial unity on the split-mindedness because of the cost of recognising it. The wish to believe causes the adoption of a strategy whose true character is masked from the agent. The suppression of the wish from the consciousness is its redescription in ways which make it assimilable by a currently held belief-policy.

According to the one-minded analysis of self-deception (for example, Szabados, 1974), the deliberateness that distinguishes self-deception from wilful ignorance or out in the open weakness of will, the deliberate irrationality or inconsistency which a person hides from himself, is to be understood in terms of a combination of at least two factors. In the first place the self-deceiver has a goal or personal stake in the avoidance of certain kinds of belief or action or emotion. Such avoidance typically has to do with comfort or pleasure or self-esteem. In the second place such a person adopts a strategy or technique in order to achieve this goal.

In the case of epistemic self-deception there is a failure to come to terms with what is a certain level of evidence available (given that person's belief-policy). The evidence may not be so strong as to make a reinterpretation of it totally implausible. Yet it is the degree of such evidence which provides one reason for regarding such self-deception as a blameworthy condition (Szabados, 1974, p. 61). Also the strategy of self-deception is one that is undertaken gradually; there is a gradual change in judgement, so that the person's overall pattern of beliefs, their self-consistency and coherence, is not overtly disrupted. The self-deceiver is accustomed to gradual shifts in opinion.

The description 'self-deception' better characterises the culmination and effect of this policy than the strategy itself. Various other factors might be at work; a principle of compensation; a tendency to procrastinate; a willingness to be distracted and to neglect to concentrate; the place of imagination. Being gradual and as yet of a purely intentional, non-behavioural character, the change in belief is not noticed.

Such failures might also be symptomatic of a failure to want to believe in accordance with one's accepted belief-policy due to a preoccupation with a more superficial want. In such a situation one believes that *p* because one wants to, but one does not want to want to believe that *p*. Nevertheless the more superficial belief prevails. The real facts may stare one in the face and are not recognised because one is operating with a belief-policy which does not recognise the facts for what they are. This may be especially true in the case of self-knowledge.

On this view, which portrays self-deception in essentially dynamic and strategic terms, evidential self-deception (that is, self-deception over the application of an evidential belief-policy to believing) is an abuse of a belief-policy, the adoption of a perverse, parasitic belief-strategy which masks from the agent a departure from an avowed belief or belief-policy. One may fail to believe that *p* at *t2*, having believed *p* at *t1*, when there has been neither forgetfulness nor psychological coercion, and where the evidential support for *p* remains unchanged.

It is not my purpose to adjudicate between the single-minded and double-minded accounts of self-deception, since our concern is not with self-deception *per se,* but with weakness of will and self-deception as they apply to believing. The parallels between action and the adoption and use of belief-policies will be made more plausible if it can be shown that there is a credible account of weakness of will in believing considered either as a case of incontinence on Kenny's understanding of incontinence, or as a person's action through self-deception, whether this is understood in either a single-minded or a double-minded way. We shall consider each of these modes of epistemic self-deception in turn.

## ONE-MINDED SELF-DECEPTION IN BELIEF

Epistemic self-deception arises at least in part because belief does not entail or require for its genuineness that there are certain incontrovertibly clear actions that are expressive of the belief. Suppose that genuine belief did require this. Then there could be no failure of match between belief and action, and the opportunities for self-deception would be much reduced. There would still be an opportunity for the agent to misidentify or misdescribe the nature of the action the belief gave rise to, and so to deceive himself. Even where there is a strong connection between belief and action, such that belief almost always issues in action, self-deception can arise through mistaking the outward symptoms or manifestations of the belief for the belief itself.

Self-deception with respect to belief about factual matters may be said to be deeper than that with respect to intention, for an agent might intend to do a particular thing, while not believing that doing that thing is the best or the most appropriate or the correct thing to do. A person may nevertheless intend this simply because what the occasion demands is an action of that type irrespective of what is believed. Intentions may be kept up even in the absence of belief, but beliefs cannot be similarly kept up.

What then is self-deception with respect to belief, the belief that $p$? It is a person's believing that $p$, while not believing that $p$ is believed; or more strongly while it is believed that $p$ is not believed. There is a useful discussion of the logical form of self-deception in Haight (1980). Self-deception is thus distinct from the occurrence of prejudice, wishful thinking or wilful ignorance because it contains, as an essential element, the purposive sustaining of a belief during disbelief. Hence the so-called paradox of self-deception.

With regard to belief about matters of fact there seem to be two avenues of self-deception. The first is self-deception about the exact character of the belief, the second about the character of the evidence for the belief. A person may be deceived about a cognitive state, mistaking an intensity of emotion for strong belief, or certain behaviour as conclusive evidence for belief.

Alternatively, a person may mistake the evidence, not through a natural gullibility or credulity which cannot properly estimate evidence, but because of an unrecognised wish to make more (or less) of the evidence than it warrants. The lack of recognition is crucial. If the wish is recognised then this is a plain and straightforward case of the falsification or exaggeration of the data in the furtherance of some interest or other, and so not self-deception.

There are numerous different strategies and combinations of strategies used to initiate and sustain self-deception. With belief and belief-policies in mind it will be useful to glance at some of these.

There may be self-deception through the admittance of a wrong description. As noted above the description under which a belief is held, or under which the evidence for it understood, is of vital importance. How do such redescriptions operate in the case of belief about matters of fact and belief-policies? There are several different cases to be borne in mind. For instance, there may be the disguised substitution of one degree of assent for another. A person may deceive himself about the strength of a belief that *p*, mistaking weak belief for strong belief or vice-versa. Again, there may be a disguised substitution of belief for no belief. I may believe myself to believe that *p* when I do not. Both of these are cases where self-deception occurs or is sustained within a given belief-policy. In addition, there is the disguised substitution of one belief-policy for another. This would be a person's wilful, but disguised, failure to recognise dispositions to believe, doxastic virtues or vices. Thus a person might describe manifest irrationality as rationality, believing it to be such.

A second strategy which initiates and sustains self-deception can be called the inexplicitness strategy. Self-deception is here sustained by a person's failing to make beliefs about matters of fact explicit without realising or fully realising this. A person might allow himself to be distracted. Here there is no need to invoke a wrong or inappropriate description of what is taking place, because the whole point of this

154

strategy is that the activity in question is reckoned to be not sufficiently developed to require a full description. Belief remains at the stage of an unavowed disposition, a disposition which is not expressed through action. There is a sense in which performing an action can make a disposition concrete or explicit. Under these circumstances, given the action, there is no denying the disposition (except of course by having recourse to another strategy, such as the redescription strategy). A belief may never have the occasion to develop itself in action, and so a person might continue with the wilful delusion that *p* is believed when this is not so, or continue with the belief that a certain belief-policy is being adhered to when it is not.

A third strategy for initiating or sustaining self-deception regarding belief concerns the disguisedly wilful mistaking of symptoms. A person may mistake the intensity of emotion, volubility (or the lack of it), certain kinds of socialising, each as being the sign of real belief when it is not.

Finally, there is what might be called the detachment strategy. Certain beliefs or belief-policies are disguisedly detached from the self so that that person comes to believe that the belief or belief-policy in question represents the position of some other individual or authority, when in fact the belief-policy in question is one which the agent subscribes to, as all objective tests reveal.

The fact that it is plausible to give detailed accounts of the inception and sustaining of self-deception regarding factual beliefs and the belief-policies which sustain them is evidence that factual beliefs and belief-policies are each subject to self-deception and are, therefore, sufficiently similar to other human conditions subject to self-deception.

There is also a similarity in the motives which may lie behind these various strategies of self-deception. The motive in factual belief and belief-policy cases will typically be that of maintaining that a person is more evidentially rational than in fact is the case. And so a person may deceive herself into thinking that she is not a Christian when she is, because openly to admit that she is would be for her to flout her own avowed canons of integrity and rationality. This is how self-deception differs from cases of straightforward prejudice and wishful-thinking – they lack the element of disguised purposive inducement of belief or of its sustaining which is characteristic of self-deception. Similarly, in the ordinary cases of weakness of will, the effort to maintain consistency does not arise. The agent knows that consistency is already gone.

### TWO-MINDED SELF-DECEPTION IN BELIEF

If we apply what might be called the Davidsonian analysis of self-deception to belief, each person's rational beliefs are formed in accordance with one overall belief-policy which the agent either explicitly or tacitly subscribes to. Or alternatively all rational belief is in accordance with one belief-policy applied at a time, since there may be quite consistently different belief-policies for different subject areas. The belief-policy which someone applies in the case of science may be different from that which is applied in religion, or that which is applied to everyday matters of fact may be different from that which is applied in the case of scientific hypotheses. This observation is not intended either as a criticism or an endorsement of such multiple policies. Weakness of will regarding belief is then explicable as an irrational rejection of beliefs which ought to be adopted in accordance with a person's belief-policy. Taking all things into account, a person subscribes to the view that beliefs ought to be formed in accordance with a certain policy, but fails to do so through the operation of a second, hidden belief-policy.

Alfred Mele (1983a) argues for doxastic *akrasia* on the following lines: that a person may believe that it is better to do A than B (better to belief *p* than not-*p*, given a particular belief-policy), but that this very belief sets up anxiety as a result of which the agent judges that it would not be better to do A than B. These cases involve a change of mind: but the verdict of *akrasia* is nevertheless justified because the change seems unreasonable. But as we have seen there are cases of weakness of will which do not involve a change of mind in this way.

According to John Heil (1984, pp. 66–7), who follows Davidson at this point, failure is due to the evidential or belief-worthy character of the proposition failing to exert its appropriate causal character in the formation of the belief, this failure being due to the agent's total psychological state.

So a person may have, let us say, the belief-policy of believing only upon sufficient evidence, yet on an occasion a belief may be formed in accordance with some whim, while the belief-policy is still firmly adhered to. So in the light of this belief-policy, the one he professes and adheres to, such a person has recognised that *p* ought to be believed, but has failed to believe because of irrationality. Weakness of will, doxastic incontinence in Heil's phrase, is a momentary rejection of this avowed policy, a policy which has indicated on this occasion that there is one proposition that is more credible or belief-worthy on evidence E than any other proposition.

Heil defines doxastic incontinence as follows

   (i) S takes P and $P^1$ to be epistemically incompatible;

   (ii) S holds R and $R^1$, and takes these to be all that is relevant to the epistemic warrant of P and $P^1$ respectively;

   (iii) S takes R epistemically to outweigh $R^1$, hence P to be more warranted than $P^1$ given R and $R^1$.

   (iv) S holds $P^1$ (and does not hold P).

If we wish to give a general account of the phenomenon of doxastic incontinence then this definition is defective because it incorporates a non-neutral account of epistemic warrant, according to which a person must, in Heil's words, be doxastically incontinent when he believes 'in the teeth of the evidence'. For this reason Heil's later characterisation, 'all he regards as having an epistemic bearing on the belief in question' is better.

Heil's initial, unqualified approach is unsatisfactory because it rules out, by definition, as not being a case of doxastic incontinence, the case of someone who has the view that certain propositions ought to be believed simply because they go against the evidence, or because they go against the evidence in some peculiar way. Kierkegaard, cited by Heil, (1984, p. 64) might be a good example of this. Despite what Heil says, Kierkegaard does not, by his view of religious belief, recommend doxastic incontinence. For Kierkegaard has reason, as he thinks, to suppose that the evidence for certain conclusions is not to be trusted to the degree of passionate intensity required by faith in God. He holds that there are certain areas of enquiry in which the gathering of evidence is irrelevant and perhaps even misleading for the formation of justified beliefs in that area. There seems to be nothing self-contradictory about such a position. For someone taking such a view incontinence would be believing in accordance with the probabilities, and the knight of faith would resist such temptation. And if, when faced with a situation which demands faith against evidence, such a person reasons in accordance with the probabilities, like a worldly person, then that is doxastic incontinence. So the phenomenon of doxastic incontinence is neutral as between the whole range of possible evidential belief-policies.

In raising the question of weakness of will with regard to belief and belief-policies one of two quite different phenomena may be in view. The more familiar one is where there is a conflict between ends, in this case between the cognitive ends of learning and discovering, and non-cognitive ends such as solitude, or money, or sensual pleasure. Having chosen one such end a person may be regarded, or regard himself, as incontinent if a lapse occurs.

It is plausible to regard at least some such conflicts as moral matters, particularly if the belief-policy adopted is due at all to one's social or professional responsibilities. And the 'weakness' in question can go either way. A person may experience weakness of will because of being drawn to cognitive pursuits when he ought to be pursuing non-cognitive ends, or vice-versa. There is nothing characteristically epistemic or doxastic about this; it is a straightforward case of a person having more than one end and having the difficult job of choosing between them. No one can seriously doubt that such choices have to be made.

The second phenomenon is one in which (as was explained earlier) there is a conflict between incompatible belief-policies. Since belief is conceptually tied to truth, belief-policies are by definition cognitive. So here what is being envisaged is a conflict between cognitive means and cognitive ends, a situation in which a controlling belief-policy (either the overall belief-policy, or a belief-policy with regard to some particular subject-matter) is abandoned because of the temporary attractiveness of another belief-policy. Finally, it is possible to envisage the extension of cases of self-deception from single beliefs or belief-policies to whole sets or webs of belief. One possible account of ideological beliefs, illusory or distorted beliefs, whether of individuals or of classes, is that such beliefs are the product of wilful distortion.

How do such belief-systems arise, and how are they sustained? One possible answer is that ideological beliefs are not irrational, but straightforwardly mistaken, due to poor evidence or undeveloped argument. Ideology is ignorance. Another possible explanation is that such beliefs are relatively true, true for the believer, but not perhaps for us the observers. Still another possible explanation is that the reasons people give for their ideological beliefs are not their real reasons for holding those beliefs, but that the reasons given are inventions of the will. This is ideology as wishful thinking or false-consciousness.

This last view is certainly a possible, if not a plausible one. Jon Elster (Elster, 1982) distinguishes between *illusory* beliefs, which arise due to the presence of bias from the sources of such beliefs, and *distorted* beliefs, the result of wishful thinking based upon, for instance, pessimism and conformism. It is only distorted beliefs which are relevant here. So wishful thinking may lead to a belief that *p* for which a person has good grounds anyway, but the belief is independent of these grounds, as when Agnes might possess good grounds for thinking her honey will win the prize, and believe that it will, not on those grounds, but through sheer wishful thinking. Nothing is hidden away from her, as in self-deception. She believes a proposition because she wants it to be true and not because of the grounds for its truth, even though there are such grounds.

All belief is formed in accordance with various belief-policies held by the agent which correspond, in the case of action-incontinence, to various different kinds of wants or needs which the agent possesses. These belief-policies may conflict. Doxastic incontinence is to be understood and explained in terms of the relative strengths and weaknesses in the holding of these policies at a time; it may be regarded as the overpowering of one standing belief-policy by the (temporary) superiority of another. Weakness of will can be revealed in conflicts between cognitive and non-cognitive goals, but also, and more relevantly for our purposes, between different ways of achieving cognitive goals. A person may be torn between the attractions of rival cognitive strategies.

## SCEPTICISM AND SELF-DECEPTION

Are some forms of *scepticism* cases of doxastic self-deception? I shall discuss this question with reference to that form of scepticism which advocates and, if successful, issues in a total suspension of belief about all matters for which either belief or knowledge are conventionally claimed. Such scepticism, more characteristic of classical sceptics such as Sextus Empiricus than of Descartes, can be expressed as a particular belief-policy: *believe only those matters of fact which there is good evidence for or which keep you from disquiet or anxiety*; or, more briefly, *believe only*

159

*what keeps you from disquiet or anxiety.* One of the goals of such scepticism was to avoid unnecessary perturbance of spirit, and to gain or retain peace of mind. It was an attempt to withdraw from the vagaries of the world. For an account of such scepticism see Penelhum (1983b).

The question is not whether such a policy succeeds, or to what extent it succeeds, but whether the belief that it succeeds to some extent, or to an appreciable extent, can be held without self-deception. Such scepticism aims to suspend all belief except what is in accord with local custom and tradition. But does such a policy itself involve belief? Does such scepticism require the sceptic to think that it does not?

M. F. Burnyeat argues that in ancient scepticism what is constrained is not belief but assent, that is a state of mind which makes no truth claims, but simply records and responds to appearances. As Burnyeat points out, this is different from Humean scepticism in which habit produces belief. Burnyeat argues that the ancient sceptics cannot consistently maintain such a position, but offers no diagnosis of why they believed that they could (Burnyeat, 1983).

According to Terence Penelhum, in the classical scepticism of Sextus Empiricus suspense of judgement comes about

upon the psychologically equivalent effects of the countervailing arguments that the Skeptic examines, and cannot be construed as an action on the Cartesian model any more readily than the way things appear to him or the quietude that suspense itself gives rise to. (Penelhum 1983b, p. 12)

Granted that such suspense is not a Cartesian act of the will, it is nevertheless inaccurate, because incomplete, to characterise it as a mere psychological effect. For this would be to forget that such scepticism is goal-centred. It is directed to the goal of peace of mind. The sceptic desires such peace above all things, and his sceptical suspense of judgement is a result of this desire, given the vagaries and unreliability (as he judges) of ordinary experience. The vagaries and unreliability of the experience would not by themselves issue in the suspense of judgement in the absence of the stated goal.

For such scepticism to be a case of self-deception it must have about it the air of inconsistency. One person can deceive another only if the belief of the person deceived is inconsistent with the truth of what is believed. I can deceive myself only if what I believe about *p* I also (in some sense) do not believe about *p*. Penelhum thinks that such scepticism is inconsistent because on a plausible view of the relation between belief and the will, being inclined to believe that *p* is a case of believing that *p*. Hence, since such scepticism involves taking certain things to be true to a degree, the opinions and utterances of others, for example, it involves both a suspension of belief and an inclination to believe. And this is inconsistent. Penelhum writes:

> But to say what seems to be true to one is to say what one is inclined to believe, which in Sextus' universe of discourse can only be to indicate what one is inclined to believe of reality. Even if the language of passivity is correct to use here (and I think it is), to say how things appear to oneself is to say what one is inclined to believe about them. If this is combined with a Skeptic suspense of judgement as to how they really are, the total state of mind that the Skeptic expresses when conforming to appearances undogmatically is one in which he inclines to think that *p*, though he suspends definite commitment whether or not *p* is so, since he has found no reasons to believe that *p* is so that are stronger than those that can be given for thinking it is not so.
>
> (Penelhum, 1983b, p. 42)

The upshot of Sextus' sceptical outlook is that he adopts the policy of being inclined to believe *p*, while suspending belief as to *p* or not-*p*. But if being inclined to believe is a case of belief this is inconsistent.

Penelhum claims that there are two alternative interpretations of the phrase 'inclined to believe'. If belief is subject to the will in some immediate and straightforward sense, then an inclination to believe can be represented as a case of inclining to act. If I can do either X or not-X, then the inclination to do X is either a desire to do X or, if X is judged improper or immoral or whatever, the inclination can be regarded as a temptation. Similarly, says Penelhum, with belief, if belief is subject to the will and is an action. If on the other hand belief is not an action, then being inclined to believe is believing to some extent. 'If belief is a passive condition, inclination toward it is a mild or early stage of that condition itself' (Penelhum, 1983b, p. 42); that is, presumably, belief upon some of the evidence that is offered for the truth of the belief in question.

Penelhum says that the matter of the consistency or otherwise of such scepticism, and *a fortiori* of whether or not it is a case of self-deception, comes down to the issue of whether or not belief is subject to the will. I shall argue that the place of the will in belief is irrelevant here, but that there is still an issue about scepticism and self-deception.

Penelhum distinguishes between belief as an effect, Humean-style, and belief as a choice, Cartesian-style. Let us accept this distinction. He says that the inconsistency in scepticism can be avoided only if belief is subject to the will. But belief is not subject to the will and so such scepticism is inconsistent. Even if belief were subject to the will the problem of inconsistency would not be avoided. For if belief were subject to the will, and the inclination to believe were then to be regarded as a desire or temptation, it is still a temptation to believe that *p*. So that the total situation can be represented as: A believes neither *p* nor not-*p* but has the desire to or is tempted to believe that *p*.

If an acceptable way of characterising the operation of the will in belief (supposing that belief is subject to the will) is in terms of desire, as Penelhum suggests, then the suspension of belief that *p* is to be understood as: A neither desires that *p* nor desires that not-*p*. But if this is an acceptable characterisation then the inconsistency remains. It is now describable as: A desires neither that *p* nor that not-*p*, but desires that *p*.

So, whether it is supposed that belief is subject to the will or is an effect, the inconsistency involved in the scepticism of Sextus Empiricus remains to be dealt with. The central issue is not whether belief is or is not subject to the will, but what the facts about the sceptic are. Can scepticism be consistently maintained? Is this a belief-policy which can be consistently maintained or is it one which will inevitably clash with other policies? And if such a policy can be maintained is one price for its maintenance, or one condition for its maintenance, that the sceptic deceives himself?

These questions can only be settled by whether there is good objective evidence that the sceptic is, despite himself, holding beliefs about those matters of fact that daily have to be reckoned with, such mundane beliefs as those regarding which parts of his environment are edible, which parts are physically resistant, and so on, and whether if such beliefs are held scepticism is only possible at the price of self-deception. The tests for the presence of self-deception would be the standard tests which are applied in any putative case of self-deception; for example, is there reason to think that the sceptic is attached to one belief-policy to such a degree that a strategy is adopted which has the effect of hiding the evidence for certain matters of fact that the sceptic possesses?

Even if it could be shown that the sceptic has beliefs about the world, and so is formally inconsistent, he may nevertheless be able to offer the following rejoinder as a palliative: although scepticism is formally inconsistent, nevertheless the beliefs about the world implied by his actions are those to which a very low personal cost is attached. So although he is not freed from all disquiet of mind, because he is not freed from all belief, he is nevertheless freed from a good deal of it.

# 7

# *Responsibility for belief and toleration*

The previous chapters have developed the thesis that all beliefs about matters of fact are the outcome of belief-policies, ways in which, for a truth-centred cognizer, believing is related to evidence. The belief-policies themselves are not determined by evidence alone. So there is a significant sense in which belief is subject to non-evidential grounds. Independently of this, it has been argued that there is a strong parallelism between believing and action such as to make it reasonable to treat the adoption of a belief-policy as an action.

If believing is a willed activity in either or both of these two senses, then perhaps we are no less or more accountable for our believings than we are for our actings. Perhaps an ethics of belief is not only possible, but inevitable. If belief is in no sense voluntary, and believing that *p* is, say, a necessary and sufficient condition for performing some action A rather than B, then the agent is not responsible for that action. Yet some philosophers have expressed dismay at the consequences of such a prospect, holding that if people are responsible for their believings, intolerance and persecution are justified.

## BELIEF, PERSECUTION AND TOLERATION

As we have seen H. H. Price held that in some sense belief depends upon the will, but he has this to say about the idea that a person may be held responsible for what he believes, and therefore may be obliged to believe certain propositions.

The consequences of this doctrine that there is sometimes a moral obligation to believe are of course pretty horrifying. The religious wars of the 16th and 17th centuries were based on just such a theory. High-principled persecutors, religious or political (and some persecutors are high-principled) would justify their actions by saying that X is morally bound to believe a proposition $p$; and if he does not believe it, or even believes its contradictory not-$p$, this 'misbelief' of his can only be due to moral wickedness, or badness of will. It is in the man's power to believe $p$ if he chooses, and he has a moral obligation to believe it. He prefers not to do his duty. Surely he deserves to be punished for this moral delinquency; and the more important the proposition in which he refuses to believe, the more drastic the punishment should be.

(Price, 1954, p. 11)

And

From this, again, a further conclusion has sometimes been drawn, though not by Descartes himself; namely that we deserve to be chastised for our intellectual errors, no less than for our moral delinquencies, and that it is no excuse in either case to say 'I couldn't help it.' This is a most alarming contention which could easily be used to justify all sorts of political and religious persecution. We may hope, for Descartes' sake, that it does not really follow from his doctrine of the freedom of assent.     (Price, 1969, p. 225)

It has not been argued that because belief is subject to the will in the sense defended, anyone may be required by another person to believe some proposition. But it may be that each person has an obligation to believe in accordance with the relevant belief-policy, his own belief-policy, and an obligation to formulate the best possible belief-policy.

Just as Price (mistakenly, as I shall try to show) held that the voluntariness of belief has led to persecution, so some have held that the non-voluntariness of belief is a ground for toleration. If a person cannot help holding the beliefs that are in fact held, social 'space' should be given to express them, and they should not be legislated against. The English Leveller William Walwyn wrote

Because of what judgment soever a man is, he cannot chuse but be of that judgement, that is so evident in it selfe, that I suppose it will be granted by all, whatsoever a mans reason doth conclude to be true or false, to be agreeable or disagreeable to Gods Word, that same to that man is his opinion or judgement and so man is by his own reason necessitated to be of that mind he is, now where there is a necessity there ought to be no punishment, for punishment is the recompense of voluntary actions, therefore no man ought to be punished for his judgment.     (Walwyn, 1933, III. pp. 67–8)

Locke echoed this when he stated in *A Letter Concerning Toleration* that

Speculative opinions, therefore, and articles of faith, (as they are called), which are required to be believed, cannot be imposed on any church by the

165

law of the land. For it is absurd that things should be enjoined by laws, which are not in men's power to perform. And to believe this or that to be true, does not depend upon will. (Locke, 1800, p. 85)

Locke's position has been influential, but it is not altogether clear, and has been the subject of disagreement.

Jeremy Waldron has argued (Waldron, 1988), that Locke's appeal to the will in his defence of toleration is incomplete, and for that reason possibly defective. He holds that Locke maintains that a person cannot will to believe that A, and therefore that such a person cannot be caused (in an evidence-less way, for example, by threats) to believe that A.

The consequence of these two claims – that coercion works through the will and that belief is not subject to the will – if they are true, would be to render religious belief or unbelief effectively immune from coercive manipulation (Waldron, 1988, p. 68). Nevertheless, although a person cannot be coerced into believing, according to Waldron he may be coerced with regard to the 'surrounding apparatus' of the formation of belief, so making it more likely that such a person will believe (Waldron, 1988, p. 83); for the surrounding apparatus is under the control of the will, even though belief itself is not.

Susan Mendus counters this by claiming (Mendus, 1989) that Waldron has not taken the full measure of Locke's position, which is an argument not merely about the causal conditions for the inducement of belief, but about the authenticity of belief. In particular, on Locke's view of religious belief, such beliefs are not mere preferences, but central and profound, 'ultimate and compelling' commitments, pervading all a person's other beliefs. Hence autonomy is not just a matter of the will, and of the presence or absence of coercive factors upon the will.

Mendus' defence of Locke tends to assimilate all religious belief to fideism, yet it is undeniable that Locke, while arguing about the toleration of religious belief, is nevertheless making a general point about belief and the will, not a particular point about religious belief as such. Moreover Waldron's argument is not specifically anti-Lockian, in that all beliefs have some causal conditions. To be anti-Lockian he would have to show that the will has a direct, sufficient role to play in the formation of particular beliefs, which he does not claim.

A reconstruction rather than an interpretation of Locke's position would be to hold that for him, while beliefs are not subject to the will, belief-policies are. Later on in her account (Mendus, 1989, p. 93) Mendus argues that autonomous rational self-determination requires a background of beliefs and values. Perhaps it is plausible to see belief-policies as incorporating such a background. If so, a recognisably Lockian case for toleration would be that it alone allows for the true development of conditions that are necessary for the formation of conscious belief-policies. And in particular that without toleration it is difficult (though not impossible) for individuals to develop doxastic freedom, a condition in which they form beliefs in accordance with their considered wants. A necessary condition for this is the ability to form views on the sorts of beliefs that there are. I shall say more on this point shortly.

In considering the relationship between belief and toleration a number of things need to be separated from each other. First is the factual question of whether the religious wars of the past were based on a sophisticated philosophical theory about the relation between belief and the will. I rather doubt it myself, just as I doubt that such a doctrine was responsible for the wars of persecution in the twentieth century, or that it was the eclipse of that doctrine which led to the relative absence of war in the eighteenth century. One motive for persecution seems to have been to save a person from the damnable consequences of even involuntary false beliefs. But settling such factual questions is happily not something that it is necessary to attempt.

Second is the need to distinguish between responsibility and punishment. The two are contingently connected; on some views even responsibility and liability to punishment are contingently connected. It may be that a person is responsible for A and ought not to be either praised or blamed for A; or not responsible for A and yet ought to be praised or blamed. This partly depends on one's theory of punishment. As Price goes on to say:

Someone might argue, I suppose, that although there is a *prima facie* duty to punish misbelievers, or suppress them by force, there is a conflicting *prima facie* duty which always, in practice, outweighs it; namely, the duty to preserve peace both within our own community, and between one community and another.                                       (Price, 1954 p. 11)

However this might be, we shall not discuss the question of whether people, if they are responsible for their intellectual errors, ought to be punished for them, but the prior question of whether or not they are responsible for them. Is such a view true, even if it has, in Price's words, 'terrifying implications'?

## RESPONSIBILITY FOR BELIEF

Beliefs occur as thoughts, and the question of whether or not thoughts should be tolerated may appear a little mad. Many thoughts are private, both in the sense that one is often one's own best judge of what one's thoughts are, and in the sense that thoughts can be kept private. And many thoughts are held by the mind in the form of dispositions that the thinker is unaware of. So the idea of tolerating or not tolerating thoughts *per se* seems rather far-fetched.

Apart from the technical Freudian sense of 'censorship' there seems to be a perfectly straightforward sense in which we can disapprove of, and even detest, the beliefs that we have, and can take steps to rid ourselves of them. Such cases include not only value-judgements, beliefs about the worth of a person or a policy or state of affairs, but beliefs of a straightforwardly factual kind. Agnes might try to rid her mind of the belief that the bees are diseased by trying to change the facts, or what are taken to be the facts. She might not like having to believe that her bees are diseased and attempt to change her belief by trying to eradicate the trouble

A second way is to shut one's mind to unwelcome facts, to ignore them and look on the bright side. And so Agnes might not like the fact that her bees are diseased and take a holiday in order to try to forget. It would not be unreasonable to describe these as cases where a person refuses to tolerate certain beliefs, and exercises a kind of self-censorship.

It is with the possibility of one person or group tolerating another person's or group's beliefs that we are concerned. And although what was said about the privacy of thoughts and beliefs remains true, it is only *as expressed* that the question of the legitimacy or otherwise of interpersonal toleration or censorship can arise.

Beliefs can be expressed with varying degrees of vigour, sophistication, rhetorical effect, and conviction; we shall be concerned with what might be called the plain, unvarnished, sincere expression of belief. For our purposes it is enough that the belief is held, and that it is expressed in a sincere, unambiguous way. In so far as beliefs are not merely expressed, but expressed with the overriding intention of gaining adherents, or of increasing the sales of a product, then even though such expressions may fall short of incitement in the formal legal sense, they are something more than mere expressions of belief. They are preachings, or verbal batterings, or exercises in propaganda.

Given that each of us has an initial endowment of beliefs, and means of generating further beliefs through the application of belief-policies, it is possible for us to reflect critically both upon the beliefs that we find ourselves with at any time, and upon the belief-policies which we have.

It has been widely assumed among those who have taken beliefs to be effects that, while a person may be responsible for the actions that follow upon belief and for goals or desires, no one can be held responsible for the beliefs themselves. And if one cannot be held responsible for the beliefs themselves then the question of not tolerating the beliefs simply does not arise. Having the beliefs is an involuntary matter, for the beliefs are events produced by evidence impinging on the mind. As Cohen says, 'Beliefs carry no commitments. They are neither intentional nor unintentional' (Cohen, 1992, p. 31).

Meiland expresses such a view as follows:

Suppose that a person holds this Nazi belief and puts it into practice by, for example, agitating for the deportation of certain racial groups. Evidentialism would allow a person to condemn this act morally, but it would not allow a person to condemn the belief because it led to this agitation. Evidentialism holds that there is a chasm between belief and action such that moral condemnation of the action which stems from that belief does not reach across this chasm and apply to the holding of the belief too. This chasm is founded on the idea that the only factor relevant to the holding of the factual beliefs is evidence. (Meiland, 1980, p. 20)

A classic (but perhaps extreme) case of passivism is that of David Hume, who wrote in the first *Enquiry* about factual beliefs

This belief is the necessary result of placing the mind in such circumstances. It is an operation of the soul, when we are so situated, as unavoidable as to feel the passion of love when we receive benefits, or hatred when we meet with

169

injuries. All these operations are species of natural instincts, which no reasoning or process of the thought and understanding is able either to produce or to prevent.                                        (Hume, 1975, V. 1.)


Hume appears to hold the thesis that not only are all beliefs about matters of fact caused, but that they are all natural instincts which are not the product of the mind (in the sense of the reason), but are produced solely by the senses and by habit.

For our purposes here we shall continue to assume the truth of *compatibilism*, that free will is compatible with at least some forms of causal determinism, and also that free will, in the sense of that expression that allows it to be compatible with determinism, is sufficient for the attribution of responsibility. It may be, as some have thought, that compatibilism, if it is true, expresses a necessary truth. If so then there can be no question of the sense of free will consistent with compatibilism only being sufficient, and not necessary for responsibility. On the other hand some have claimed that at best compatibilism is an empirical truth, in which case it might be that compatibilism is sufficient for free will, and not necessary. I shall not take sides on the issue here. It is sometimes held that a person, while not responsible for believing, is responsible for not having considered the evidence with the thoroughness that it merits. Cohen holds (Cohen, 1992, pp. 43–4) that we are responsible for belief to the extent that our beliefs arise from a failure to acquaint ourselves with the evidence we ought to. There is a problem with this half-way position, however. Not to acquaint oneself with evidence is partly to believe that such evidence is not relevant, interesting or whatever. But on Cohen's view for these beliefs, as for all beliefs, our minds are passive. Alternatively it might be held that we simply *find ourselves* becoming acquainted with the relevant evidence. But this is hardly a satisfactory basis on which to hold anyone responsible for believing

Swinburne holds that belief is not subject to the will, but that we have a duty to investigate the truth (Swinburne, 1981, p. 26; also pp. 54, 75f.) But if someone is responsible for investigating, and the results of the investigation are causally sufficient for some belief, it would appear that that person is responsible for that belief. That is, if enquiring is causally sufficient for believing, then the investigator is responsible for believing.

The further assumption is that the relevant sense of responsibility is not merely that a person is responsible for A if praise or blame would either reinforce a tendency to perform A-like actions, or weaken the tendency. It is the sense of responsibility in which it is appropriate to praise or blame someone for having done A irrespective of the effects of praising or blaming. A person can hold beliefs which he ought not to, and fail to believe what he ought. For a person may hold beliefs that the evidence which is available to him, personal evidence, does not warrant. As a result of being partial, or biased, or weak-willed in some way beliefs are held for which there is no evidence, or for which there is less evidence than for some other proposition which is not believed, or beliefs for which there could be no evidence against. Given certain facts about a person's situation there are beliefs which that person could be expected to hold, and for which he may be held responsible.

Often the ascription of responsibility to people for beliefs occurs, or only receives attention, when the holding of the belief is a part of some situation of moral significance. It may be that believing that P has done such and such leads Q to commit some act against him, and Q may be culpable because of a lack of epistemic entitlement to believe what he did about P. But the fact that cases of the ascription of responsibility only surface in situations of straightforward moral praise or blameworthiness does not mean that they are not themselves praise or blameworthy.

This basic idea of responsibility for beliefs does not depend upon the power to will a belief from scratch, but upon the ability to reflect upon and to review beliefs, and to ask whether the belief is reasonable given the evidence; to reflect upon a belief in the light of one's belief-policy, including one's estimate of the importance of acquiring true beliefs about a particular matter.

Such responsibility is a function not only of the evidence possessed by a person, but also of that person's evidence-gathering and evidence-appreciating capabilities. This is akin to the idea of physical and psychological capacity in other cases of responsibility. A person is not responsible for neglecting evidence if it is beyond her powers, or outside her experience, to appreciate it, just as a person is not responsible for failing to do whatever is beyond her physical strength. But as a person may be responsible for the lack of physical strength, though not responsible for what that lack of strength prevents, so a person may be responsible for a lack of intellectual and sensory awareness and capability, though not for failing to do what, given this incapacity, cannot be done.

We are no more or less responsible for many beliefs about matters of fact than we are for our actions. We are responsible for some of our actions, for others, for example, those produced by drugs, or hypnotism, or done in certain kinds of ignorance, we are not. Similarly while there are ways of a person gaining beliefs that render that person not responsible for those beliefs, there are other ways of gaining beliefs that imply that responsibility for them. For example, hypnotism or brainwashing produce beliefs in a person for which a person is not responsible, while paying careful attention to the evidence produces beliefs for which a person is responsible.

One argument against responsibility for individual beliefs, the argument from passivity, has already been noted. According to this view beliefs are the effects of empirical data, real or imagined, upon the mind. If the receptive mind has sufficient evidence for a particular belief, then that belief will follow automatically. On this view perhaps the recognition that there is preponderating evidence for $p$ *is* the believing that $p$. Similarly, if there is insufficient evidence, or what is taken to be insufficient evidence, then it will follow that the mind will not believe the proposition concerned.

This empiricist–evidentialist position ignores the place of assent in belief. However minimal a role assent plays, it does play a vital role. Believing is a matter of judgement. Even if the cat is on the mat, the person is standing in front of them, with senses in good working order, and knows what a cat and a mat are, it does not follow that the judgement that the cat is on the mat will follow. For the situation has to be recognised, to be judged, and so it is unsatisfactory to say that the conditions just mentioned are logically sufficient for the making of the judgement. They may all be present, but the appropriate belief may not ensue because a person is distracted or absent-mindedly predisposed. If it is objected that whether or not I choose to assent, or to direct attention, is itself governed by the evidence, then the argument reverts to classical libertarian–determinist issues. If our believings were totally passive we would not be responsible for them. But they are not totally passive.

It is often the case that ignorance excuses. If so we can impale the opponent of the view that people are responsible for their beliefs on the horns of a dilemma. Take the following: someone may believe that the Ming vase is in fact a crude reproduction and give it away to the jumble sale. Either there was no reason for the person to have known that the vase was a Ming, because of a lack of knowledge of vases or of antiques, in which case it looks as though ignorance is going to excuse from responsibility in this and every similar case, or the person ought to have believed that the vase was a Ming. But, if the person ought to have had certain beliefs, then he is responsible for his ignorance. He is responsible for not believing those propositions that it was reasonable to suppose, in the circumstances, he should have known. This might be expressed as the claim that in the forming of their beliefs people have duties to the evidence. People can believe irrationally, or whimsically, and their motive in what they do may be a motive that has little to do with truth-seeking. But though a person's motives may be suspect and affected by irrationality, this ought not to be so. So such a person has a basic duty, as a cognitive agent, not to be irrational. In these circumstances irrationality is culpable irresponsibility.

In a similar way a person can be held responsible not merely for believing that *p* but for believing *p*, to a certain degree. A person may be held responsible for credulity or for scepticism.

Even if, for whatever reason, no person is responsible for coming to hold any belief about any matter of fact, a person may be responsible for retaining beliefs. Suppose the most extreme case, that at a given time a person finds himself with certain beliefs about matters of fact, the products of certain stimuli, and of the giving of assent of which that person had previously been unaware. A person who finds that he believes that *p* may nevertheless ask whether the belief that *p* ought to be retained, and attempt to answer the question by reference to his belief-policies.

It was noted earlier that there is a perfectly straightforward sense in which the will directs belief, in that the attention can be directed to certain evidence, to neglect other evidence, and so forth. Even if belief is not immediately subject to the will, at least some beliefs are subject to the will in this indirect way. For example, someone might, after long research, come to believe some previously disbelieved proposition about the anatomy of the honey-bee. Such a person is responsible for coming to believe that proposition. This is signalled by his willingness to defend it by argument and by the adducing of evidence. As it is possible to excuse one's action by indicating that one was drugged or tired, so it is possible to excuse one's belief by saying that one had not had the opportunity to consider the evidence, or that one was misled by someone who was otherwise trustworthy, and so forth – that is, that on such occasions it was not possible for one fully to exercise one's belief-policy by forming beliefs in accordance with it.

This fact is closely connected with a remark of Bernard Williams in his treatment of Descartes on the will cited earlier, (Williams, 1978, p. 179). Williams claims that the very idea of critical reflection requires a person to suspend judgement. Suspending one's judgement that *p* is coming to believe that *p* may be true or may be false on the evidence available. That is, suspension of belief entails belief. Beliefs that are arrived at after the use of such critical processes – suspending judgement, reviewing the evidence, reflecting upon the strengths and weaknesses of the evidence – are paradigm-cases of beliefs that one is responsible for, just as overt actions in similar circumstances are actions that one is responsible for.

At least some of our actions are caused by our beliefs, in the sense that such beliefs are *ceteris paribus* sufficient causal conditions of the action. For example, given a desire to keep the bees alive through the winter Joe may give them sugar in the belief that otherwise they will not survive. In such cases (unless there was an intervening set of special exculpating conditions) Joe would be regarded as being responsible for the action of procuring sugar for the bees. If this is so, then it is paradoxical to suppose that Joe is responsible for an action performed because of certain beliefs, but not responsible for the beliefs. Of course Joe is not responsible for every causal condition that is necessary for the success of an action. For example, he is not responsible for sufficient oxygen being present in the atmosphere. But such causally necessary conditions are not properly described as things that Joe does, whereas believing is. It would surely be odd to say that Joe was responsible for giving sugar to the bees because he was responsible for a desire for the bees' well-being, but not responsible for believing that the bees need the sugar.

Suppose that Joe, through no fault of his own, is misled about the bees' condition. Joe's friend Jim has a malicious desire to harm the bees. He knows, but Joe does not, that the condition that the bees are in would mean that extra sugar could harm them. Joe, believing that this harmful sugar will in fact benefit the bees, gives it to them, for he wants the bees to prosper. In such circumstances Joe would be relieved of a good deal of the responsibility for the worsening of the bees' condition, because the action was the outcome of a false belief for which he was not responsible. Therefore the responsibility for an action is a function not only of the beliefs that give rise to it, but also of whether those beliefs are held responsibly.

It seems perfectly reasonable to raise the following sort of question about a person's belief: given that a person has normal perceptual abilities, the abilities of the average person, is committed to a particular belief-policy, and is confronted by such and such data, ought that person to believe that *p*? It might be asked if a person has normal visual abilities, of focussing, range of visual field, colour discrimination, and the normal linguistic and conceptual abilities of the average English person in 1994, and if she is seated in front of a beehive, ought she to believe that there is a beehive in front of her?

Whether or not she ought to believe, even if it is blindingly obvious that she ought, such an enquiry seems to be entirely proper, and it parallels the sort of enquiry that is frequently made in the case of action. About action we ask – suppose that a person has normal physical abilities, the sort of abilities that the vast majority of human beings have, and suppose that he has certain beliefs and desires, then we can ask: Is such a combination of factors causally sufficient for that person to perform a particular action, or not? Suppose that, in such circumstances, the person does not perform the action, then it may be because, though he desired certain things, other things were desired more. Or it may be that our supposition that the person had normal physical abilities is incorrect. Similarly, suppose that in such a situation the person does not believe that there is a beehive directly in front. This may be because, though having normal perceptual abilities, such a person is at the time preoccupied with some problem, and though in some sense she sees the beehive she does not see that it is a beehive.

That the same considerations can be raised about action and about belief provides additional presumption for the claim that as certain sorts of action are under our voluntary control so certain sorts of belief are, and that as we are responsible for certain of our actions, so we are responsible for certain of our beliefs. There are standards of attainment in belief that it is reasonable to expect people to achieve, and they are blameworthy if they do not.

### RESPONSIBILITY FOR BELIEF-POLICIES

So far our discussion has been mainly about responsibility for single beliefs or sets of beliefs. But what about responsibility for belief-policies?

It has been argued by Harry G. Frankfurt (Frankfurt, 1988) that what count in assessing responsibility for action are not so much issues of causation, determinism, and the existence of alternative possibilities as the question of the ownership of actions, of wholeheartedness or indifference of commitment to what one wants, at the deepest level. I shall attempt to show that the same sorts of claims can be made for belief-policies. If responsibility for one's actions turns on what one cares about then, once again, we are no more or less responsible for our beliefs and the belief-policies which give rise to them than we are for our actions.

Wants are both wide-ranging in their character and of greatly differing degrees of strength. A person can want to X without believing that she does; she can want to X while not wanting to X; she can want to X while believing that she does not want to X, and so on. As regards strength, a want to do X may or may not be decisive; A may want to X and not X, being quite content not to X. But A may also want to X and as a result of wanting to do X, X is done (Frankfurt, 1988, pp. 13–14).

It is only when wanting is decisive, when it is (in Frankfurt's terminology) a 'volition' and not a 'desire', that it is to be identified with the will. The will is an effective first-order desire, one that issues or results in the action wanted (unless frustrated by adventitious factors) because it is wanted. A second-order want, that sort of want which is characteristic of a person, according to Frankfurt, is simply a volition to do X where X stands for a first-order want or desire. A second-order want is thus a wanting to want. According to Frankfurt this is to be understood as follows

The statement (viz. that 'A wants to want X') means that A wants the desire to X to be the desire that moves him effectively to act. It is not merely that he wants the desire to X to be among the desires by which, to one degree or another, he is moved or inclined to act. He wants this desire to be effective – that is, to provide the motive in what he actually does.          (*Ibid.*, p. 15)

Suppose that a man wants to be motivated in what he does by the desire to concentrate on his work. It is necessarily true, if this supposition is correct, that he already wants to concentrate on his work. This desire is now among his desires. But the question of whether or not his second-order desire is fulfilled does not turn merely on whether the desire he wants is one of his desires. It turns on whether this desire is, as he wants it to be, his effective desire or will. If, when the chips are down, it is his desire to concentrate on his work that moves him to do what he does, then what he wants at that time is indeed (in the relevant sense) what he wants to want. If it is some other desire that actually moves him when he acts, on the other hand, then what he wants at that time is not (in the relevant sense) what he wants to want. This will be so despite the fact that the desire to concentrate on his work continues to be among his desires. (*Ibid.*, p. 16)

According to Frankfurt a person does not merely have second-order desires, desires to have desires, but wants a certain desire to be his will. A person who has first-order desires, but who has no desire that that desire should be his will (a 'wanton' in Frankfurt's felicitous terminology) may reason or deliberate about what he wants to do; what marks him off from being a person, according to Frankfurt, is that 'he does not care which of his inclinations is the strongest' (*Ibid.*, p. 17). It is important to note that the characteristic of an individual who is not a wanton is that he cares about which of his inclinations is the strongest, not that he necessarily succeeds in making those inclinations he wants to prevail actually to prevail.

So Frankfurt wishes to maintain that the distinctiveness of being a person lies not in reason, but in will. Reason is necessary for being a person, but non-persons such as the wanton may also reason. What is needed in addition for personhood is the will in the sense defined; the caring about a person's first-order wants or desires.

These rather abstractly delineated distinctions may be illustrated as follows. A habitual liar may experience a struggle between telling a lie and telling the truth. On the one hand the liar wants to tell a lie, while on the other hand the liar wants to tell the truth. Such a description can cover two different cases. One case is where the struggle is accompanied by a hatred and detestation of lying. Such a hatred may in turn be accompanied by a struggle against lying which is in this case, let us suppose, ineffectual. The individual in question wants to want not to lie, though to no avail. The other case is where lying or not lying do not issue from a preference of not lying over lying. It makes no difference to the wanton which conflicting first-order desires are in fact satisfied. A person, however, makes one of them more truly his own and withdraws himself from the other.

Because of this it is natural for those who have such a second-order volition to use the language of externality about the desire which they do not identify with; the desire is alien, intrusive, and so on. In the case of the wanton

it makes no difference *to him* whether his craving or his aversion gets the upper hand. He has no stake in the conflict between them . . . when a person acts, the desire by which he is moved is either the will he wants or a will he wants to be without. When a *wanton* acts, it is neither.     (*Ibid.*, p. 19)

It must not be thought from these examples that Frankfurt intends that his account of second-order volitions is concerned only with moral matters. They could apply to what is trivial, and a person may form or retain second-order volitions without serious thought, or for capricious reasons. The point is that according to Frankfurt we all have such second-order volitions; or at least we do if we are persons.

It is possible to think of beliefs as engagements that are already entered in an epistemic diary. We may not only enter or delete such engagements, but also conduct a review of the sort of engagements we permit ourselves to make, the standards for accepting or turning down prospective engagements. My chief purpose in drawing attention to Frankfurt's insights is to take this idea further.

Among the things we want are that certain of our beliefs should be true, just as we want certain of them to be false. For instance Joe might want the belief that the bees are about to swarm to be false, but the belief that they will produce a good crop of honey to be true. For the belief that the bees will produce a good crop of honey to be true, they will have to produce the crop, that is, the world will have to change in certain significant respects. And in wanting a belief to be true a person is wanting the world to be changed in appropriate ways. The desire for the belief to be true, or for it to be false, just is, in normal cases, the desire for the world to be changed.

So it is possible, in these relatively straightforward ways, to connect wanting (in its many different strengths) with believing (in its many different strengths). To want a belief to be true is to have, in Frankfurt's terminology, a first-order want or desire.

Suppose that the belief that I want to be true is one that I have formed on the basis of what I take to be good evidence in accordance

178

with my current belief-policy. In that sense it is a reasonable belief, and I want this belief, and my beliefs in general, to be reasonable beliefs. In an endeavour to gain a better purchase on the truth (supposing that the person's overall motivation is truth-centred), and to be free as much as possible from error, a person is typically led to reflect upon the appropriateness of the epistemic standards adhered to. It is now possible to raise the question, granted that I want my belief to be true, do I want to want my belief to be true? But what precisely does this question mean?

In this case, a person may ask, Do I want to be true only those propositions for which there is good evidence? Are those the sort of wantings to believe that I want to have? Or do I want to have wantings to believe for which there is less than good evidence? Or for which there is no evidence? Or (like Kierkegaard's knight of faith) for which there is evidence against? These are questions about second-order desires or wants, in Frankfurt's sense. Similarly it is possible to distinguish between (in Frankfurt's terminology) the doxastic wanton and the doxastic person. A doxastic wanton is someone who has wantings to believe, but who does not care what those wantings are, which wantings to believe are to prevail.

We may ask ourselves whether we are believing the sorts of things that we want to believe. In asking this question we will have in mind some evidential standard or other. We may be asking whether we have in fact accepted too stringent or too lax a standard of evidence, whether we are being too sceptical or too credulous in terms of the belief-policy we want to operate consistently.

Or a person may be raising questions about epistemic importance. For given the adoption of a particular belief-policy a person may come to recognise that there are myriads of beliefs which a person could painlessly come to possess by operating a particular belief-policy, but that these beliefs would be of less doxastic importance than other beliefs. May it not sometimes be a person's duty to seek to acquire beliefs which are harder to acquire than others?

The parallel with action is clear. A person may ask whether she is wanting what she wants to want. She may want to want intellectual pursuits rather than the pursuits of sensuality. And once a person has decided what are, in broad terms, the sorts of things she wants to want she may also decide which among these things are more important than others.

The doxastic wanton is someone who does not advance further than accepting or rejecting epistemic engagements. Sometimes these engagements are straightforward; at other times accepting one engagement is at odds with accepting another and a choice has to be made. But the wanton, in settling the choice, does not have in mind any overall conception of the sort of beliefs he wants to want. If there is a conflict between believing a proposition on good evidence and believing some alternative on less good evidence the wanton does not mind which prevails.

Suppose that someone has formulated a second-order decision only to believe propositions of a certain type upon evidence of a certain type and strength. Let us suppose that evidence of that type and strength is obtained, but that nevertheless a person wishes to believe some proposition for which the evidence is of a poorer type and strength. Can the person decide to believe not-p? A decision to believe not-$p$ is an expression of an unprincipled want. A person is, at that point, behaving wantonly.

Harking back to the earlier discussion of weakness of will we may say that a doxastic incontinent is someone who has a set of appropriate second-order volitions. That person's will is identified with certain doxastic standards. However, though that person has standards about engagements, none the less engagements continue to be accepted in accordance with other standards. The person's doxastic will is constituted by an acceptance of certain standards; but there is a persistent failure to believe, (in a way which may or may not involve self-deception), in accordance with these standards and instead belief in accordance with other standards with which that person does not identify.

So if, as Frankfurt claims, responsibility for action depends not on the existence of libertarian choice between alternative possibilities, nor even upon the degree of control a person exercises over action, but upon the conformity of one's second-order volitions and one's first-order wants, then there is reason to think that one is responsible for at least some of one's belief-policies. (For criticism of Frankfurt's views, see Fischer (1986).)

## DIFFERENCES BETWEEN BELIEVING AND ACTING

We have been concentrating attention upon similarities between believing and acting, and upon responsibility for the adoption and retention of belief-policies. But are there not significant differences? For activity is marked by an agent's initiative, the intention that something shall happen, by his foresight, and so forth. It is argued, belief is not subject in this way to a person's active control. Rather, belief (about matters of fact) is governed by a conceptual connection with the truth, and by openness to evidence.

As we have already seen it is frequently asserted that it is impossible to believe at will. But this appears to be no more or less true of beliefs than of actions. Except in the case of what Arthur Danto has called 'basic actions', it is impossible to act at will either, since non-basic actions require the co-operation of other factors over which the agent may have no direct control.

> Certain simple perceptual judgments are forced upon me by my present sensory experience, and I *cannot* believe something with which they conflict. This does not imply that belief is not subject to the will. Larceny presumably is; and if I am sitting in a warm bath in my own bathtub, in my own home, I cannot steal. (Van Fraassen, 1988, p. 146)

And even the much-trumpeted passivity of belief may be the result of the development of sensitivity · and receptivity to evidence and argument which have had to be worked for, and on which amounts of concentration and self-discipline have been expended.

Sometimes beliefs come upon us unannounced and unsought. We find it impossible, on occasions, *not* to believe certain propositions about the world around us, if, for example, we have been trained or educated in certain ways. Surely this at least is sufficient to demarcate these beliefs from actions, and to show that we cannot be responsible for them? But as we cannot, under certain circumstances, stop ourselves believing that *p*, so in certain circumstances we cannot stop ourselves acting to bring about A. There are habitual actions and consciously learned routines, which one can, only with considerable difficulty in some cases, control or modify.

There is at least one significant asymmetry between belief and action. Responsible actions are those which are performed with awareness of their likely consequences. It is impossible to foresee what, when one begins an inquiry about the truth of some matter, one will come to believe. For if, before one entered into serious inquiry, one already knew the outcome, what would be the point of the inquiry?

It might be replied that a person can foresee or anticipate belief on some future occasion without believing now (Stocker, 1982).

To foresee that I will believe *p* for certain reasons, and yet not believe now, shows an extraordinary level of detachment. If I foresee that I will believe *p* I must have grounds for this foresight, and these grounds must have to do with coming to believe that the reasons which I at present regard as bad reasons will turn out to be good reasons. If I have grounds for this, then I already believe, or am beginning to believe. In the case of action, foresight is relevant to the issue of responsibility in so far as it is foresight of the consequences of the action. In the case of belief, it is the belief itself which is foreseen.

Acts of discovery and creativity, such as looking for a swarm or designing a beehive, are the sorts of action the end of which cannot be foreseen, but which are nevertheless clear cases of responsible action. The agent is able to use certain skills and such use implies foresight, as Michael Stocker points out (Stocker, 1982, p. 402). Yet the would-be discoverer does not foresee the specific results of the voyage of discovery until land is reached. In so far as a person is acting with the first kind of foresight then that person is responsible even if the second kind is necessarily lacking, for intelligence and skill are being used, though for an end that is as yet unknown.

## TOLERATION AND BELIEF

It is initially puzzling that writers advocating toleration should insist that what is expressed and is to be tolerated should be sincerely held. For it would appear that sincerity is irrelevant to the public effects of holding a belief. There are some beliefs which are not to be tolerated however sincerely held, and some may be tolerated even if held insincerely, particularly if the community comes to know that the beliefs are held insincerely.

If what one is concerned with in toleration is not the mere allowing of the expression of certain views, but with the fostering of certain attitudes through such expression, then sincerity becomes central, for it is only *bona fide* beliefs that one can assess and foster or discourage.

There seem to be two levels at which it is possible to discuss and defend toleration. One is on the grounds that one person's opinion is at least as likely to be true as any other's, and is therefore entitled to be held and propagated. This comes to the view that a person's opinions are an expression of individuality, and that expression is to be tolerated as part of the enjoying of that freedom of expression. Various relativistic or subjectivistic theories of truth would be compatible with this view. Closely allied to it is the claim that the agent of toleration, the state or some other body, has a concern to promote social peace and stability and hence that any expression of opinion, however irresponsible, is allowable provided that it does not endanger social peace.

Toleration may also be advocated as a necessary condition for fostering and maintaining true belief in a society. On this view toleration is desirable because it allows and encourages beliefs to be formed upon reasons, and it also encourages people to reflect upon their doxastic wants (in the sense already discussed). We shall be concerned exclusively with this second type of defence of toleration.

Such a defence will be consequentialist in character. Toleration is beneficial; it permits and even encourages the development of certain intellectual traits which are necessary for the achieving of much that is good in itself, the acquisition of truth and the elimination of error. Toleration invokes respect for persons, but the reasons for toleration are not simply respect for persons. Rather a policy of toleration will likely further the epistemological ends of cognitive agents.

On this view, to tolerate is to ensure or at least to allow what is tolerated to come under full critical scrutiny. It is only in the clash of opinions, and of the data (or the lack of such data) which support each one, that the truth of one view will emerge, and such clashes are not likely without a policy of toleration. To tolerate is not merely to allow an opinion to be expressed, but to place that opinion in the market-place of ideas. The value of toleration is that it makes possible the free, in the sense of politically or socially uncoerced, acceptance of the truth.

Toleration of the expression of belief allows the flourishing of epistemic virtues such as the need to be impartial, the use of checking and re-checking procedures, and the suspicion of one-sided evidence. It discourages situations in which there is not a free exchange of information, permitting second thoughts. It makes it harder for inquirers to close their minds to hitherto-overlooked possibilities, to surprising facts and surprising connections between facts.

Such toleration could not *ensure* that these virtues flourish, since they also depend for their flourishing on the desire for such virtue, and on data to enable argument and experiment to proceed. Nor is toleration necessary, since intellectual virtue could flourish on a desert island. However, while toleration is neither strictly necessary nor sufficient for the inculcation of such virtues, it helps to produce them by enlarging the appropriate opportunities.

Some of J. S. Mill's central arguments for toleration can be understood as supporting this view. In *On Liberty*, particularly chapter 2, 'Of the Liberty of Thought and Discussion', Mill provides four main arguments in favour of toleration.

Mill argues that it is possible a priori that any belief is true. To hinder or prevent the expression of that belief is to claim to know in advance that it is not true, which is to assume a position of infallibility. That is, either one claims in advance of any discussion whatever that one's belief is true, or one allows discussion. If the former, then one is claiming infallibility.

This seems to be an argument for a limited degree of toleration, unless Mill is taking up a sceptical position. For there will come a time in the discussion of many questions when it will be possible to say, beyond reasonable doubt, that $p$ is true and not-$p$ is false, or that $q$ is a self-contradiction, sheer nonsense, or whatever. And at that point Mill would presumably say that the toleration of the clear falsehood should cease, or at least that intolerance is more excusable in such situations. Mill would say this if he were to take this sort of consideration to provide both a necessary and sufficient condition of toleration. But of course he does not.

The second argument is offered as another sufficient condition. Let us suppose that some opinion is manifestly erroneous, a flagrant falsehood. Mill argues that even a flagrant falsehood may contain some truth. And if it may then it ought to be heard, for 'it is only by the collision of adverse opinions that the remainder of the truth has any chance of being supplied'. The flagrant falsehood may contain some truth that the obvious truth does not (Mill, 1912, p.65).

Mill presumably means by this not the nonsense that any false proposition is in some sense true, but that any false proposition has logical presuppositions some of which are true. Probably his remarks are meant to cover sets of propositions; a set which is overall false may contain some unnoticed truths. A conjunct may be true even while the conjunction is false. Does it seem reasonable to suppose that in a clash between complex hypotheses even those maintaining the false position have seen something which those maintaining the true view have not? Let us suppose that this is so. Mill makes the proposal that in the event of such a possibility it is only in the public clash of opinions that the truth in the false hypothesis 'has any chance of being supplied'.

This seems to be rather extreme. Why should not someone who holds the true opinion refine and elaborate that view, either by further private investigations (if this is appropriate) or by thought experiments and the creation of counter-examples, if this is appropriate? Then there would be a collision of opinions, but one that is entirely private. Public collision does not seem to be necessary. At the most, Mill is saying that toleration has been, or might be found to be, necessary in order to produce the intellectual clashes necessary for progress. Whether this is so or not will depend, once again, upon empirical investigation.

Each of the arguments so far considered has to do with the conditions under which true belief may emerge. A social ethic of belief-formation is implied in this, roughly that people ought to be placed in those conditions in which their beliefs are tested and questioned. The general benefits of allowing toleration have to do with the improved prospects, under toleration, for the discovery of truth.

Mill's third argument has to do with toleration as a necessary condition for the holding of beliefs with an understanding and appreciation of the grounds on which they are held. Here Mill is concerned with the influence of toleration upon the *way* in which a truth is held, not merely with the fact of gaining truth. He is combatting the idea that it is sufficient for proper belief that A believes *p*. Mere assent to the truth of the true proposition is not sufficient. A must know how the proposition is rationally supported, and for this the toleration of contrary opinions is necessary in order that the ability to defend the belief against objections may be developed and alternative candidates for belief be seriously entertained. The possessing of evidence for a belief is as much a matter of developing a skill as is the knowledge of certain supporting propositions of the

185

belief in question. That is, Mill seems to be offering an analysis of responsible belief as follows: that A responsibly believes *p* if and only if: (i) A believes that *p*; (ii) A is able to give reasons for *p* and refute objections to *p*; and (iii) A is able to refute the reasons for holding not-*p*.

He who knows only his own side of the case, knows little of that. His reasons may be good, and no one may have been able to refute them. But if he is equally unable to refute the reasons on the opposite side; if he does not so much as know what they are, he has no ground for preferring either opinion. The rational position for him would be suspension of judgement.

(Mill, 1912, p. 46)

Mill endorses the following belief-policy: *One ought to believe only those propositions which one possesses good reason for, and only when one possesses good reasons against any known alternative.*

Their conclusion may be true, but it might be false for anything they know: they have never thrown themselves into the mental position of those who think differently from them, and considered what such persons may have to say; and consequently they do not, in any proper sense of the word, know the doctrine which they themselves profess.                       (*Ibid.*, p. 47)

So Mill endorses an internalist account of epistemic justification, and links toleration to it.

Leaving aside the empirical questions, Mill makes toleration to be a necessary condition for the proper acquiring of beliefs. Toleration is not a right that a person can expect in virtue of having a belief to express, not even a prima facie right, it is one of the epistemic conditions that is necessary for acquiring a properly based belief. It is not a consequence of the will being exercised in belief, it is a necessary condition of the will being properly exercised in the formation of belief.

Voluntariness is given even greater emphasis in the final argument for toleration that Mill provides, that discussion and the toleration it presupposes are necessary in order for a person who has a certain belief to retain a proper understanding of it.

The fact, however, is, that not only the grounds of the opinion are forgotten in the absence of discussion, but too often the meaning of the opinion itself. The words which convey it, cease to suggest ideas, or suggest only a small portion of those they were originally employed to communicate. Instead of a

vivid conception and a living belief, there remain only a few phrases retained
by rote.                                                                    (*Ibid.*, p. 49)

Here Mill has moved from defending the general desirability of
toleration to defending the necessity of controversy. It is consistent
with a policy of toleration that as a matter of fact incompatible ideas
live side by side and never engage each other in debate. Mill seems to
be saying that controversy is necessary for the proper formation and
retention of beliefs. Toleration provides the conditions in which
controversy can take place, so toleration is a necessary condition for
the continuation of belief with understanding.

The following general connection can be drawn between toleration
and belief-policies. If A has a truth-maximising belief-policy, for
example, then it would follow that any restriction on the general
freedom of expression which would limit the carrying out of that
policy would be unacceptable. It would not be the same with a
falsehood-minimising policy, for a person who is concerned to hold as
few beliefs as possible (lest any of them turn out to be false) will not be
exercised by the fact that the evidence on which beliefs ought to be
based is less than it could be.

Thomas Scanlon defends (Scanlon, 1972) what he calls a Millian
principle of freedom of expression not by a consequentialist argument
but by an appeal to human autonomy. 'The powers of a state are
limited to those that citizens could recognise while still regarding
themselves as equal, autonomous rational agents' (Scanlon, 1972, p.
215). According to Scanlon an autonomous, rational person is
sovereign in deciding what to believe, and in weighing competing
reasons for action. To coerce a person in such a way as to prevent that
person carrying out these functions is to flout the canons of rationality.

So intolerance makes impossible, or difficult, or unlikely, the proper
formation of the belief that is not being tolerated, and the beliefs that
are formed as a result of a policy of intolerance may not be formed in
appropriate ways, but in ways that do violence to the proper notion of
belief. Beliefs ought to be formed only by those considerations that are
consistent with the belief-policy adopted by that person. It may be, as
Mill suggests, that toleration is necessary for the evidence properly to
come to light and to be appreciated in all its manifold ramifications,
but toleration is also necessary so that the belief can be properly
formed upon the evidence presented. What is true of the place of

toleration in the formation of beliefs is true *pari passu* in the formation of belief-policies.

So, I suggest, what Mill is doing in his celebrated defence of toleration, as regards at least some of his arguments, is to describe (and, to an extent, to prescribe) the conditions under which responsible believing and its associated intellectual virtues can flourish.

# 8

# *Fideism*

Fideism has, in general, received a bad philosophical press. It has become a synonym for un-reason and dogmatism, and classic fideistic thinkers, such as Pascal and Kierkegaard, have been given an unsympathetic treatment. In this final chapter I wish to bring together epistemology and religion by reflecting upon fideism in the light of our development of the idea of a belief-policy

## WHAT IS FIDEISM?

The *Shorter Oxford Dictionary* defines 'fideism' as 'A mode of thought in which knowledge is based on a fundamental act of faith', while in his article on fideism in *The Encyclopaedia of Philosophy* Richard Popkin defines it as the claim that 'truth in religion is ultimately based on faith rather than on reasoning or evidence' (Popkin, 1967, pp. 201–2). From these definitions it is clear that, according to the fideist, faith provides knowledge. Such knowledge, either knowledge in general or within some particular area of inquiry, is not acquired through the reason or the senses, or by some combination of the two, but by trust, usually by trust in God. It is as a result of that trust that data become available which are otherwise not available, data which remain hidden from those not willing or able to exercise faith, but which are commonly available to all who do.

An alternative view is that a fideist is someone who holds that one may justifiably form a belief supported by insufficient evidence for the truth of what is believed or even unsupported by evidence, or even in the teeth of evidence against; or that one may justifiably give a greater degree of strength to a belief than is warranted by the evidence for the proposition that is believed. What is unsupported in the forming of the belief may none the less be supportable; the fideist seeks to make the point that it need not be supported to be justified; perhaps even that evidential support rules out justification.

These initial characterisations of fideism indicate that it is both a more complex and a less clear doctrine than is commonly believed, and that different members of the fideistic family make very different claims. It is one thing to say that reason or sense-experience cannot give knowledge of some proposition, but that faith can, quite another to say that evidence for the truth of a proposition is contained in a special divine revelation the only epistemic access to which is through faith. It is another thing to say that although there is evidence for a proposition one is justified in believing that proposition in ignorance of that evidence, or to a degree not warranted by the evidence.

Besides the questions that individual versions of fideism raise, there are also interesting issues of a more general kind. For instance, there is the question of whether total fideism is consistent. Total or global fideism is the view that all justified belief is acquired by faith, that no knowledge comes through the senses and the reason apart from faith. I shall, in due course, in considering how fideism can be justified, consider global fideism. If it can be plausibly argued that Alvin Plantinga's Reformed epistemology is a version of fideism, then perhaps it is an example of global fideism.

How is fideism possible, and how can it be justified? The first of these questions concerns the intelligibility of claiming to be justified in believing things not by reason or evidence, but by an act of will, an act of commitment, for fideism typically understands faith in voluntaristic terms.

The second question has to do with how it is that a person is entitled to hold beliefs not justified by evidence, as according to the fideist he is. It may seem strange, even paradoxical, that a rational defence can be offered for a view which is so often characterised as irrational. I shall try to show that this possibility is one of the factors which makes fideism an interesting and philosophically enduring position.

## THE ATTRACTIONS OF FIDEISM

Why is fideism, a position which appears to fly in the face of evidential rationality, attractive in the first place? It is unsatisfactory to answer this question merely by pointing to a common human tendency to backslide into irrationalism. I shall offer two or three types of possible answer; one has to do with subject-matter, the other with method. According to the first type of answer, certain areas of human interest and enquiry are susceptible only to a fideistic approach. For example, and typically, a fideistic approach has been attractive in religion because of the intrinsic difficulty of the putative object of belief, because by definition God transcends the boundaries of our normal experience.

Another possible answer has to do with human nature. In the face of scepticism or radical uncertainty some philosophers have preferred a policy of risk rather than of damage limitation. The reason for the risk may be the possible personal gains from gambling on the truth of some propositions – one thinks here of Pascal and James – but there may also be confirmation in experience of the epistemic fruitfulness of taking chances. While this supports the rationality of taking chances, it does not eliminate the chanciness unless past and present chancy situations are strongly analogous. And some have advocated the type of risk that may occur not in the absence of any evidence, or that goes against the evidence, but that may occur in a situation where there is not sufficient evidence. Augustine's treatment of scepticism is a case in point.

Often what has made religion a focus of fideistic attention is not the transcendent subject-matter as such, but the related fact that this transcendence has led to perpetual debates about the true way of gaining religious knowledge. This has in turn led to the second reason that has made fideism attractive, not only in religion, but more generally, the presence of methodological confusion about a particular area, and the consequent rise of scepticism.

In fideism there is a dislocation of the normal relations between believing that something is true, and having evidence for that thing's being true. In previous chapters reference has been made to various possible forms that these relations can take, for example, 'The wise man proportions his belief to the evidence.' In fideism the dislocation can take one of two forms; the belief can be of a proposition which is not, in terms of such an individual belief-policy, sufficiently belief-worthy, or it can be of a proposition which, on such a policy, one ought positively to reject.

A fideist may believe *p* even though *p* is improbable when judged by some evidential belief-policy. Or he may believe it *because* it is improbable when thus assessed. There have even been cases where propositions have been believed *because* they are logically impossible. This most extreme form of fideism has sometimes been attributed to Tertullian. Tertullian said, 'The Son of God died; it is by all means to be believed, because it is absurd. And He was buried, and rose again; the fact is certain, because it is impossible' (Tertullian, 1870. ch.5). But, as Bernard Williams says, 'If you do not know what it is you are believing on faith, how can you be sure that you are believing anything?' (Williams, 1955, p. 209). Perhaps a more plausible case of such fideism is the Russian philosopher Lev Shestov:

Where reason proclaims *ineptum* (absurd), we shall say that it is precisely this that preferentially deserves our complete trust. And finally where it raises its *impossible* we shall oppose our 'It is certain'. (Shestov, 1968, p. 288)

Such extreme fideism has been held on the grounds that since only an omnipotent God can make what is logically impossible to be true, it is a sign of grace to believe such propositions.

The absurdity of Shestov's view serves to raise certain other matters which need to be discussed in order to develop the full picture. One is that it is extremely difficult to maintain most forms of fideism consistently as belief-policies across the whole body of a person's beliefs. The other is that there is sometimes, in fideism, a distinctively ethical strand. A reason sometimes given for fideism is not that our evidence may fail or be inappropriate in areas where we need or are impelled none the less to believe, but that reliance upon such evidence leads to, or is a manifestation of, pride or complacency or some other spiritual or ethical failure.

The Tertullian–Shestov view might be called conceptual fideism. Normally a precondition of belief is understanding; what is believed is not a meaningless form of words or a mere set of sounds, but something that has a definite sense. But according to the conceptual fideist in the case of at least some matters relating to God one ought to believe what one cannot understand; not merely cannot fully understand, but cannot understand at all. In some cases the distinction between conceptual fideism and what might be called evidential fideism is one of emphasis, in that one reason for a person being an evidential fideist is that the meaning of what is believed is opaque, and therefore the question of the evidence or reasons there might be for its truth cannot properly be considered.

Another factor that needs to be taken into account is that fideism has reason-giving and reason-less forms. Suppose that the fideist asserts

(a) Despite all the evidence against *p*, and the fact that there is no evidence for *p*, or less evidence than for some alternative, I nevertheless believe *p*.

The fideist is here asserting that *p* is to be believed without evidence; but it does not follow from this that the fideist has no reason for accepting (a). There may or may not be a reason for (a). A person may have a reason for believing a proposition which cannot be supported by reasons. This is not only true of belief in the narrow sense, but applies to action as well. A person may have a perfectly good reason for behaving irrationally; irrational behaviour may be part of a game, or a piece of dissimulation. It follows from this that fideism cannot be written off as sheer irrationality and nothing more. Certain forms of fideism may be dismissed in this way, those that have no reasons for believing in the absence of reasons, or for believing against all reason; but fideisms which appeal to reason at the second-order level may not be dismissed so easily.

Fideism of the type outlined in the previous paragraph is in no different case than, say, intuitionism in ethics. The view that the recognition of ethical distinctions, and even the acceptance of ethical truths, is based upon human intuition, is often regarded as being the abdication of human reason. It need not be. The intuitionist may have reasons for intuitionism; reasons, that is, for holding that the acceptance of ethical propositions is not a matter of reason, but of intuition. It may even be argued that any view to the effect that there are basic propositions, propositions which either do not need, or which cannot be provided with, a further justification is in precisely the same logical boat as that of the intuitionist and the fideist.

The distinction between reasoning and reason-less forms of fideism is thus another significant division in the fideistic family. A further, but less basic, division can also be made. The role that reason and evidence play at the second-order level can differ significantly, corresponding to the two roles that reasoning can play in establishing the truth or otherwise of propositions.

The more central and familiar role that reason plays (and included in reason here is the intelligent accumulation and testing of evidence) is that of establishing grounds for believing the truth of a proposition.

A rational person typically provides reasoning in support of a proposition, or evidence is marshalled in its support. Thus $p$ is true because $q$ is true and $p$ follows logically from $q$. Or $p$ is true because there is good evidence for $p$. A rational person may also accept the truth of a proposition because all the known objections to believing it have been rebutted. Not because there is reason for belief, but because there is no reason against belief. Richard Popkin refers to this belief-policy as 'moderate fideism'.

The picture is beginning to look decidedly complex. 'Fideism' is now seen to be the name of a family of philosophical positions, some at least of which can be called rational and evidential in character in that the fideist may be moved by evidential considerations at the second-order level in defending his fideism. 'Fideism' is not synonymous with an unreasoning act of the will in blindly accepting the truth of a proposition, though there are fideisms of this kind.

There is one final complication to be noted. One example of fideism given earlier is the view that belief may go beyond what is warranted by the evidence. According to Arvin Vos (Vos, 1985, p. 64) Aquinas held that faith was a certitude that was strictly speaking not warranted by the evidence, since the evidence went beyond our true or full understanding. Nevertheless, faith that God exists is justified, not so much by the evidence, and certainly not by the evidence alone, but by the goal of faith, its end, and by the acceptance of authoritative testimony.

Even in this it can happen that what is an object of vision or science for one person, can be an object of belief for another who does not have proven knowledge about it.

Matters set before the whole community for belief, however, are in no instance the object of any science, and these are the object of faith pure and simple. In these terms faith and science are not about the same object.

(Aquinas, 1974)

It is somewhat surprising, perhaps, that on this understanding of fideism Aquinas was among the fideists, for he held that the transcendent subject-matter of much theology necessarily goes beyond the human understanding, only a little theology being accessible to demonstration and therefore to be regarded as scientific in the strict sense, at least to those who are capable of following the relevant arguments. Faith is always relying upon what cannot be demonstrated, while the principles of science are accepted by natural light. Unlike Descartes for example, Aquinas held that all acceptable belief did not rest upon one foundation, but upon at least two separate foundations, what is discernible by natural light and what is supported by divine revelation.

However, if fideism is defined as the holding of a proposition on faith alone, without evidence, or in defiance of the evidence, then Aquinas was not a fideist, since for Aquinas there is *some* evidence for faith (Vos, 1985, p. 61).

There are obvious questions to be raised about the place of the will in fideistic belief, for what all fideistic positions share in common is that a person may choose to believe either in the absence of sufficient evidence or against the evidence or beyond the evidence. However, it will be taken for granted that the place of the will in the acceptance of propositions and the formation of belief-policies has been sufficiently discussed and vindicated in the previous chapters. We shall concentrate upon elaborating fideism as a family of distinctive belief-policies worthy of serious intellectual consideration.

## GLOBAL FIDEISM

According to some non-Cartesian versions of scepticism the familiar sceptical arguments arising from the weaknesses and distortions of the senses and the intellect ought not to lead to rationalism (as they did in the case of Descartes), but to a total suspension of belief. Yet such sceptics do not doubt the reality of the external world, only the capacity of the human mind to know that world with objectivity and certainty. Because of the confusing welter of opinions, none of which can be established with certainty, the function of scepticism is to clear the mind of them all.

In a way such scepticism is more radical than that of Descartes' in that it extends not only to the senses and the knowledge of the external world, including the body, as it does in the *Meditations*, but also to belief. In such scepticism reason cannot come to the rescue to reconstruct the edifice of human knowledge *more geometrico*. Rather, when, faced with the confused Babel of opinions, the wise person follows the sceptical path in order to induce belieflessness (and not, as with Descartes, with the aim of arriving at rational belief ).

Faced with the equilibrium of belieflessness, what ought the sceptic to do? The answer given by certain sceptics is: to pursue a belief-policy of having no beliefs, one based not upon evidence (which, for the reasons given, is out of the question), but upon detachment. The sceptic ought therefore to assent to (without believing) only what a particular group, however identified, believes, to follow the crowd, to accept the consensus. Such fideism manifestly does not claim to provide knowledge, but to provide a justification for belief in epistemic adversity, a justification, however, which is not based upon evidence. Only by adopting beliefs on this policy will anyone achieve the intellectual stability and tranquillity which is sought, but which the rational pursuit of the truth cannot provide due to the inadequacy of human evidence-gathering and evidence-assessing powers.

Such a stance is characteristic, in religion, of a sceptical attitude such as that of Montaigne (and also of Pierre Bayle), and was for a period used as an apologetic strategy by Roman Catholic evangelists (Popkin, 1964), in rather sharp contrast to the later (and earlier) emphasis upon natural theology. There is no reason why a no-belief belief-policy cannot operate in other areas of human inquiry.

One might regard Hume's response to his own scepticism as a case of global fideism, though not of no-belief fideism, in pursuit of the following belief-policy: *In the face of the inability of reason and the senses to provide any knowledge of anything except relations between ideas I ought to believe only what I find myself believing by habit.*

As we saw earlier when discussing scepticism as a belief-policy one might raise the question whether participation in the local customs, and acquiescence in the local opinions, is a case of genuine belief. But why should it not be? In the face of scepticism, and out of a desire to avoid inner conflict, one might genuinely believe what others believe, simply on the grounds that others believe it. What they believe might, after all, be true, and, while one has no reason for believing any alternative set of propositions, one does have a motive – the desire for inner peace and harmony – to believe what they believe.

Similarly with Humean habit. Hume does not merely say that one ought to believe what one finds oneself believing by habit, but that one ought to continue to believe what one habitually believes; that, for example, when an event of a certain kind occurs, an event of another kind will immediately follow, or that the next piece of bread will not be poisonous. For Hume these are genuine beliefs, and in the face of scepticism they ought to be indulged despite their rational groundlessness.

What is perhaps open to question in the case of Hume is whether the will plays or could play any part in the acceptance of the propositions believed. Hume's stress upon habit would suggest that the will plays no part, but this suggestion is not quite correct. For in so far as Hume's view can be rationally reconstructed in terms of a belief-policy, then the will may be said to play the part not of originating a belief-policy, but of sustaining it. In the face of turbulence induced by philosophy Hume may be taken as saying that he ought to accept the belief-policy of continuing to believe those propositions that habit, through the *de facto* regularity of experience, has produced in his mind.

Scepticism is, historically, the most important reason for fideism, both for particular fideism, and for global fideism. Terence Penelhum has brought out the parallels between a certain kind of faith and philosophical scepticism in an interesting way (Penelhum, 1983a). He has also shown that in some instances, such as that of Montaigne, scepticism has been incorporated into a person's view of religion and of faith ('conformist scepticism') while in the case of others, for example, Pascal and Kierkegaard, scepticism has acted as a propaedeutic to faith ('evangelical scepticism').

The local sceptic takes the view that, while reason is capable of arriving at knowledge in many areas of enquiry, it is incapacitated in religion, for example, either because of the influence of sin, or because of God's transcendence. And that in order to minimise theological divisiveness a fideistic policy of believing what the church teaches or the legislature prescribes (say) ought to be adopted.

So far the focus of our discussion has been upon global fideism and upon local fideism in religion and theology because such fideism is the most prominent in the literature. But there are other possible local fideisms. Fideism in ethics, for example. Some might take the view that, though there are ethical truths, it is impossible to know which ethical propositions are true and which are false, and that the only recourse in this situation, if one is a cognitivist in ethics, is to commit oneself to the truth of certain propositions, say, those that one has been brought up to accept. Such a person might combine ethical scepticism with a marked lack of scepticism in other areas, science for example. It may thus be claimed that one can know scientific truths, but that we do not know any ethical truths. In such a situation a person may, or must, believe, i.e. without reason or grounds that certain propositions are true, or adopt the ethical views of one's neighbours.

A philosophical objection to such fideistic strategies, either global or local, arises from an alleged incoherence in the nature of faith on such accounts. Penelhum, for example, raises the question, already touched upon, of whether conformity to local custom is belief of any kind (Penelhum, 1983a, pp. 291–2). He also asks why, in the case of Pascal or Kierkegaard, the believer believes in this God rather than that.

Except on a behaviourist account of belief it is very difficult to equate conformity to custom with belief, the intellectual acceptance of certain propositions as being true. But in the case of someone who, like Kierkegaard or Pascal, commits himself to God in a sceptical situation, a defence of such a commitment as involving belief is more promising. Penelhum says

I have suggested that the Skeptic suspense of judgement can be ascribed to someone even in the face of lapses into conviction. The converse is clearly true for the person of faith, whose conviction can still be acknowledged despite periods of doubt. For doubt can occur within faith and need not destroy it. It will not destroy it if the doubter *contends* with the doubts that he has . . . Faith also is a normative notion, and one shows one deserves to be credited with having faith when one acknowledges that one does not have it strongly enough and accepts the obligation to deepen it. The norm excludes doubt, but the state does not, any more than the state of courage excludes all fear. (*Ibid.*, pp. 300–1)

It is not clear that these comments quite address the force of the objection that can be made against the fideist. It is not so much whether a person can fight against doubt as what entitles a believer to have conviction in the first place. Clearly a fideist cannot have general grounds for belief, nor personal grounds, though such a possibility will be explored further later in this chapter. He can believe without any grounds at all; this is what fideism is. But then can the believer be said to believe? This is possible if one distinguishes faith from assured faith. The fideistic believer may commit himself to God while content to live in a situation in which that faith is totally ungrounded.

But why faith commitment to *this* God? If faith were mere belief the question would be unanswerable. Religious faith is not mere belief, it is a propositional attitude (or perhaps a personal attitude)

198

which is such that only an object with the properties of the God of classical theism – transcendence of space and time, immutability, omnipotence, immaculate holiness, and so on – can satisfy. For it is only such a God who is beyond all evidential vicissitude, a fit object, the only fit object, for that faith commitment which does not rely upon empirical grounds – for there are no empirical grounds – but which gambles on the existence of the one who is necessarily hidden from all ordinary human enquiry.

Such a notion of faith is similar in many respects to a Kantian *postulate*. For Kant the existence of God was a requirement of his morality, and so God was postulated, a God whose character, as one would expect, fitted Kantian morality like a glove; a moral God who transcended space and time, whose commands were perceived as duty, and who was capable of being the rewarder of virtue and the punisher of vice.

For the fideist weakness of will may show itself when the scepticism which forms the justification of the fideism is to any degree modified or abandoned. The fideist may be tempted to adopt a dogmatic stance; to believe there is real knowledge of an external world and not merely to accept the habit of living as if there is one. And in an effort to avoid weakness of will the fideist must continually be fortified by reminders of the strength of the sceptical arguments and by resisting any pressure to dogmatise. As Penelhum puts it, the sceptic and the fideist must be committed to

cultivating a habit of suspense which undermines our inclination to share the beliefs that surround us. This policy is indeed one he can follow, and which will express his real stance in spite of those occasions when he may lapse into conviction like the rest of us. (*Ibid.*, p. 299)

Just as in the more central cases of weakness of will it is possible to represent the conflict which gives rise to such weakness as a clash between two 'selves', the flesh and the spirit, or duty and desire, so in the case of the fideist's weakness of will there is a distancing or externalising of some deep inclination. That inclination is repudiated as not being a part of the real self, but an alien intrusion. The fideist will see the tendency to be convinced that (say) there is an external world as a temptation, as something which is deeply undesirable and which may be resisted by carrying through the policy of reaffirming the arguments for scepticism, which forms the basis of that intellectual position.

So epistemological scepticism provides a general argument for fideism, for that second-level version of fideism which offers reasons for not having reasons for belief. But as was noted earlier there may also be moral arguments for fideism, arguments which involve identifying the epistemic practice of the rest of humanity, whether that practice is one of full religious conformity or of avowed unbelief, as being immoral in some way, the product of pride or self-satisfaction or worldly conformity. In discussing the connection between epistemology and ethics in the opening chapter the suggestion was made that there may be ethical preconditions to knowledge; what now follows is a case in point.

### THE MORAL FIDEIST

The reasoning offered in favour of fideism (in religion, or in some other distinct area of human interest) may involve a characterisation of human reason as 'worldly wisdom'. This critique may take various forms; for example, a kind of moral non-conformity, part of a general critique of the temptations of worldliness, a refusal to drift with the crowd and to accept what everyone else accepts, and to adopt instead a kind of intellectual bohemianism. And since the crowd, or at least many in the crowd, accept that reason or evidence are the only guides in matters of religion, it follows that as a matter of fact they cannot be such guides, and the alleged 'findings' of reason or evidence in the matter of religion cannot be accepted. But if the crowd came to accept some kind of fideism, then presumably the principle of non-conformity to the world would demand a reversal of the strategy. Matters of religious truth ought now to be approached by the use of the reason, or by assessing evidence.

It is likely in view of this last point that the moral fideist would support such a position by another argument; by claiming, in general, that the use of the reason or the appeal to evidence leads inevitably to self-deceit. Reason feeds human conceit, and misleads the reasoner into looking for the wrong things, and in the wrong places. Such a view might be made more plausible if it were believed that the knowledge of the self is directly connected with the knowledge of what is being enquired into; the nature and existence of God, for example. It might be said that confidence in the powers of human reasoning or evidence-gathering is both a cause and a strengthening of pride, and that human pride prevents people from coming to an appreciation of the nature of God and his relationship to themselves. Because of this those ways of knowing which minister to human pride must be avoided, and the lowly road of evidence-less trust in God must be taken instead (Gooch, 1987, ch. 2).

Such a view accepts that there are moral preconditions for acquiring knowledge; if the use of the reason is incompatible with the existence of such moral preconditions then it will follow that not only is reason of no use in the establishing of truth in religion, it can be of no use in elaborating that truth once it is acquired by faith. In other words, the claim that the unbridled use of reason leads to conceit and self-deceit is a general claim about reason; if it is valid it not only requires some version of fideism for acceptable belief in God it also rules out the Augustinian *credo ut intelligiam* view of the place of reason in religion.

Whether or not the use of reason ministers to pride and conceit and self-deceit is presumably a matter for empirical inquiry, inquiry which, though it may be difficult to carry out, the second-order fideist should at least welcome. In addition such a fideist might conceivably argue that investigating whether the use of reason has moral consequences and conditions is itself a moral matter and so not open to evidence.

The claim that there are moral preconditions for knowledge by no means leads logically to fideism. Someone might argue that the connection is such that once a person has a true appreciation of the limitations of human powers it is not the moral merits of fideism that will be recognised, but the merits of the use of reason in acquiring truths which previously he had disdained. Or that a proper appreciation of oneself will clear the mind to realise that the knowledge of God acquired through reason ought to lead to the acceptance of a certain source as the authoritative repository of divine revelation.

Another argument of a moral kind for fideism can go as follows; for the believer in God to argue (say) for the existence of God is to adopt the standpoint of the unbeliever, either genuinely or for dialectical reasons. If one genuinely adopts such a standpoint then, whatever one's motives in arguing for the existence of God, one has deserted the faith. If one adopts it dishonestly or disingenuously then one is being less than fully sincere.

To argue for the existence of God requires that one assume that God does not exist, for the arguments that one constructs and considers are all arguments that have as premises propositions whose truth is acceptable to the non-believer. So on this view the believer who accepts the strategy of natural theology is indulging in a kind of weakness of will; for the believer accepts without these arguments, prior to them, that God exists. Why then adopt a strategy which allows acceptance of the proposition that God exists to be suspended upon the success or otherwise of a rational or evidential argument for his existence?

This is not so much a moral argument for the adoption of fideism, as a moral argument for its retention. The argument is that a certain moral stance is incompatible with a faith already in exercise.

## FAITH, EVIDENCE, AND PROOF

In order to strengthen the case for treating fideism as a family of belief-policies I shall discuss two recent contributions to religious epistemology, those made by O. K. Bouwsma and Alvin Plantinga.

In a paper 'Faith, Evidence and Proof' (Bouwsma, 1984) O. K. Bouwsma sets forth, in effect if not in intention, a belief-policy for the acceptance of Christianity. Characteristic of Bouwsma's approach is that he holds that there cannot be evidence for the central tenets of Christianity. The impossibility is not, he maintains, a physical impossibility, nor is it epistemic. It is not that we cannot reach God as we cannot reach the outskirts of the physical universe; nor is the impossibility due to the fact that we do not know where to look nor what would count as evidence. It is that it is logically impossible for there to be evidence for such matters as the existence of God, or any of his deeds.

But neither we nor Abraham could have evidence that God either spoke to him or did promise him anything; not even Abraham could have evidence of this. In making or insisting on the distinction I do not mean to say that we have any evidence that Abraham did anything . . . I am interested in emphasising that the religious belief of Abraham, namely, that God commanded him to go and promised him a future, this belief is of an altogether different order. For this there can be no evidence. I dare scarcely say that we can understand this, I mean, understand what Abraham believed.
(Bouwsma, 1984, p. 9)

Later in the same paper, writing of Jehovah's appearance to Moses at the burning bush, he writes

Belief is possible. And such belief! Is there now no evidence possible that the angel of Jehovah appeared to him in a flame of fire? There is no evidence and no evidence possible. It is not that evidence is lacking. Evidence is inconceivable. (*Ibid.*, p. 11)

And again

And what is the evidence? Admitting, however, that the urge to persist in this question, almost as though one scanned the landscape to search for the evidence, is extremely powerful, the problem arises as to how it is that we do this. It is not, remember, that we can look for what is not there. Neither is it like looking for air in a vacuum. There might be air in the enclosure which is supposed to be a vacuum. It is rather like looking for air in joy, in kindness, in anger. It is said that oil and water do not mix. And so it is with evidence and faith. (*Ibid.*, p. 18)

So Bouwsma holds that there are cases of belief for which evidence is impossible. These are not pathological cases; they are paradigms, model cases of belief for Christianity; Abraham and Moses. It may be that he would say that such cases are of belief 'in', belief in God, or even of believing God, rather than of belief 'that'. But there is no reason to think that Bouwsma would deny that such cases involve beliefs 'that' – the belief that God exists, for example.

Bouwsma gives two main reasons for taking this position. I shall call these the *ontological* and the *religious* reasons. The ontological reason has to do with the fact that God is not a part of the physical universe, and cannot be. 'We are like people who lie in an enclosure behind walls, and the question "Is there a God or not?" is a question about what is behind the wall' (*ibid.*, p. 4). In the story of Abraham or Moses, Bouwsma maintains that there is a human part and a divine part. There can be evidence about the human part, but no evidence about the divine part.

So for Bouwsma nothing in the world can provide evidence for (or against) whatever is outside the world. Evidence is only relevant in cases which are 'analogous to cases in which we know both what corresponds to the evidence in this case and what we come to know by way of that evidence' (*ibid.*, p. 7). And presumably whatever is outside the world is God; hobgoblins and other foul fiends are creatures. Perhaps evidence for such creatures is thin, perhaps there is none at all. But, if it is impossible to gain evidence of hobgoblins, this is not for the same reason that evidence for God is impossible. So one cannot have evidence for God, the divine mind, as one can, say, for creaturely minds.

The religious reason provided by Bouwsma has to do with the relationship between evidence and trust. We can ask how much evidence there is, whether it could be better, whether it has been properly weighed, and so on. But

> We are not to say that since Abraham believed that God called him and that God promised, it must be so or very likely to be so . . . The Scriptures say, 'And Abraham went', and later, 'And Abraham believed'. They do not say, 'After having taken all the reasonable precautions about being taken in and after making sure that he would be able to give a good account of himself to his friends, he decided to obey the order.'                    (*ibid.*, p. 8).

So there is something *sui generis* about true religious belief. Such belief is conceptually connected with obedience.

> 'Who art thou, Lord?' is said by one who in saying it does not make a discovery, as though he noticed something and inferred that Jesus was after all someone important, perhaps Moses or Elijah, as men had said earlier. In this utterance Saul becomes a servant, certainly not knowing what the end would be, and as he would have said, 'through the grace of God'. It is a mistake to regard Saul as believing at one moment and obeying the next – as though he then said, 'Well, I had better.'                    (*ibid.*, pp. 12–13)

The reasons that Bouwsma gives for the way in which he regards belief in God have a bearing on the question of what kind of belief-policy we are dealing with here. They place a great strain on the very idea of a belief-policy. For such policies, as we have so far considered them, have to do with standards of evidence; but standards of evidence are the very thing that, according to Bouwsma, are not applicable in the case of faith. In this respect Bouwsma's view of religious belief forms a kind of limiting case of a belief-policy. As we have already seen the place of the will in the forming of beliefs has partly at least to do with the fact of there being different possible standards of evidence to which one might appeal in support of the belief that a particular proposition is true. This limiting case appears to have very little to do with the will. It is not as if Abraham or Moses chose to believe, or believed in accordance with a particular belief-policy that they had chosen; they were constrained to believe. Perhaps it is more accurate to say that they found themselves believing.

Yet the will plays a negative role. For on Bouwsma's account Abraham rejects the very idea of evidence; his belief-policy is not to consider evidence; it is not allowed to enter into his thinking. Not even, presumably, evidence that it is God who is speaking. There may be evidence of, say, sounds of thunder. But there is no way in which sounds of thunder could be evidence for God's speech.

In such an enclosure as I have described and in which such a conversation may take place there are not only dummy doors which tempt people, but there are also doors, or at least one door, which opens only from the outside of that enclosure. And when that door is opened – it is obviously opened only by what is outside the wall and does not even show from inside the enclosure – and one sees what is to be seen, naturally he has no interest in those other doors others try so hard to open. (*Ibid.*, p. 4).

There is no positive policy that one can conceivably adopt in such circumstances, for policies are exercised with respect to doors with visible handles. They are concerned with the problem of the best way of opening the door. One can have no door-opening policy with respect to a door which is invisible and which in any case opens only from the outside. Bouwsma reinforces this point by stressing that Christianity is not a discovery, that is, something made acceptable through evidence and the exercise of belief in accordance with a certain belief-policy.

I am emphasising that Christianity is something that happened and not a theory or an explanation or a set of doctrines in order, at the outset, to make sure of what sort of evidence one might look for were one tempted to look. So too it is not anything that someone discovered, as though one stood behind a tree and then later reported, 'I saw it with my own eyes.' (*Ibid.*, p. 6)

So we must say that the question of whether A ought to believe *p* or may do so does not arise in the case of Christian belief, according to Bouwsma, and *a fortiori* the question whether belief is exercised because the evidence for *p* is logically impossible, or even though it is, does not arise.

We are now in a position to answer the question whether Bouwsma's account of the paradigm-cases of Christian faith are fideistic or not in any of the senses discussed earlier. The answer must

205

be that his account is not that of a first-order fideist, for he provides reasons for the impossibility of obtaining evidence, and for exercising faith in the absence of evidence. Also Bouwsma is not advocating that people believe *p* when there is no evidence for *p*, or when the evidence for or against *p* is evenly balanced, or when there is less evidence for *p* than against. He is arguing that in this case evidence, of whatever kind and in whatever strength, cannot apply. And the fact that he is arguing in this way means that he has second-level reasons for regarding evidence for a certain type of first-level belief as involving a kind of category-mistake.

The issue of which belief-policy is not entirely irrelevant, however. For one of the prime reasons for Bouwsma drawing attention to the peculiar features of religious belief as he understands them, and emphasising them, is to counter the view that all belief is evidential belief-policy belief. There are those, Bouwsma says, in whom the urge to persist with the question, 'And what is the evidence?' is very powerful.

In seeking for evidence, [they] are misled by the Scriptures themselves, to which Scriptures they are devoted, and are under the illusion that in seeking for evidence they 'do God service', helping along the cause of the Scripture by a straw or two straws here and there.          (*Ibid.*, p. 19)

The problem, as Bouwsma sees it, is that 'belief' is normally and properly used in contexts in which questions of evidence are relevant. 'Generally if the belief in question is a belief of any moment, concerning something important, we will want to know what reasons there are for his believing that' (*ibid.*, p. 20). But it is a mistake to think that all belief is like this.

Now the temptation ensues. How can one believe without evidence? So one looks for evidence. One cannot believe anything of this sort without the crutches of a few words on the side. Evidence is the crutch of belief. But faith with a crutch is not faith.          (*Ibid.*, p. 20)

A person may think that he is an earnest seeker after truth, but deceive himself because he has misunderstood the sort of belief religious belief is. Bouwsma believed that in his writings Kierkegaard was preoccupied with attempting, in various oblique ways, to unmask this self-deception. One way we could express this preoccupation is: Kierkegaard was attempting to replace any of the various evidential belief-policies by which people attempt to establish the truth of Christianity with a policy of having no evidential belief-policy at all.

It is difficult to state Bouwsma's position in the form of a belief-policy, since it is at the extreme of involuntarism. Moreover this is not the involuntarism of Humean naturalism or evidentialism, but that which arises from the priority and sufficiency of God's gracious activity. Yet for Bouwsma, faith is not, as it is for Kierkegaard, a passionate leap beyond or against or apart from any evidence, for it is not a leap of any kind. Perhaps the belief-policy would have to be something like: *if faith in God arises in your mind, do not resist it, but resist any attempt to ground such faith in evidence.*

## FAITH AND FOUNDATIONALISM

Alvin Plantinga's religious epistemology is couched explicitly in ethical or normative terms, in terms of what a person *may* or *is entitled to* believe, in terms of the norms to which the mind ought to conform. In the absence of a rational proof of God's existence is a person obliged to espouse atheism or agnosticism? No more, says Plantinga, than in the absence of a proof of atheism or agnosticism a person is obliged to espouse theism. But in the absence of a proof of God's existence a person may believe that God exists, for the proposition that God exists may quite properly find a place in the set of that person's basic propositions, those propositions which are accepted without evidence or argument. So, as we noted earlier, Plantinga defends the reasonableness of theistic belief by adopting a permissive belief-policy.

Central to Plantinga's argument is a critique of classical foundationalism. According to such a foundationalist there are certain propositions which are logically necessary, and others which are evident to the senses. Such propositions are basic; they form part of the justification for all non-foundational propositions and are themselves incapable of further justification. So for any non-foundational proposition to be rationally acceptable according to the foundationalist there has to be evidence for it; it must ultimately rest upon a foundation of truths which are evident to the senses, or on a set of propositions, intermediate propositions as we might call them, which themselves rest upon a foundation of self-evident propositions.

We may think of the foundationalist as beginning with the observation that some of our beliefs are based upon others. According to the foundationalist a rational noetic structure will *have a foundation* – a set of beliefs not accepted on the basis of others; in a rational noetic structure some beliefs will be basic. Non-basic belief, of course, will be accepted on the basis of other beliefs, and so on until the foundations are reached. In a rational noetic structure, therefore, every non-basic belief is ultimately accepted on the basis of the basic beliefs.                                    (Plantinga, 1983, p. 52)

There is not much that is wrong with foundationalism, according to Plantinga. The trouble lies rather with the conditions or criteria of proper basicness. The appeal of the classical foundationalist is to the incorrigibility or self-evidence of certain propositions. Plantinga offers several arguments against such a criterion; for example, he points out that if we accept it then most of our everyday beliefs are not probable (*ibid.*, pp. 59–60). He also argues that there are many propositions which we accept without further evidence which are not properly basic by the criterion of the classical foundationalist; for example, the proposition that I had lunch today (*ibid.*, p. 20). Not only does classical foundationalism fail to justify many everyday beliefs, many such beliefs do not require foundational justification.

Plantinga's central argument is as follows. Take any criterion of proper basicness advanced by the classical foundationalist. It is something like the following: a proposition is properly basic for a person only if that proposition is self-evident or incorrigible for that person, or evident to the senses of that person. But what is the status of the statement of the criteria of proper basicness that has just been given? To be acceptable to the classical foundationalist these criteria must themselves be either self-evident or incorrigible or evident to the senses. Plantinga says, they are far from being any of these things. So while classical foundationalism may appeal to self-evidence or incorrigibility, classical foundationalism itself is far from being self-evident or incorrigible (*ibid.*, p. 60). Just as there are second-order arguments for fideism, so there are second-order arguments against foundationalism.

From this argument Plantinga concludes that classical foundation-alism, with its appeal to criteria of self-evidence and incorrigibility, is flawed. It follows, therefore, that there is nothing to prevent another proposition, for example the proposition *God exists*, from appearing in the foundations of a person's belief. For, while that proposition may not be self-evidently true, it does not need to be in order to appear in the foundations. It could be among the propositions that that person accepts without evidence, as the classical foundationalist accepts certain propositions without evidence, the so-called incorrigible truths.

As we noted earlier, in *The Retreat to Commitment* W. W. Bartley III accused a host of philosophers and theologians of defending their respective positions by employing an argument which he regarded as disreputable and which he called the *tu quoque* argument. The trouble with foundationalism, according to Bartley, is that it involves a 'retreat to commitment' for it relies upon a person's non-reasoned commitment to certain foundational truths and thus has no answer to any irrationalist who may, in turn, be basically committed to irrationalism. According to Bartley, the classical foundationalist epistemologies of rationalism and empiricism are in the same dialectical boat as that occupied by the most dire irrationalist:

(1) For certain logical reasons, rationality is so limited that everyone must make an irrational dogmatic commitment; (2) therefore the Christian has a right to make whatever commitment he pleases; and (3) therefore, no one has a right to criticise him (or anyone else) for making such a commitment.

(Bartley, 1984, p. 72)

Just as the foundationalist appeals to certain propositions as being self-evident or beyond rational dispute, and builds an epistemological structure upon them, so any irrationalist may choose anything as a foundation and cite the example of the classical foundationalist as a justification for doing so. Any foundationalist is thus a fideist.

Is Plantinga guilty of using the *tu quoque* argument? It is hard to see that he is, for the simple reason that he does not defend his view by saying that he is entitled to accept God into the foundations of his noetic structure merely because the classical foundationalist accepts certain supposedly self-evident truths as foundational. Rather, as we have seen, Plantinga provides *arguments* for his view, arguments based upon the fact that the classical foundationalist's belief-policy (the 'criteria for basicality' as Plantinga calls them) is not self-evidently true, and upon his own claim that certain truths are justified while being ungrounded.

What is true of Plantinga in relation to the *tu quoque* argument will be true of every second-order or rational fideist; for it is characteristic of this view that it provides reasons or arguments for fideism. To be sure these arguments concern the inadequacies of non-fideism, but nevertheless they involve a reasoned consideration of the philosophical merits of respective positions. So while the *tu quoque* argument may have validity against first-order fideism it is hard to see that it makes any impression on rational or second-order fideism.

There is reason to think that the *tu quoque* argument is not such a flawless weapon as Bartley claims. Not only is it inapplicable to Plantinga's argument it is also, as we saw earlier, pretty useless against the more dogmatic versions of fideism.

According to Plantinga there are propositions for which we do not have grounds, but which we are entitled to believe; or more accurately perhaps, there are propositions which we are entitled to believe in ignorance of any grounds that there may be in support of the truth of those propositions.

While Plantinga does not fall foul of the *tu quoque* argument, he may yet be a fideist. In order to get a clearer view of Plantinga's philosophical method it will be helpful to consider an objection to his proposal for a foundationalism that is less than strict, one which readily comes to mind, and which he himself considers.

If belief in God is properly basic, why cannot just any belief be properly basic? Could we not say the same for any bizarre aberration we can think of? What about voodoo or astrology? What about the belief that the Great Pumpkin returns every Halloween? Could I properly take that as basic? Suppose that I believe that if I flap my arms with sufficient vigour, I can take off and fly about the room; could I defend myself against the charge of irrationality by claiming this belief is basic? If we say that belief in God is properly basic, will we not be committed to holding that just anything, or nearly anything, can properly be taken as basic, thus throwing wide the gates to irrationalism and superstition? (Plantinga, 1983, p. 74)

In other words, is not the permissive ethic of belief or belief-policy adopted by Plantinga too permissive, positively anarchic and antinomian in character?

Naturally enough Plantinga rejects this objection out of hand, arguing that what a person is entitled to take as properly basic depends on circumstances (*ibid.*, p. 74). Because no criteria of justification are self-evident it does not follow that just anything can count as being basic; the next best thing to self-evidence is accepting propositions as properly basic. And the proper epistemological strategy is to proceed not a priori in terms of some general criterion of epistemic justification, but a posteriori, in terms of actual cases of propositions which are properly basic to a person at a time.

We must assemble examples of beliefs and conditions such that the former are obviously properly basic in the latter, and examples of beliefs and conditions such that the former are obviously not properly basic in the latter. We must then frame hypotheses as to the necessary and sufficient conditions of proper basicality and test these hypotheses by reference to those examples. Under the right conditions, for example, it is clearly rational to believe that you see a human person before you: a being who has thoughts and feelings, who knows and believes things, who makes decisions and acts. It is clear, furthermore, that you are under no obligation to reason to this belief from others you hold; under those conditions that belief is properly basic for you. (*ibid*, p. 76)

The significant move in this argument is from the rejection of general criteria of rationality to the acceptance of *personal* or *community* criteria; the step from 'It is self-evident that *p*' to 'It appears to me (or to us) to be self-evident that *p*'. Plantinga's appeal to personal or community criteria of the acceptability of propositions certainly removes most if not all of the initial shock-value of his proposal. For Plantinga's belief-policy is not, *You may believe the first thing that comes into your head*, but *Believe only what is properly basic for you, and whatever validly follows from this.*

In 'Is Belief in God Rational?' (Plantinga, 1979) Plantinga sets himself the task of discussing the question of whether it is rational or reasonable or rationally acceptable to believe in God. Considering W. K. Clifford's ethic of belief, Plantinga asks what propositions form the evidence on which, according to Clifford, one ought to believe any further proposition; could the proposition that God exists form a part of that evidence? It is widely held that it could not, that it is possible only to believe that God exists, never to know it.

But why should the theist concede these things? Suppose he grants that there is a foundation to his noetic structure: a set F of propositions such that (1) he knows each member of F *immediately* and (2) whatever else he knows is evident with respect to the members of F. Suppose he concedes, further, that he does know other things, and knows them on the basis of his knowledge of these basic propositions. (Plantinga, 1979, pp. 19–20)

And in 'The Reformed objection to Natural Theology' (Plantinga, 1980) he says that, according to John Calvin, belief in God

need not be based on any other propositions at all; under these conditions he is perfectly rational in accepting belief in God in the utter absence of any argument, deductive or inductive. Indeed, a person in these conditions, says Calvin, knows that God exists, has knowledge of God's existence, apart from any arguments at all. (*Ibid.*, p. 52)

And later in the same paper

Calvin claims that one who takes belief in God as basic can nonetheless know that God exists. Calvin holds that one can *rationally accept* belief in God as basic; he also claims that one can *know* that God exists even if he has no argument, even if he does not believe on the basis of other propositions. A weak foundationalist is likely to hold that some properly basic beliefs are such that anyone who accepts them, knows them. More exactly, he is likely to hold that among the beliefs properly basic for a person S, some are such that if S accepts them, S knows them. A weak foundationalist could go on to say that other properly basic beliefs can't be known, if taken as basic, but only rationally believed; and he might think of the existence of God as a case in point. Calvin will have none of this; as he sees it, one needs no arguments to know that God exists . . . Now I enthusiastically concur in these contentions of Reformed epistemology. (*Ibid.*, p. 58)

Plantinga repeats this more recently

On Calvin's view, properly functioning human cognitive capacities will indeed produce belief in God; the modules of the design plan governing the production of these beliefs are indeed aimed at truth; belief in God taken in the basic way, therefore, does indeed have warrant. Hence natural theology is not needed for belief in God to have warrant; the natural view here, in fact, will be that many people *know* that there is such a person as God without believing on the basis of the arguments of natural theology.

(Plantinga, 1991, p. 311)

There are certain difficulties with some of these statements as they stand. By them Plantinga, following Calvin, at least as Plantinga understands Calvin, advances two claims; that the proposition that God exists is properly basic both for him and for Calvin, and that 'one who takes God as properly basic can also know that God exists'

(Plantinga, 1980, p. 58). The 'can' in the last sentence is a bit awkward, for Plantinga surely means that one who takes the existence of God as properly basic *does* know that God exists.

What are the difficulties? As philosophers typically understand the concept of knowledge, if a proposition *p* is known then *p* is true. Unless a different concept of knowledge is being used, from the fact that Calvin and Plantinga know that God exists we can infer that it is true that God exists. If anyone knows that God exists then it is objectively true that God exists. God exists for everyone, whatever their epistemological starting-point or ending-point may be. And, according to Plantinga, both Calvin and himself know that God exists because that proposition appears in the foundations of each of their noetic structures.

Had Calvin and Plantinga been strong or classical foundationalists then there would be no problem. For, if the proposition that God exists is a properly basic proposition for a strong or classical foundationalist, then that proposition is incorrigible or evident to the senses, and incorrigible propositions are both true and indubitably so. But, as Plantinga is at pains to point out, neither Calvin nor he are strong foundationalists, and so the problem remains.

The difficulty can be sharpened up as follows. Suppose there is another weak foundationalist, another person who accepts that knowledge has a foundational structure, but who believes himself entitled to accept the proposition that God does *not* exist. Perhaps acceptance of such a proposition arises from his experience of meaninglessness or tragedy. It would follow, by parity of reasoning, that such a person knows that God does not exist. While Plantinga and Calvin know that God exists, and therefore it is true that God exists, true for everyone, this other weak foundationalist knows that God does not exist, and therefore it is true, true for everyone, that God does not exist. Note that the objection is not to the weak foundationalist being entitled to include either of these propositions in his foundations. It is not a question of such an entitlement, but of what follows from the entitlement. And what cannot follow is the conclusion that God both exists and does not exist.

Plantinga insists that it is one of the features of any foundational proposition that it is accepted without argument. For both strong and weak foundationalists hold in common the view that in every rational noetic structure there is a set of beliefs taken as basic (Plantinga, 1983,

p. 72). Nevertheless, when he clarifies the view that the proposition that God exists is properly basic Plantinga argues that although it is basic it is not *groundless*. For whether a proposition is accepted as basic or not depends, among other things, upon the circumstances of the person concerned.

Consider the belief that I see a tree: this belief is properly basic in circumstances that are hard to describe in detail, but include my being appeared to in a certain characteristic way; that same belief is not properly basic in circumstances including, say, my knowledge, that I am sitting in the living room listening to music with my eyes closed.          (*Ibid.*, p. 74)

So a belief is properly basic only in certain conditions, conditions which it may be difficult to specify in detail and exhaustively.

Now similar things may be said about belief in God. When the Reformers claim that this belief is properly basic, they do not mean to say, of course, that there are no justifying circumstances for it, or that it is in that sense groundless or gratuitous. Quite the contrary Calvin holds that God 'reveals and daily discloses himself in the whole workmanship of the universe', and the divine art 'reveals itself in the innumerable and yet distinct and well ordered variety of the heavenly host'. God has so created us that we have a tendency or disposition to see his hand in the world about us.          (*Ibid.*, p. 80)

Plantinga needs to be able to make out a distinction between having an argument for a proposition and having a ground for a proposition; he needs to be able to do this because he has to say that the Reformed epistemologist may accept the existence of God without argument but that there are grounds for the belief that God exists since acceptance of God's existence is not arbitrary; it is not like belief in the Great Pumpkin, for example.

No doubt Plantinga can make out this distinction. But success in being able to make it out carries interesting consequences. Once it is asserted that there are grounds for properly basic propositions then, as we noted earlier, the philosophical shock value of Plantinga's claim that the existence of God may be properly basic diminishes considerably. The claim that one does not need arguments in order rationally to believe that God exists, or even to know that God exists, is transmuted into an appeal to personal experience. Plantinga's Reformed epistemology is a variant of the argument from experience to the existence of God. It is no worse for that, of course; such arguments have a long and honourable tradition.

214

The moral to be drawn from this discussion is not about natural theology, but about belief-policies. Earlier in the book it was argued that there can be no knock-down proof of the superiority of one policy over all the others. Plantinga's Reformed epistemology underlines the sorts of constraints that arise in the choice of a belief-policy; they are the familiar constraints of logical consistency and freedom from arbitrariness. The discussion of Plantinga's views reveals that while it is possible for there to be a wide variety of foundationalist belief-policies, not just anything can function foundationally without the rapid appearance of a *reductio ad absurdum* if not of a *tu quoque*.

The views of Bouwsma and Plantinga have in common a position which makes religious faith, trustful belief in God, discontinuous from any rational grounding which appeals to criteria operative in rational man as such. In Plantinga's case, because there are no such criteria; in Bouwsma's because such criteria necessarily exclude faith in God.

So is Plantinga's Reformed epistemology fideistic? Plantinga himself demurs at the suggestion on the grounds that according to the Reformed epistemologist reason and faith do not clash (Plantinga, 1983, p. 89). But this may not be the determining characteristic of fideism. For Bouwsma, as we noted, reason and faith, or at least evidence and faith, cannot clash, because evidence cannot be used to support faith or to weaken it. Furthermore, according to Plantinga it would be inaccurate to suppose that taking certain propositions as basic is taking those propositions on faith; or at least, such faith – if we wish to call it that – is not the faith of the fideist. A person is only a fideist, according to Plantinga, if he 'holds that some central truths of Christianity are not among the deliverances of reason and must instead be taken on faith'. This is certainly sufficient to distinguish Plantinga from Bouwsma.

The problem – once again – lies in getting clear what are the deliverances of reason and what are not. They must include, according to Plantinga, 'basic perceptual truths (propositions "evident to the senses"), incorrigible propositions, certain memory propositions, certain propositions about other minds, and certain moral or ethical propositions' (Plantinga, 1983, p. 89). But why should the deliverances of reason not also include the belief that there is such a person as God and that we are responsible to him? If so, then the Reformed epistemologist cannot be a fideist because there is for him no conflict between faith and reason. This is because one central proposition of the Reformed epistemologist's religious faith is included within the propositions of reason.

Finally, there may be another feature of Reformed epistemology which makes it a close relation of fideism, the fact that the grounds for taking the belief that God exists as basic are person-relative (Mavrodes, 1970a), or community-relative. In this sense they are not general, accepted by all and every rational person. This is certainly an important feature that both the fideistic family and Plantinga's Reformed epistemology have in common.

# References

Adams, R. M., 1987a, 'Kierkegaard's Arguments Against Objective Reasoning in Religion', in Adams 1987d, pp. 25–41.

1987b, 'The Leap of Faith', in Adams 1987d, pp. 42–7.

1987c, 'The Virtue of Faith', in Adams 1987d, pp. 9–24.

1987d, *The Virtue of Faith and Other Essays in Philosophical Theology*. Oxford, Clarendon Press.

Alston, W., 1988, 'The Deontological Conception of Epistemic Justification', in Tomberlin (ed.), 1988, pp. 257–99.

Anscombe, G. E. M., 1979, 'What is it to Believe Someone?', in Delaney (ed.), pp. 141–51.

Aquinas, Thomas, 1974, *Summa Theologiae*. 2.2ae, trans. T. C. O'Brien. London, Eyre and Spottiswoode, pp. 22–7.

Armstrong, D. M., 1973, *Belief, Truth and Knowledge*. Cambridge University Press.

Audi, R., 1979, 'Weakness of Will and Practical Judgement', *Nous*, 13, 173–96.

Augustine, 1873, *On the Trinity*. trans. A. W. Haddon. Edinburgh, T. and T. Clark.

Bartley, W. W. III, 1984, *The Retreat to Commitment*. Revised and enlarged, La Salle, Open Court.

Bouwsma, O. K., 1984, *Without Proof or Evidence: Essays of O. K. Bouwsma*. Eds. J. L. Craft and R. Hustwit. Lincoln, University of Nebraska Press.

Braithwaite, R. B., 1950, 'Moral Policies and Inductive Policies' London, *Proceedings of the British Academy*, 36, 51–68.

Brandt, R. B., 1985, 'The Concept of Rational Belief', *The Monist*, 68, 3–23.

Brown, S. C., 1989, 'Christian Averroism, Fideism and the "Two-Fold" Truth', in *The Philosophy in Christianity*. Ed. G. Vesey. Cambridge University Press, pp. 207–23.

Burnyeat, M. F., 1983, 'Can the Skeptic Live His Skepticism?' in Burnyeat (ed.), pp. 117–48.

Burnyeat, M. F., (ed.), 1983, *The Skeptical Tradition*. Berkeley, University of California Press.

217

Charlton, W., 1988, *Weakness of Will*. Oxford, Blackwell.

Chisholm, R. M., 1976, *Theory of Knowledge*. Second Edition. Englewood Cliffs, Prentice-Hall.

1982, *The Foundations of Knowing*. Minneapolis, University of Minnesota Press.

Clifford, W. K., 1970, 'The Ethics of Belief', in Mavrodes (ed.), pp. 152–160.

Coady, C. A. J., 1992, *Testimony: A Philosophical Study*. Oxford, Clarendon Press.

Code, L., 1987, *Epistemic Responsibility*. Hanover, University Press of New England.

Cohen, L. J., 1992, *An Essay on Belief and Acceptance*. Oxford, Clarendon Press.

Davidson, D., 1963, 'Actions, Reasons and Causes', *Journal of Philosophy*, 60, 685–700.

1982, 'Paradoxes of Irrationality', in *Philosophical Essays on Freud*. Eds. R. Wollheim and J. Hopkins. Cambridge University Press, pp. 289–305.

Delaney, C.F., (ed.), 1979, *Rationality and Religious Belief*. Notre Dame, University of Notre Dame Press.

Descartes, R., 1968, *Discourse on Method and The Meditations*, trans. F. E. Sutcliffe. Harmondsworth, Penguin.

Edgley, R., 1969, *Reason in Theory and Practice*. London, Hutchinson.

Elster, J., 1982, 'Belief, Bias and Ideology', in *Rationality and Relativism*. Eds. M. Hollis and S. Lukes. Oxford, Blackwell, pp. 123–48.

Feldman, R., 1988, 'Subjective and Objective Justification in Ethics and Epistemology', *The Monist*, 71, 405–9.

Firth, R., 1952, 'Ethical Absolutism and the Ideal Observer', *Philosophy and Phenomenological Research*, 12, 317–45.

1956, 'Ultimate Evidence', *Journal of Philosophy*, 53, 732–9.

1959, 'Chisholm and the Ethics of Belief', *Philosophical Review*, 68, 493–506.

1978, 'Are Epistemic Concepts Reducible to Ethical Concepts?' in *Values and Morals*, Eds. A.I.Goldman and J. Kim. Dordrecht, Reidel, pp. 215–29.

Fischer, J. M., (ed.), 1986, *Moral Responsibility*. Ithaca, Cornell University Press.

Foley, R., 1988, *The Theory of Epistemic Rationality*. Princeton University Press.

Frankfurt, H. G., 1988, *The Importance of What We Care About*. Cambridge University Press.

French, P. H., Uheling, T. E. and Wettstein, H. K. (eds), 1980. *Studies in Epistemology, Midwest Studies in Philosophy*. Minneapolis, University of Minnesota Press.

# References

Gale, R. M., 1980, 'William James and the Ethics of Belief', *American Philosophical Quarterly*, 17, 1–14.

Goldman, A., 1980, 'The Internalist Conception of Justification', in Tomberlin (ed.) (1988).

Gooch, P., 1987, *Partial Knowledge*. Notre Dame, University of Notre Dame Press.

Haight, M. R., 1980, *A Study of Self-Deception*. Brighton, Harvester.

Hare, R. M., 1952, *The Language of Morals*. Oxford, Clarendon Press.

1963, *Freedom and Reason*. Oxford, Clarendon Press.

Harman, G., 1986, *Change in View*. Cambridge, Harvard University Press.

Hayek, F., 1967, *Studies in Philosophy, Politics and Economics*. London, Routledge and Kegan Paul.

Heal, J., 1988, 'The Disinterested Search for Truth', London, *Proceedings of the Aristotelian Society 1987–8*, 88, 97–108.

Heidelberger, H., 1963, 'On Defining Epistemic Expressions', *Journal of Philosophy*, 60, 344–8.

Heil, J., 1983a, 'Believing What One Ought', *The Journal of Philosophy*, 80, 752–65.

1983b, 'Doxastic Agency', *Philosophical Studies*, 43, 355–64.

1984, 'Doxastic Incontinence', *Mind*, 93, 56–70.

1992, 'Believing Reasonably', *Nous* 26, 47–61.

Hodgson, D. H., 1967, *The Consequences of Utilitarianism*. Oxford, Clarendon Press.

Hume, David, 1911, *A Treatise on Human Nature*. London, Dent.

1975, *An Enquiry Concerning Human Understanding*. Ed. P. H. Nidditch. Oxford, Clarendon Press.

James, W., 1970, 'The Will to Believe', in Mavrodes (ed.), pp. 161–83.

Johnston, M., 1988, 'Self-Deception and the Nature of Mind', in McLaughlin and Rorty (eds.), pp. 63–91.

Kekes, J., 1988, 'Some Requirements of a Theory of Rationality', *The Monist*, 71, 320–38

Kenny, A., 1975, *Will, Freedom and Power*. Oxford, Blackwell.

Kvanvig, J. L., 1989, 'Conservatism and Its Virtues', *Synthese*, 79, 143–63.

1992, *The Intellectual Virtues and the Life of the Mind*. Savage, Rowman and Littlefield.

Lakatos, I., 1965, 'Falsification and the Methodology of Scientific Research Programmes', in Lakatos and Musgrave (eds.), *Criticism and the Growth of Knowledge*. Cambridge University Press, pp. 91–196.

Levi, I., 1970, 'Probability and Evidence', in Swain M. (ed.), *Induction, Acceptance and Rational Belief*. Dordrecht, Reidel, pp. 134–56.

Locke, J., 1800, *A Letter Concerning Toleration*. A new edition, London, J. Crowder for J. Johnson.

219

1961, *An Essay Concerning Human Understanding*. ed. J. W. Yolton. London, Dent.

Macintyre, A., 1981, *After Virtue*. London, Duckworth.

McLaughlin, B. P., and Rorty, A. D. (eds.), 1988, *Perspectives on Self-Deception*. Berkeley, University of California Press.

Malcolm, N., 1952, 'Knowledge and Belief', *Mind*, 51, 178–89.

Mavrodes, G. I., 1970a, *Belief in God*. New York, Random House.

(ed.), 1970b, *The Rationality of Belief in God*. Englewood Cliffs, Prentice Hall.

1982, 'Belief, Proportionality and Probability', in *Reason and Decision*. Eds. M Brodie and K. Sayre. Bowling Green, Bowling Green State University, pp. 58–68.

1983, 'Jerusalem and Athens Revisited', in Plantinga and Wolterstorff (eds.) pp. 192–218.

Meiland, J., 1980, 'What Ought We To Believe? Or, The Ethics of Belief Revisited', *American Philosophical Quarterly*, 17, 15–24.

Mele, A. R., 1983a, 'Akrasia, Reasons and Causes', *Philosophical Studies*, 44, 345–68.

1983b, 'Self-Deception', *Philosophical Quarterly*, 33, 365–77.

Mellor, D. H., 1971, *The Matter of Chance*. Cambridge University Press.

(ed.), 1980, *Prospects for Pragmatism*. Cambridge University Press.

(ed.), 1990, *F. P. Ramsey: Philosophical Papers*. Cambridge University Press.

Mendus, S. (ed.), 1988, *Justifying Toleration*. Cambridge University Press

1989, *Toleration and the Limits of Liberalism*. Cambridge University Press

Mill, J. S., 1912, *On Liberty, Representative Government, The Subjection of Women*. London, Oxford University Press.

Millar, A., 1991, *Reasons and Experience*. Oxford, Clarendon Press.

Milton, J., 1834, *Prose Works*. London, Westley and Davis.

Mortimore, G. (ed.), 1971, *Weakness of Will*. London, Macmillan.

Nathan, N., 1987, 'Evidential Insatiability', *Analysis*, 47, 110–15.

Oakeshott, M., 1962, 'Rational Conduct', in *Rationalism in Politics*. London, Methuen.

Pascal, B., 1961, *Pensées*, trans. J. M. Cohen. Harmondsworth, Penguin.

Passmore, J., 1978, 'Locke's Ethics of Belief', London, *Proceedings of the British Academy*, 64, 187–208.

Pears, D. F., 1984, *Motivated Irrationality*. Oxford, Clarendon Press.

Penelhum, T., 1983a, 'Scepticism and Fideism', in Burnyeat (ed.), pp. 287–318.

1983b, *God and Scepticism*. Dordrecht, Reidel.

Plantinga, A., 1979, 'Is Belief in God Rational?' in Delaney (ed.), pp. 7–27.

1980, 'The Reformed Objection to Natural Theology', *Proceedings of the American Catholic Philosophical Association*, 54, 49–62.

# References

1983, 'Reason and Belief in God', in Plantinga and Wolterstorff (eds.), pp. 16–93.

1988, 'Positive Epistemic Status and Proper Function', in Tomberlin (ed.), pp. 1–50.

1990, 'Justification in the Twentieth Century', *Philosophy and Phenomenological Research*, 50, Supplement, 45–70.

1991, 'The Prospects for Natural Theology', in Tomberlin (ed.), pp. 387–415.

Plantinga, A. and Wolterstorff, N. (eds.), 1983, *Faith and Rationality*. Notre Dame, University of Notre Dame Press.

Popkin, R., 1964, *The History of Skepticism from Erasmus to Descartes*. Revised edition. New York, Harper and Row.

1967, 'Fideism' in *The Encyclopaedia of Philosophy*. Ed. Paul Edwards. New York, Macmillan, III. pp. 201–2.

Potts, T. C., 1971, 'Aquinas on Belief and Faith', in *Inquiries in Mediaeval Philosophy*. Ed. James F. Ross. Westport, Greenwood, pp. 3–22.

Price, H.H., 1954, 'Belief and Will', London, *Proceedings of the Aristotelian Society*, 53, 1–26.

1969, *Belief*. London: George Allen and Unwin.

Putnam, H., 1981, *Reason, Truth and History*. Cambridge University Press.

Quine, W.V.O., 1969, 'Epistemology Naturalized', in *Ontological Relativity and Other Essays*. New York, Columbia University Press.

Quinn, P.L., 1991, 'Epistemic Parity and Religious Argument', in Tomberlin (ed.), pp. 317–41.

Ramsey, F. P., 1990, 'Truth and Probability', in Mellor (ed.) pp. 52–94.

Scanlon, T., 1972, 'A Theory of Freedom of Expression', *Philosophy and Public Affairs*, 1, 204–26.

Shestov, L., 1968, *Athens and Jerusalem*. Trans. B.Martin. New York. Simon and Schuster.

Sosa, E., 1980, 'The Raft and the Pyramid', in French, Uehling, and Wettstein (eds.), pp. 3–25.

Stocker, M., 1982, 'Responsibility Especially for Beliefs', *Mind*, 91, 398–417.

Stroud, B., 1981, 'The Significance of Naturalized Epistemology', in *The Significance of Scepticism*. Oxford, Clarendon Press, pp. 209–54.

Swinburne, R., 1973, *An Introduction to Confirmation Theory*. London, Methuen.

1979, *The Existence of God*. Oxford, Clarendon Press.

1981, *Faith and Reason*. Oxford, Clarendon Press.

Szabados, B., 1974, 'Self-Deception', *Canadian Journal of Philosophy*, 4, 51–68.

Tertullian, 1870, *De Carne Christi*, trans. Peter Holmes, *The Writings of Tertullian*. Edinburgh. T. and T. Clark., V1, chapter 2, section 5.

References

Tomberlin, J. (ed.), 1988, *Philosophical Perspectives 2, Epistemology*. Atascadero, Ridgeview.

(ed.), 1991, *Philosophical Persepctives 5, Philosophy of Religion*. Atascadero, Ridgeview.

Van Fraassen, B.C., 1973, 'Values and the Heart's Command', *Journal of Philosophy*, 70, 5–19.

1984, 'Belief and The Will', *Journal of Philosophy*, 81, 235–56.

1988, 'The Peculiar Effects of Love and Desire', in B. P. McLaughlin and A.E.Rorty (eds.), pp. 123–56.

Vos, A., 1985, *Aquinas, Calvin and Contemporary Protestant Thought*. Grand Rapids, Eerdmans.

Waldron, J., 1988, 'Locke, Toleration and the Rationality of Persecution', in Mendus (ed.), 1988, pp. 61–86.

Walwyn, W., 1934, 'The Compassionate Samaritane', in *Tracts on Liberty in the Puritan Revolution 1638-1647*. Edited with a comentary by William Haller. New York, Columbia University Press, III, pp. 67–8.

Warnock, G. J., 1971, *The Object of Morality*. London, Methuen.

Watkins, J., 1984, *Science and Scepticism*. London, Hutchinson.

Williams, B., 1955, 'Tertullian's Paradox', in *New Essays in Philosophical Theology*. Eds. A. G. H. Flew and A. C. Macintyre. London, SCM Press, pp. 187–211.

1973, 'Deciding to Believe', in *Problems of the Self*. Cambridge University Press, pp. 136–51.

1978, *Descartes: The Project of Pure Enquiry*. Harmondsworth, Penguin.

# Index